Addi

A Peter Panelli Novel

Stephen Liosi

based on a true story

Copyright © 2023

All Rights Reserved

LCCN: 2022922716

ISBN: 9798392974016

Published by

Montebellier, Ltd.

Dedication

For Maria and Frankie, who saw and felt it all

Acknowledgment

I thank my San Jose State University Creative Writing Professor and Novelist, Rob Swigart, for giving me an A+ in Creative Writing 101. And I thank the late Ann Sanford, California poet laureate, for her kind words of encouragement when I studied under her at Cal State Northridge University. And I thank John Updike and Charles Bukowski for giving me stuff to read, think about and emulate.

Contents

Dedication iii

Acknowledgment v

Preface xi

Part ONE 1

Twenty Years Later 5

| 1 | 5
| 2 | 16
| 3 | 23
| 4 | 32
| 5 | 43
| 6 | 52
| 7 | 67
| 8 | 79
| 9 | 89
| 10 | 101
| 11 | 113
| 12 | 130
| 13 | 145

⌊14⌋	161
⌊15⌋	173
⌊16⌋	182
⌊17⌋	188

Part TWO 199

⌊1⌋	199
⌊2⌋	208
⌊3⌋	215
⌊4⌋	222
⌊5⌋	236
⌊6⌋	245
⌊7⌋	256
⌊8⌋	261
⌊9⌋	274
⌊10⌋	281
⌊11⌋	290
⌊12⌋	297
⌊13⌋	307
⌊14⌋	320

	15		326
	16		333
	17		339
Part THREE	349
	1		349
	2		356
	3		365
	4		373
	5		384
	6		393
	7		403
	8		416
	9		425
About the Author	430

Preface

I began writing this novel in 2018 while homeless and living in my car before transitioning into various motels and hotels. I didn't end up in the gutter because of the kindness of a couple dear friends -- David Ruyle and Gabriel Velasco. And I didn't end up divorced because of my wife's celestial capacity for forgiveness. It's 2022 as I write these very words, and I'm still homeless.

ADDICT'S WAY

Part ONE

Whenever God sends angels my way, they seem to be the lazy ones, too afraid to fly into my darkest hours . . .

I got the stuff. This time, it was a little yellower than usual. I drove a couple of blocks to a nearby alley just off Hoover. Dog shit, human shit, litter everywhere. Homeless people resting, sleeping, and shooting up. Gang graffiti, the relentless swarming of flies. Skinny stray dogs. Rats scurrying about like cockroaches among the cockroaches. I parked between two trash dumpsters, which shielded me from passing cars. Just south of Dodger Stadium, all the alleys in the Hoover-Pico District looked the same. I knew almost all of them. I took a slice of tin foil from the glovebox, wrapped it around the Bic pen, twisted one of the ends shut, then pulled the aluminum cylinder off the pen. I used the blunt end of the pen to make a small crater in the makeshift pipe. Then I used the pen's tip to make four holes in the mini-crater and dropped a piece of the stuff inside it. My brain couldn't wait for me to unleash the pleasure of the stuff by engulfing it with the flame of a cigarette lighter so that it could spread through my lungs and everywhere else, including my brain. Before I took a hit, I used my cell phone to call Cheryl back. "My water broke!" she shrieked. "Nathan's coming! Head to St. Jude's!"

"Now!?"

"Yes, now."

"What happened?"

"*It* happened."

"Okay, but it's rush hour."

"Just get here," she said.

"All right."

"How'd court go?" she asked.

"It's worse than the fucking DMV. I hate being a lawyer."

"Okay, come as fast as you can," she said. "Where are you right now?"

"I'm on my way."

I looked around for cops. Then I took a couple of hits of crack from the foil pipe, trying to revisit the early days of my use, where it was only pure pleasure that I had felt. Over 85% percent of users eventually segue into paranoia. Still, they use to feel the glory of the first few hits again. I was one of those users. Suddenly and viciously, I was in full-blown paranoia after less than a minute of pleasure. I made my way to the 110. There was an invisible soldier of Satan in the backseat. There was a serial killer in my trunk. There were members of L.A.P.D. on the roof of my car. I had to keep driving so none of them could get a hold of me. At one point on the 60, I thought an 18th Street gang member was hanging on the undercarriage of my car. He would be ready to kill me as soon as I stopped. I quickly glanced at the gas gauge: I had enough gas, but I was really worried about a flat tire.

I headed toward Montebello, the city where I had spent most of my childhood. I knew more than a few cars on the freeway were undercover FBI and CIA. They were tracking my every move. Every helicopter overhead was following me. On the 57, the paranoia had dissipated a little. The drive suddenly became bearable. I wanted another hit, but I decided it would be best to wait until I was in the hospital parking lot.

I got to St. Jude's Hospital, a medical icon of sorts in Fullerton. It was dark out. I stayed in the parking lot for over an hour before walking into the hospital. I smoked some more crack while I read tomorrow's Racing Form. I was worried hospital security might see the flash of my Bic lighter from time to time and investigate further.

ADDICT'S WAY
Twenty Years Later . . .

| 1 |

I didn't have any bottles of water with me. I didn't want to go back into the room to get one, not with Alison in there. Her monthly hormonal frenzy had just crash-landed, which always turned her into a foaming-at-the-mouth lunatic. About to collapse, I kept on walking.

As usual, my head was pounding, the left side of my face was tight, and the constant headache above my left eye was in full force. I felt like I was inside the sun itself. I thought I might fall to the ground. I slowly hurried to the nearest structure. It happened to be the large banquet hall of a nearby seasonal golf course. In the summer, the fairways were nothing but heat-singed grass: yellow and brown with only a little bit of green. I stepped inside the banquet hall. Thankfully, it was air-conditioned. The ceilings were 30 feet high. The walls had been painted an Easter-egg light-blue pastel. The carpeting was an off-white burnt-orange, looking like a spill of rusted water. Six cheap-looking chandeliers were hanging about ten feet off the floor. Blah wooden-paned windows tracked the perimeter. Collections of fake plants gathered at every corner. The place was a veritable eye-sore, but it was quickly being turned into a makeshift church. Young and old Black people, all of them well-dressed, were lining up rows of chairs, putting a mahogany podium in place, and setting up an altar with a black-and-gold crucifix. They were doing everything needed to get the place ready for Mass.

I quietly made my way to the back wall that faced the crucifix. I had my laptop, my duffel bag, and several hangers of clothes with me. I was drained from the little time I had been in the heat. I sat down on the floor and leaned against the wall. I put my elbows on my knees, my face in my hands. The unsightly banquet hall wasn't helping my mood. I needed the comfort of opulence. I felt headed to madness.

I wasn't by myself for long. A light-skinned Black man walked up to me. He was in his late 50s. He had a short Afro that sported blotches of grey. He asked me how I was doing. He extended his hand to be shaken. He was smartly dressed: black slacks, black wing-tipped shoes, a black-and-grey, short-sleeved shirt, which looked like a dressy bowling shirt. His deep-set brown eyes were a bit cautious, almost empty. I shook his hand. I took a few steps back. "I'm not doing too well," I said. I didn't say anything else. He didn't need all the details. At least not yet. I did not mention that I wanted to snort an ounce of cocaine, drink an entire bottle of scotch, jump off a high-rise, and so forth. I kept that a secret. I know how to win friends and influence people.

"I'm John. Can we pray for you?" he asked. Before I could answer, he waved over a small group of Black men. We all joined hands in a circle. I told them what had happened to us in generalized detail. All the men, except for John, were in full-blown suits. A couple of them donned hats. All of them handed me a 5-dollar bill. One of them said, "You didn't end up in the back of this church by accident. I'll tell you that much." Everyone agreed. Even I did.

ADDICT'S WAY

It was a sign. I calculated the chances of walking into a church that didn't have the façade of a church in place or a cross on its rooftop. I figured the odds of something like this happening had to be lottery-like. Had my mother's prayers finally been answered? I didn't believe in the power of prayer, but it felt good knowing my mother was always praying for me. It gave me the courage to act destructively. Her prayers weren't keeping me alive. God hated me. It was part of His plan to keep me miserable for as long as possible. Longevity is my cross to bear.

I took my seat up by the altar. The seats were metal card-table chairs. A man was singing and playing the piano off to the side. He looked exactly like CeeLo Green. He could have been a tribute singer. He was talented. The song was upbeat and catchy. John danced over to me. He was full of unusual energy. "Would you like to share today?" he asked. "You know, share your story?"

"All right. Thank you," I said.

Inside this makeshift church, people surrounded me who loved and adored God. They were much happier than I was. That isn't saying much – most goldfish are happier than me. I say most because I assume some aren't. I assume some aren't into the whole stuck-in-a-bowl thing. In any event, I've always envied those who had a relationship with God. I was too shy to introduce myself.

When I shared, I felt all eyes on me. Everyone knew I was a beaten-down loser with a broken brain, destined for skid row or the madhouse. "My name is Peter Panelli. I want to say that this is one of the best days of my life," I began. I was speaking in front of about two hundred people. All of them were black, except for a handful of Mexicans and Filipinos. "Here I am, a white man in an all-Black church, but I am so warmly greeted. You know, it's not like in the news. There just isn't that much hatred in the world. The media would make you believe that I would be killed, being here today."

I paused. I looked over my shoulder at the small crucifix as a nervous fidget. "Anyway, I was in a car crash a couple of years ago. My skull cracked my windshield at a 40-mph impact. I suffered a traumatic brain injury." I surveyed the crowd. I made eye contact whenever I could. I smiled as much as I could. They were good listeners. "I haven't been able to work for almost two years now. My wife and I have lost everything," I said. "We've been homeless and broke for four months now. I've thought about taking my life. The devil wants to kill us. I believe this." Some of us believe in Satan but not in God. That's because Satan is the better marketer. There's still time for me to believe in God. "The devil wants to destroy everything good in us and around us. When things get bad, he wants us to blame God. I can't do that. I can't kill myself. It would kill my wife, and it would kill my son, and it would kill my mother. I have to endure and pray and hope that God intervenes."

A baby cooed. Someone's cell phone rang. Police sirens wailed in the distance. "I'm a lawyer, and my wife's a lawyer, too," I said. "Homeless lawyers. Dead-broke. Living in our car. Sometimes, cheap motels. I never thought this would be my life. I have no idea what to do.

I pray everything gets back to normal sooner than later. I feel bad for my wife, who is suffering from full-body arthritis during all this. We do need a miracle. Thank you for listening. Amen."

I walked back to my seat. The pastor walked back to the podium. He was wearing a black suit with a red shirt and a white tie. The suit seemed a bit too small for him. He looked like a former football player who had stopped caring about his physique and ate anything he wanted after his playing days. His midsection protruded noticeably like a circus ringmaster who would have trouble darting away from an angry lion if it came to that. He had a friendly, penetrating set of eyes as if he knew what you were thinking. He had a commanding presence. It was obvious he had found his life's calling. His spirit was genuine. He had been fully engaged the moment Mass began. "Thank you for that wonderful and heartfelt share," he said. "We need to be missionaries for Brother Peter. We need to walk the walk. We need to pass around the basket for Brother Peter. Put whatever you can in it for Brother Peter and his wife. Amen."

He turned his attention to me. He gestured for me to stand up. I did. Some people clapped. There was a standing ovation for a natural-born loser. Only in church. "Brother Peter, I am Pastor Ricky. I hope this isn't the last time we see you here. You're walking in here today has made us a better church, a better congregation. You brought meaning to the words I spoke today. You brought meaning to the songs we sang today. You walked in here for a reason today. You walked in here today to help all of us be better people. Amen."

Without warning, he started singing – "Can you hear it? Can you feel it?" – in a voice worthy of a record deal. He was as good as the CeeLo Green lookalike. Everyone stood up and began singing, clapping, and swaying side-to-side. I did my best to join in, but I did not sing. I sing awfully. I only sing when I'm alone inside my car on an empty street. I smiled and made eye contact with everyone who smiled and looked my way. I was famous this Sunday. When the song ended, everyone began moving outside. You could hear the happy small talk and idle chatter.

I walked over to my stuff. I was greeted by an overweight man who was about 70 years old. He was sitting in a Hoveround. He shook my hand and slipped me a twenty-dollar bill as he did. He smiled at me. "This nigger's just trying to help you out."

"Thank you so much," I said. I felt like a charity case.

"Things will work themselves out, Peter," he said. "They always do, somehow. My name is Bill. Pastor Ricky's my cousin. How are you, my son?"

"Things could be worse," I answered.

Bill was nothing but happy. There was something playfully cartoonish about him. He didn't have a care in the world. He was a human rainbow. I was a collection of black rain clouds. There wasn't anything bothering Bill. He was a black Charlie Brown in both temperaments and looks. I liked Bill. "Things could be worse. You could be black." He laughed. "Things will work out."

I nodded in agreement, thinking the exact opposite. "Right. I know."

"Do you need a place to live?" he asked.

Before I could answer, an elderly woman materialized. She was dressed in her Sunday best, wearing long white gloves and a long black dress. She handed me an oversized-sized manila envelope. She smiled. "This is for you. I hope this helps."

"This is amazing," I said.

"This is my wife, Ann," Bill said.

"Oh. Hi, Ann," I said. "It's nice to meet you."

Bill's wife had an air of pompous royalty to her. It was as if she was the Queen Mother herself, doing her best not to offend the peasants. Her features were soft and gentle. Her skin was ashen. There was a bit of Goth to her. Like John, there was something mildly unsettling about her. Robotic and calculated were words that came to mind. Friendly and easy-going didn't.

"Honey, we have some rooms available, don't we?" Bill asked her.

"Yes, we do," she said matter-of-factly.

"I'm thinking about Brother Peter and his wife."

"That would be fine," Ann said. Then, she invited me for dinner. "Show up tomorrow evening at about seven o'clock. That'll give me time to get home from work and have some food ready. We'll set you up and give you the keys."

"If you want to come earlier, I'll be home," Bill said. "This nigger is retired. I'll be sitting on my ass in this thing, watching Gunsmoke reruns."

I smiled at both of them. "Okay," I said. "Thank you both so much. Me and Alison will be there. I want her to meet the two of you. I can't wait to tell her about what happened today."

I shook Bill's hand and smiled at Ann. We exchanged cellphone numbers. I turned to my belongings. I hoped the offer from Bill and Ann would be something that could help us. If we could live rent-free for at least a little while, that would help tremendously. The money we had been pouring into hotels was keeping us in a frightening cycle. The eviction on our credit report, because of the car accident and the gambling, was keeping us poor. You had to be a nearly-perfect human being just to rent someplace to take a shit and take a shower. Awful world.

As I was at the back wall counting the money in the envelope, Pastor Ricky came over to me. "Brother Peter, tough times don't last for those who have faith. Keep the faith. I hope we see you here again. Come to our Bible study Tuesday night."

"Here?"

"No, not here," he said. "Ann and Bill will tell you where. It's at their house. Right now, you and your wife need community. You need to be with people of faith." He smiled and slowly waddled away. Because of his girth, it was difficult for him to keep his balance. He looked like he was holding onto an imaginary handrail while walking a tight rope with no safety net below. I knew how that felt.

John quickly took Pastor Ricky's place. "Peter, we are in a position to help," John said in a tired voice. He was almost lifeless, barely able to stand. The unusual energy he had earlier was gone. "And we want to help. Ann is my mother. Bill is my stepfather. Bill and my mother own the home with the rooms. I manage the rooms. You need to get out of that motel world."

I finished counting the money. One-hundred-and-forty-five dollars had been put inside the envelope, not including some loose change. Five people had put in twenty-dollar bills. Indio is a poor city. I was pleasantly surprised. I was touched by the generosity. I couldn't wait to tell Alison.

When I got back to the room, she was sitting cross-legged on top of her bed, looking at a magazine. She was wearing a pair of pink Victoria's Secret sweats, looking beautiful. She has perfect alabaster skin, framed by jet-black hair, with the angular, rare features of a supermodel. Her eyes are deep-set and the color of turquoise-green tidal pools. They still splash sadness on me whenever I look deep into them. Her lips are full and inviting. Her cheekbones are high. It took me less than a second to fall in love with her. It'll take me a million years to fall out of love with her. Unfortunately.

"I can't believe that happened," she said drably. There was zero enthusiasm in her voice. This wouldn't be a pleasant afternoon.

"Give me that envelope! How much did you get?!"

"I said $145 and some change."

Her tone was suddenly belittling and demeaning: "How much exactly?! How much to the penny? You're an idiot! When are you going to go through life with precision?!"

Dread swirled through me. "Stop treating me this way. You're always so exhausting."

She threw her magazine across the room with a quick, wicked flick of her wrist. Her voice became nastier: "You're such a loser! You're the reason we're in this position! I know the story you tell about your brain injury! There wasn't just a brain injury! It's a lie the way you tell it! Tell everything!"

Alison always kept her hotel rooms like a second home, no matter how long we were booked. For example, she brought her microwave, refrigerator, and even her bedspread. Her microwave and refrigerator were needed because the ones provided by the hotels were too noisy and had to be unplugged, though I could never tell the difference.

Her bedspread was needed because hotels never changed them; only the sheets were changed. And we always needed two rooms because she needed space and was embarrassed by the sleeping-and-waking rituals she must perform due to her arthritis and fibromyalgia. She feels extremely uncomfortable knowing there is someone in the room that will look her way from time to time, even though I always do my best not to look in her direction. It only causes problems when I do, especially when she walks out of the shower. Since the eviction, it seemed like we were always arguing in a stranger's apartment.

She smiled wickedly like she was possessed. "Boohoo, Peter. Boohoo. Nobody's crying for you. Tell everyone you were a compulsive gambler who destroyed our entire family. All our dreams shattered, just like my heart."

"All you want to do is be a cruel bitch. You're just like everybody else. And you're awful this time of the month. Boy, did I hit the lottery."

Fuck you, Peter! I'm the one who hit the lottery with your addictions that ruined us, that ruined everything I was working for! You completely obliterated me! What did I even do?!"

"I stopped."

She started crying. Her voice grew weak. "You stopped too late. Now, look at us. Now, look at us. I lost my health insurance. I lost my Enbrel. I lost all my medicines. I want my Enbrel back. I'm going to end up in a wheelchair. I always get the short end of the stick."

| 2 |

We stopped at Walmart for some ultra-thin Kotex pads before we made our way to the seven o'clock dinner at Bill and Ann's. Their home had been built in the 1980s by Bill himself. In his prime, he was a general contractor. The floorplan's main focus was an expansive kitchen next to a sizable TV-viewing area, which featured a large colorful throw rug. Bill found comfort in a black reclining soft leather chair, which propped up his feet at a relaxing angle. There were TV trays on both sides of the chair, full of popular brand-name snacks designed to kill us all. Bill had earned himself a coveted piece of nirvana. Good for him.

Still dressed in her light-green nurse fatigues, Ann apologized for not having time to cook anything homemade. While we waited for Italian food to be delivered, we handled the necessary paperwork at the circular kitchen table for the room we'd be staying in. Even though everything would be free, we had to complete a rental application and let John take a picture of our driver's licenses. "This is just a formality," Ann said. "You will not owe us a single penny of rent. Years ago, we set up a non-profit to house the needy. We've been funded by grants ever since."

After a hearty dinner of spaghetti, garlic bread, and red wine, we were each handed a set of keys. There was one for the front door and one for the bedroom. We went back to the hotel and loaded all our stuff into the Navigator. Then we came back to the nightmare. Either Satan or God was messing with us – or both were. Sometimes, they collude and conspire with one another. They're not mortal enemies. They often work in concert.

Later that night, I clicked on the kitchen light in our new digs. Cockroaches scurried about in a frenzied fashion, like fleeing felons running from a barrage of police helicopter lights. I was barefooted, so I resisted the urge to smash any of them with my feet. What would it matter if I had cockroach insides on the soles of my feet? I thought. I hadn't showered in four days. Like an unwanted snowfall, dandruff was all over my black t-shirt from the constant, nervous scratching of my scalp. The gooey insides of cockroaches on the sole of my feet would seem a fitting accessory.

I didn't remember why I had walked into the kitchen. It was just to have something to do to avoid falling asleep. Lately, every time my eyes opened upon awakening my thoughts turned to suicide. Should I use a gun, a knife, rat poison, or just find a bridge high enough? The last thing I'd want is to end up paralyzed because I didn't find a high-enough bridge. With my luck, I'd end up living the life of a vegetable who could hear all the bullshit talk around his hospital bed. I'd be wide awake in a coma, trying to yell out, "Will somebody just fucking kill me already!?" Hell really is mostly other people.

The free room made it seem like there was nothing but doom in front of us, hanging there like a web of dirty fog. It had to have been spawned from a demonic mechanism. Yesterday, church. Today, this? It's never like in the movies. Your head does not spin around.

Pea-soup-colored vomit does not spurt from your mouth onto the crisp, black outfit of a priest trying to send the demons elsewhere with all his might. It's rarely that obvious. God works in mysterious ways. So does Satan. On planet Earth, Satan is the victor. Even the Bible says it. The possessed are among us. They're everywhere. We're all living a life of quiet desperation, but it's not our fault.

Alison was thirsty. That's why I had walked into the kitchen, which was a small junkyard of broken and barely-working appliances with a noisy refrigerator. There was no linoleum or tile, just concrete full of hairline cracks, which seemed to serve as streets for all the cockroaches. Alison and I were in were in a crack house. Young children were living in it. Some of them were just babies who crawled around smiling, cackling with glee. They were chased by mothers who wore their dissatisfaction with life like thoughtlessly-applied makeup. "It is what it is," these mothers seemed to be thinking. "At least we're not out on the streets." There was a suppressed fear in the eyes of these Black women. They did their best to keep this fear from spilling outward and always smiled. They wanted to shield their children from all the ugliness. These mothers knew they'd never be part of the one-percenters. Even the crawling babies seemed to know. The house owned by the Trubbles was nothing but a monument of sorrow and pain. America is full of houses like this. And Alison and I were in this one. I'm glad I met her, but I wished Alison had never met me. That's how much I loved her.

When we had pulled up earlier, Alison was wearing a stylish sundress, which looked like a piece of modern art hanging in the lobby of a 5-star hotel. It was a wonderful blend of turquoise, gold, and muted orange with random black specks. The black specks looked like distant crows flying toward a sun that was slowly losing its luster. I was wearing a suit because I had just finished a court appearance. Like two locomotives over a swelling sea, we looked out of place. We landed here because of the madness of addiction and the many sirens of self-destruction.

Eddie Rodriguez was the first person I had met. Eddie was a clean-cut, 20-something, light-skinned, Mexican dope dealer living in the house with his gang-banger girlfriend, Heather. They were in the room next to ours. Helping us bring our things inside, Eddie wanted to know why two lawyers were moving into a place like this. "I was in a car crash, and my skull cracked the windshield. My seatbelt didn't work. The airbag didn't deploy," I explained. "I suffered a traumatic brain injury. I haven't been able to work in over two years. We lost everything."

"It's like a movie, you guys being here," he said.

"Like a horror movie. I'm just starting to feel ready to get back into the courtroom," I said. I lied. No lawyer with any kind of soul wants to get back into the courtroom. Lawyers are patron saints of misery, with most of them hating what they do for a living. I wasn't starting to feel ready to get back into the courtroom. I was beginning to feel ready to start drinking and writing. I was Arturo Bandini, a tortured soul destined for madness.

"Ahh, man. That's why," Eddie said. "Yeah, everyone's wondering what two lawyers are doing here. Well, yeah, that makes sense. I'm sorry, man."

"Yeah, there just wasn't any backup. People whom I thought I could rely on just didn't come through for us. That's life."

Eddie seemed like a good person with a good heart. Like many of us, he was simply stuck in a web of mediocrity, not knowing how to untangle himself. We're the fly; life is the spider. Eddie was an uneducated dope dealer who worked part-time in the restaurant industry as a kitchen helper. He and Heather got EBT for food. They just hadn't yet figured out there were better options – maybe there weren't any. "Do what you can to get out of here, Eddie."

"Yeah, man, we're not going to live here forever."

It was easy to tell Eddie didn't necessarily believe that. Defeat and pain had painted his face with a shade of subtle panic. Like a dull glaze over a piece of pottery that was once shiny.

"We've been living here two years. That's enough," he said.

"Yeah." I nodded. I thought two hours was enough. Alison would think two minutes was enough.

"My Dad was living here before me. That's how I found out about the place," Eddie said. "He's in an apartment now with his fiancé, just about two miles away."

ADDICT'S WAY

So, this is America, I thought, looking at Eddie. He was standing there like a lost soul, fear and dread in his eyes. This was all a bad dream. From the President of my law school graduating class to living in a cockroach-infested crack house in Indio. Like all tragedies, there were reasons behind the fall.

Eddie and I were vastly different people. I had been born into privilege and prosperity, while Eddie had been born into a life with few options. We're all born equal but not with equal opportunity. I tried explaining this to my father once. Born in 1927, part of the Greatest Generation, George Panelli would have none of what I was saying whenever I was saying it.

"You think your grandson, Paul, doesn't have more opportunity than a Black kid born in Watts?" I had asked him once. "Paul lives on the sixth hole of a private country club with two lawyers for parents."

"That's bullshit, Peter," he said. "You work hard. You can make yourself a great life without putting yourself on others. No more nonsense. It's time for dinner."

He's 90 years old now and a green-eyed Paul Newman lookalike – except for the eyes, of course. He's an intelligent man, mostly with street smarts. He can't be bullshitted by anyone, not even himself. But he's not someone whom I'd call cerebral. You won't find him reading literature or poetry that doesn't rhyme. He's not a touchy-feely man by any means. Whenever a conversation between us turns to emotion, he'll simply stand up and walk out of the room mid-sentence. Odd to me. Emotion is where love and madness live side-by-side. Some people, like my father, preferred the false ledge of logic. I learned to not share much with my father when it came to my weaknesses and confusion. Our conversations were usually superficial, focusing mostly on sports and world events. He didn't want to hear about your problems because he didn't care about your problems. He lost friends in WWII. They were shot dead right before his very eyes. He had no tolerance for the struggling.

At 2 a.m., loud ghetto music was blasting from the living room. I walked out of our bedroom. I wondered who'd be so rude. It was Eddie. He was swaying back and forth and jumping up and down to the music. He was taking deep hits from a see-through glass bong. The dirty bong water was splashing around from his dancing and jumping.

"Hey, Eddie, I'm dealing with a bad headache from the brain thing. Could you please lower the music?" I asked. "My head's pounding worse than the music."

"I got you, bro," Eddie said. "I got you. Sorry, man."

"Thanks, Eddie," I said.

I slowly walked back to our bedroom. I flicked a cockroach off my mattress before I sprawled across it.

| 3 |

It was 4 a.m. I could hear distant traffic, lazy crickets, and Alison snoring softly. I still couldn't believe everything. As little as two years ago, we'd be able to stay at any hotel we wanted. Three hundred dollars a night was not out of the question. We didn't have to think twice. Alison would simply go online and find a nice weekend getaway for us. Once, we stayed in Sausalito, just north of the Golden Gate Bridge, for seventeen straight days and nights. We ate wherever we wanted. We did whatever we wanted. That was then; this is now. We only have money for food because of the generosity of Pastor Ricky's congregation.

I was feeling hopeless. Everything irritated me. God was an accomplice in all this evil and madness. I found some music that would sustain my low mood. I wasn't in the mood for Somewhere Over the Rainbow or What a Wonderful World. I put my headphones on. "You got a fast car, I want a ticket to anywhere. Maybe we make a deal. Together we can get somewhere. Any place is better. Starting from zero, got nothing to lose ..." I started to think about a particular summer day in the late 1970s.

In college, my father got me great-paying summer jobs. He was a high-up executive with the phone company. I didn't have to work hard. I was just on the payroll. My job was to confiscate the phones of people who couldn't pay their phone bills. This was before we were able to buy phones. Back then, all you could do was lease a phone. One summer, I confiscated phones from Skid Row. I took telephones from drunks, pimps, and prostitutes.

I'll never forget one flea-bag flat I visited. It was a small, pay-by-the-week bungalow full of cockroaches and rats. I had to deal with the property owner because the tenant had died. He was fat, balding, and smelled of alcohol. His hair was black and unruly. There was a gold yarmulke floating on top of it. He said, "She killed herself. The beauty-school dropout killed herself. Three months' rent gone. At least there's no court date anymore." He pushed open the door and walked away. I walked inside. The first thing I noticed was a bullet hole in the wall of the den. There was a coagulated stream of blood stuck on the wall, ending in a petrified pool on the brown shag carpeting. A few maggots tried to squirm about, but they were hopelessly stuck.

That night, I told my best friend about the ungodly scene. "I'll never kill myself," I said. "There's too much to live for. It should never get that bad. You just need to keep going." I had only been giving myself a pep talk to deal with all the senseless emptiness. Those were the naïve words of a 17-year-old boy hoping for the best. I was acting like a football coach in a Hollywood movie who was trying to inspire his team: "There's still time. We're only losing by forty-nine points. Dig deep." I wondered where the hairdresser was today. I wondered if anyone had ever placed flowers on her grave. Probably not. I took the phone and left. There was a little blood splatter on it.

ADDICT'S WAY

Alison was in total shock from sleeping on a mattress in a crack house. Her arthritic pain was spiking and draining her energy. I had recently developed pain in my frontal lobes. There was a constant painful electrical fluttering across my forehead and eyes. I couldn't wake up in the mornings with any noteworthy energy. I wanted to collapse in the street somewhere and become a ward of the state. Sometimes, we both slept until six o'clock in the evening. We slept through every kind of noise. We slept, and babies were born, people were killed, and everything in between. We missed very little.

I reluctantly attended the Bible Study at Ann and Bill's. I went for the free food Preacher Ricky had promised. However, there was the small hope Jesus might possess me. If Satan can do it, why not Jesus? Why doesn't God just send an army of angels inside my heart and end all this madness? He doesn't seem like a merciful God. Look at the news. Look at the world. God is on vacation. He always gets a free pass. He does absolutely nothing, and prayers aren't answered, but the righteous will ignorantly defend Him: "God knows what He's doing." There's just no accountability. If God had a Yelp! Page, I'd give him one star.

Ann and Bill live in a modest five-bedroom, single-story, white-stucco home. Through the years, the stucco had turned pale grey, like many white-stucco homes in Indio. An accumulation of all the dust spewed from the nearby empty land. The dust travels freely in gnat-like clusters. You can taste the dust in the air, but the people of Indio have better things to do than worry about dust-stained stucco.

There's the meth, the heat, the crime, the killings, the poverty, and the police brutality.

Alison didn't come to the Bible Study. A Bible Study put on by people like Ann and Bill – slumlords, as far as she was concerned – would be a farce. "They're slumlords," she said. "They're not good people." Plus, Alison's a devout Catholic who can't stand the anti-Catholic stance most Christians take. There's usually some criticism about praying to statues and worshiping saints as if Christians are superior to people who call themselves Catholics. She wasn't in the mood for anything like that.

I arrived at the Bible Study a little early. Bill was watching Gunsmoke. We small-talked for a bit. Then, I asked him about the history of the boarding house (aka the crack house). "I built that house myself," he said. "I built it about 40 years ago. It used to be a Boy's Home for juvenile delinquents. Instead of the judge sending the kids to jail, they'd stay next door. All that stopped when they started putting the kids into foster homes. That was far worse for most of the kids. After that, we rented it out to people in need."

Bill was sitting deep in his soft leather recliner. He was wearing blue sweatpants, an oversized burgundy t-shirt stained with various food droppings, and black-leather slippers. He was eating a plate of Chinese food. It seemed like every fifth forkful fell onto his shirt or his lap, but he couldn't care less, or he didn't notice. "I started early," he said. "You can grab some from the kitchen counter if you want. There's some pizza on the way, too."

"I'm okay for now," I said.

Bill pointed to a picture on the mahogany mantel above the big-screen television. "See that nigger up there?" he asked.

I nodded. "That's you."

He smiled, remembering. "It is," he said. "I was 17 years old. Believe me, that handsome face got loads of pussy back in the day. Now, I'm 72, and I don't get shit. Not even from Ann. But who can blame her? I'm a fat, ugly nigger now."

We both laughed. When Bill laughed, the rolls of fat around his mid-section jiggled as if the fat itself was laughing, too. "How do you stay so skinny, nigger?" he asked me.

I told Bill the whole story. I couldn't seek the proper medical treatment after the car accident because I had no health insurance. Because I couldn't afford any. It was almost $1,800 a month for someone my age – because of the Obama Care campaign lie, which was not supposed to raise anyone's rates. So, instead, a friend of mine, with a medical practice in Banker's Hill, just above downtown San Diego, put me on a cocktail of drugs to try to help. Adderall, testosterone shots, and vitamin B-12 shots. It turned out that was the same cocktail given to the morbidly obese. In a matter of a few months, I went from 225 to 163. I lost sixty-two pounds and looked like a methhead.

At my father's 90th birthday party, my Aunt Carmella said to Alison, "We need an intervention. Peter looks awful." Everyone had assumed I was doing crack again, and my sister Amanda ran with this faulty assumption. Because of her, my entire family thought I had returned to the drug. If I ever expressed the need for money, she told my family, "Do not give him one red cent! He's a drug addict and a gambler!" Therefore, all sorely-needed funding sources had been cut off. As a result, we ended up living in our car in a Walmart parking lot for three months before we transitioned into flea-bag motels. That's my sister for you, a true Narcissist. Condemnation without investigation. It's how she, and people like her, move through the world. My entire family followed her lead, cousins included, but not all of them. My Cousin Michael knew better. So did my Cousin Daniel.

"They didn't understand," Bill said, "because they didn't want to understand. They did not want to help you."

"Yes," I said.

"Yes," Bill said, "sometimes, it goes like that."

"It sucks," I said.

"Try going through life as a real nigger. You're just a nigger in proxy right now, son. I have stories that'll blow your mind."

Bill told me he had built 186 single-family homes in Indio during his career as a general contractor. He could have built well over a thousand homes, except, according to him, he ran into too many all-white city councils in the 60s and 70s. They purposely blocked projects to put a ceiling on a Black man's wealth. I believed him. "I used to dress as sharp as a trial lawyer and drove around in a Stutz Bearcat," he said. "Nigger, I was a white man's nightmare. They kept me down as much as they could. Who knows what kind of house we'd be sitting in right now if it wasn't for that cleverly-disguised oppression? 'Oh, it's in the hands of the Planning Commission. Oh, it's in the hands of the Community Redevelopment Agency.' No, nigger, it's in your white hands. Just say it to my face."

"That's awful, Bill," I said.

"You got that right, nigger," he said. "I'm sure that shit still goes on today."

We both turned our heads to the sound of the opening front door. Pastor Ricky walked in with boxes of pizza in one hand and a Bible in the other.

He held up the Bible for me to see. "Brother Peter!" he said.

Soon enough, the kitchen, the dining room, and the living room had filled with the Bible Study crowd. I met most of them at the Mass on Sunday. The ones I hadn't met, I recognized from the Mass. For about thirty minutes, there was eating, drinking, and socializing. Everyone asked me how I was holding up, and I was handed five-dollar bills by several people. Ann put some food aside for me to take back to Alison.

Pastor Ricky started the Bible study by having us all join him in saying the Our Father. After that, I tuned out. I didn't hear a word.

I was thinking about The Baseball Days. Even though Nat lived with his mother, we were with each other 5-6 days a week. I'd rather be on the road with Nat heading out to a baseball tournament in Arizona than be inside some courtroom battling over nothing in front of some stuffy Judge who neither cared about you nor the outcome of your case. Sometimes, I'd reschedule court appearances just to see Nat play. Other times, I wouldn't show up to court at all for the same reason. I missed the days when I was one of my son's best friends.

I hadn't seen him in over four months because his mother, Barbara, felt it was best he didn't see me like this. "Do not bother him until you get yourself sorted out. He needs to become a young man and not have to worry about you," she had callously e-mailed me.

Like many women, she was purposely intent on creating an emotional chasm between my son and me. How else do you get back at a man who left you for a younger, more beautiful woman? How else do you get back at a man who left you for someone he *really* loved? Nat's mother did the same thing to the father of her daughter, Courtney. Courtney was born out of wedlock when Nat's mother had been attending junior college. "Forget about him," she told Courtney, who was twenty at the time. There's always a pattern and practice in place, no matter how old the children are. That's why Family Law is such an awful area of practice. It's mostly the women who make it that way, including the female Judges. I call it Dysfunctional Family Law.

"Brother Peter, do you have any thoughts about the passage?" Pastor Ricky suddenly asked me.

I didn't have any thoughts. I couldn't stop thinking about Nat. I didn't hear a word of the passage.

Alison missed Nat, too, but she was upset with him. "He's a little shit if you ask me," she said one evening. "He's nothing but a self-centered, narcissistic millennial. After all you and I did for him, this is how he treats us? I never saw a better father in action than you. And I was a stepmother any kid would dream of having. I loved him and raised him like he was my son. And he was my own. His mother's doing to you what she did to Courtney's father. Any mother worth a damn would make sure her son had a relationship with his father. Especially a father like you. What, you should be ostracized because you're an addict? No, that's not how it works. What Nat's doing to me and you, forget about him for now, Peter. It's sad, and it breaks my heart, but he's just not acting like a good person right now."

I brought back the food Ann had packed up, but Alison had fallen asleep. I placed it in the corner of the room on top of my shoes to make it harder for the cockroaches to get to.

| 4 |

There are many choices. You can jump off a bridge or a high-rise. You can put the barrel of a gun against your temple and pull the trigger. You can overdose on opiates. You can use rat poison. You can slit your wrists with a sharp steak knife. I had a friend starve himself to death. The police found Chuck Badgely's body in his rented Las Vegas mobile home. People nearby had reported a smell. They also discovered weeks' worth of meals hidden underneath his bed. The meals had been prepared for him by a mutual friend who had been helping him get through a tough patch. Chuck had been involved in an awful custody battle. He not only lost his children, but he also lost his will to live without them. He became someone who didn't care about anything, especially himself. He's not the only man who's lost more than his children to a custody battle. There was nothing about Chuck that should have kept him from his children. It was just another murder by a family law judge and an ex-wife.

I had been thinking of jumping off a high-rise. I'd have to get very drunk to do it. Downtown San Diego has many inviting ones. That's where we had been living before the eviction sent us packing. There, I could have a view of San Diego Bay as I fell to my death. How would it feel knowing I had just jumped off a building to end my own life? Would I close my eyes, or would I take in the scenery on my way down as my hair blew in and around my eyes? Would I be elated, or would I wish I could take back that moment of jumping off? Should

I wear a football helmet to keep my brain intact for an autopsy so my family can see that I really did suffer a brain injury?

Years ago, I started to write a novel called, Racing with Nat. It's one of many unfinished novels on my hard drive. It was about me trying to get my life together before Nat realized I was a loser. I lost that race. I'm a 60-year-old man with nothing to his name. I'm living in a crack house now with my wife, who deserves better.

Before we had ended up living in our car, Alison came at me with uncontrollable rage one night. She flailed her fists at my face and chest. She kicked at my knees and shins. "What middle-aged man has absolutely nothing to his name!?" she yelled. "No money!? No house!? No nothing!? Why do I always get the short end of the stick!? Why did I meet you!?"

When Alison finally woke up today, she said, "You need to ask your family for money, Peter. We need to get out of this Godforsaken place."

I watched a cockroach aimlessly scurry across the rug. I named it Rex. "I know," I said.

Alison rubbed her eyes awake. "We don't need any more piddly amounts. We need to get out of us this mess. I still can't believe they did nothing when they knew we were being evicted. That's just cruel. That's unforgivable."

"That's them."

"They just don't care," she said. "They don't love us. That's not how you treat people you love." She stood up and started stretching, as her arthritis doctor had ordered. "We need to go today, or we don't eat," she said. "All we have is the money from the church."

I sighed. "All right," I said.

I thought about how much money I had lost through the years, about how much time I had wasted in the pursuit of the impossible. Another cockroach caught my eye. It disappeared from our bedroom into the hallway through the space underneath the door. What's the purpose of these ugly insects? On the Seventh Day, when God was resting, Satan took his turn with everything. Cockroaches were one of his many awful contributions – like child molesters and narcissistic siblings.

Alison was driving in the slow lane of the 10 freeway on the way to my parents. "That crack house is like a prison, Peter," she said. "Fucking Heather, Eddie's slutty girlfriend. Do you see how she walks around the place, always half-naked, like a prostitute? Also, her stupid pots and pans. The other day, I used one of her pots to heat some soup. The next day, she posts all those stupid signs on the kitchen walls. She's territorial. Like a prison inmate, trust me."

Alison glanced in the rear-view mirror. "And, Jesus Christ, Eddie, get a life! You have a 5-year-old daughter, and you're living in a crack house and smoking pot all day long and busing tables. No wonder your daughter's mother is constantly taking you to court. Lowlife."

She turned and looked at me. "And because of the great Peter Panelli, I'm living with these people."

"Make sure you don't miss the 60," I said.

"I know where I'm going!" Alison barked. "You sure don't!"

"I'm going to the top of a high-rise."

"There you go with the suicidal stuff."

"I'm not suicidal. I just envy anyone who's not alive."

Alison slowly shook her head, eyes on the road. "How are you going to lead us out of this darkness when you're so addicted to darkness? You pursue sadness. The Pursuit of Sadness, by Peter Panelli."

I stared at the dying ice plant on the side of the freeway. "Just keep driving," I said. "I can only imagine what I'll be walking into."

"If your sister's there, you'll be walking into hell."

In the 70s, when America was fixated on Watergate and Pet Rocks, my father had moved us to an exclusive, upscale community called Friendly Hills in the city of Whittier. It was a country club community with a mixture of expensive tract and custom-made homes, many of them lining the fairways of the private golf course there,

Friendly Hills Country Club, which was the social center of everything for those who could afford to join. We soon became members.

Relatives told my father he was crazy for taking on a mortgage that was three times the state average, but the move had to be made. Especially after my friend, Jimmy Alegria, had found a man stabbed to death in the ivy of the Montebello Fire Station, only two blocks from our modest post-war home.

"We need to get the hell out of here," my father announced at dinner one evening. The next morning, he hammered a for-sale-by-owner sign into the middle of the front lawn. It was the only house I had ever known. It was where I was told I had been adopted; where I woke up to the news that Senator Bobby Kennedy had been killed the night before; where I watched Neil Armstrong take that step; where I cried when Mickey Mantle announced his retirement from baseball.

Not long after the sign had been put in place, we were living on the fourth fairway of Friendly Hills Country Club in a fancy 4-bedroom house. From my bedroom window, you could see Catalina on a clear day and a lot of shitty golfers.

Friendly Hills is where my father earned the nickname Crazy George from our neighbors. He was always yelling hysterically at the top of his lungs at something or someone – usually my poor mother. After spending the weekend, Nat would usually say, "Grandpa is mean to Grandma. He always yells." Yeah, he was only nice to neighbors and members of the country club. He was trying to present an image of a likable guy who had it all – enough money and a beautiful wife. I knew better. That's why I'd always dread hearing the garage door open, signaling he was home from work.

Anyway, asking my father for money was always unpleasant. Even when I simply needed gas money in high school. Today, it's still like that: "You need to just get off your ass and stop talking about the brain injury. It's been almost three years since that car crash."

"And I'm still affected by it," I responded. "Are you even listening to a word I've said? Jesus Christ! What don't you understand about my head cracking my windshield? How hard would I have to slam your head against your windshield to crack it? Pretty fucking hard!"

"You don't even know if you have a brain injury," my brother-in-law, Jay, had chimed in. Jay was balding and overweight now but had looked like Kevin Costner when he began courting my sister. He had snuck into the conversation, unannounced, through the backyard sliding glass door. He was holding his laptop in his hands like it was a television tray full of food.

"What in the fuck are you saying!?" I asked him. "That car crash ruined my life!! What in the fuck are you and Amanda trying to say to me!? What is wrong with you people!?"

"Peter, watch your language!" my mother yelled from upstairs.

"Irene, stay out of this!" my father yelled back.

"I'm in the middle of saying a Rosary for you, Peter!" she yelled back down, her words echoing slightly against the walls of the entryway.

I pictured my mother up in her bedroom, kneeling at her bedside, with her wrinkled hands clutching her Rosary beads against her chest. I imagined she was staring at the mirrored closet, looking at her sad face, wondering what had gone wrong with everything.

I'm sure she wanted to blink her eyes and go back in time to forty years when there was still a life that could have been crafted differently by all of us.

Only a few months from ninety, you could tell she was once a beautiful woman. But now, her chestnut-brown hair was pink from years of dying. Her brown eyes, which once had the shine of melting chocolate, were now a dull brown like powdered Hershey's chocolate past the expiration date. I missed those days when her vibrance was undeniable and when she turned the heads of most men. Mostly, I missed her – she was the only one I missed. She wanted to help, but she was a throwback to women who had married in the 50s: "I don't have access to large amounts of money, Peter."

"Where's Alison?" Jay asked. "Why isn't she here?"

"She doesn't need to be here," I answered. "I'm here."

Alison was waiting for me at the nearby Target on Whittier Boulevard because she didn't want to see my family. "I'm done with them," she had pronounced many times.

"All I'm hearing about is the brain injury," Jay continued.

"Uh. Yeah. I. Suffered. A. Brain. Injury. Jay," I said as if I were speaking to a retarded child.

Jay's return tone was condemning. "Did you get an M.R.I.?" he asked.

"No, I could not afford an MRI."

"How about a CAT scan?"

"No, I don't need a CAT scan, or an MRI, to know that I suffered a brain injury," I said. "My skull cracked my windshield. I couldn't get out of bed for two years. We ended up homeless, living in a goddamned Walmart parking lot for nine months. What happened to you, Jay? Oh, I know twenty-five years of life with my disgusting sister."

"Hey, come on, Peter," my father pleaded.

"Peter! Please!" my mother shouted from upstairs.

"Amanda wants to see medical documentation, Peter," Jay said with an unusual amount of indignation. He was now my sister's lackey.

"Fuck you guys," I said. I quickly stood up and quickly walked toward the front door. "Fuck this. This isn't a deposition, Jay. You can go to hell. I don't deserve to be treated like this. Neither does Alison. Fuck you."

I could hear my mother running from the master bedroom to the top of the stairs. "Please, don't leave, Peter!" she yelled. "We will help you and Alison!"

"Shut up, Irene!" my father shouted. "Do not put words in my mouth!"

"You shut up, George!" my mother shouted back. "You're 90 years old! You don't need any money!"

"All right. Look, how much do you need?" my father asked. "You always need help, Peter."

"Especially now," I said. I slowly walked back into the den. I sat back down on the big couch. It was across the small couch Jay was sitting on.

"What's the plan moving forward, Peter?" Jay asked.

I heard my mother walk back into the bedroom.

"We need help getting into an apartment," I said. "Right now, we're living in a cockroach-infested crack house. However, we are living rent-free. That's a plus."

"Look, how much do you need?" my father asked again.

"Seventy-five hundred," I answered.

My father held up an envelope from Chase bank. "How about five thousand? I have five thousand right here," he said.

"That's too thin to be five-thousand dollars, Dad," Jay said.

"That looks more like five hundred," I noted.

Jay took the envelope from my father and opened it. "It is five hundred," he said.

"I need more than five hundred, Dad."

"Just give him the seventy-five hundred, George!" my mother shouted from upstairs.

"Shut up, Irene!" he shouted back.

"You shut up!" my mother shouted back. "Drive to the bank right now! Get him the money, George!"

"How about five thousand?" my father asked again.

"Dad, I really need seventy-five hundred. I haven't had any real income for over two years now. You just don't understand."

"Just give him the seventy-five hundred, George!" my mother shouted from upstairs.

"You be quiet!" my father shouted back.

"What's the plan moving forward, Peter?" Jay asked.

"To get everything back in order," I told him. "That's all I can say right now. I'm just hoping for the best. I was harmed by that car accident. Nobody seems to believe that. I've got a lot of symptoms that you can't see. It's not a matter of trying harder. You could see if I had a broken leg, right? But you can't see a broken brain. Trust me, Jay, I'm fucked-up."

"All right," my father said. "Let's go to the bank."

Jay's cell phone rang. "Wait a minute," he said. He walked outside to the far-left end of the backyard.

"You should call us more often, Peter!" my mother shouted from upstairs. "I don't know how many years me and your father have left!"

"Shut up, Irene!" my father shouted. "Don't be so goddamned morbid!"

Jay quickly walked back inside. He looked at me.

"That was Amanda," he said. "She does not want to give you seventy-five hundred. She doesn't want to give you a single penny. You'll either buy drugs or gamble it away. It's what she said."

"Fuck that bitch!!!" I screamed. "Fuck that fucking bitch!!! I hope she rots in Hell!!! Who in the fuck is she!?!"

We all made our way to Chase. I stayed in the car. My father handed me a Cashier's check. It was made payable to Alison Panelli – for $5,000.

| 5 |

I felt unusually calm. I slowly sat up on my mattress, Indian-style. "I'm serious."

Alison laughed. "Your sister deserves to die. I'll be the get-away driver," she playfully offered.

A cockroach crawling on the rug caught my eye. I beat it to death with both fists. Like I was in jail-cell fighting for my life.

I wanted to go back to sleep and set my alarm for some time next month, next year. "It'll be a murderous rage. I'll do time on Death Row. It'll be worth it. That's the cockroach I nicknamed Amanda."

"All right," she said matter-of-factly. "Get the dead body out of here. Wash your hands, Peter. That's gross."

I flushed the dead cockroach down the toilet. The toilet had been left full of feces by the previous user. "Fucking lowlifes," I muttered.

I headed back to our room. I walked through the hallway full of Taco Bell and McDonald's wrappers and smashed cups that nobody had bothered to place inside trash bags. "Fucking lowlifes," I muttered again.

I told Alison about the fecal gift left behind: "That's disgusting."

I slowly lowered myself onto my back, looking up at the dirty ceiling. "Yeah," I said.

Alison was doing her morning stretching. "Well, the five-thousand dollars didn't do much for us," she said. "We're behind on the storage, the Lincoln is about to be repossessed, and decent hotels cost almost two hundred dollars a night."

"Yeah."

"Life is about cause and effect, Peter. I hope you know that now."

"Yes, I plan on writing children's books about that very concept: The Diary of a Fucked-Up Loser."

Alison was no longer stretching. Now, she was using her hands to illustrate a point. "Look, Peter," she said. "You're IQ is up here, and you're living way down here. Something's seriously wrong. Just like your cousin Michael said."

"We need to stay here a few months. Try to save as much money as we can."

"Are you out of your mind?!"

"Yeah," I said. "Look, maybe now it's time for you to ask your family for some help. All we're doing is asking mine."

"I don't even know them," she said. "I can't ask them for anything."

Alison escaped home right after she had graduated from Chula Vista High School in 1991 when she was only 17 years old.

Her father, Thomas Tradgett, had created a horrible household for all of them. He was an emotionally-compromised man who had been the victim of unspeakable child abuse involving switches, dark closets, and forced sodomy. Through the years, he had often beaten Alison's mother to a bloody pulp. Almost monthly, the police and paramedics were summoned to wherever they happened to be living at the time. The walls of where they lived were often stained with blood splatter, serving as a fitting wallpaper, an artistic testament, if you will, to the suburban horror Alison, merely an innocent bystander, endured until the end of her senior year. One beating, in particular, made her leave home for good. Still in uniform, she had just finished cheerleading practice and made the usual walk home through the semi-rough streets of Chula Vista, a mostly impoverished town full of enough gang members to make anyone feel uneasy or unsafe. The city was not too far from the Mexican border. Alison's spectacular beauty, which she shared with her mother, often incensed the young cholo boys and men of the neighborhood. Constantly, she was harassed on her walks to and from school. Alison had always walked around town staring down at the ground, careful not to make eye contact with anyone.

One afternoon, however, her eyes quickly moved from the sidewalk to her home on E Street. She knew something was very wrong. She had never seen yellow police tape draped across the front yard of anywhere she had lived. Until today. She ran to the scene and was greeted by Officer Lopez, who had become a family friend because of all the domestic violence calls through the years. "Did he kill her?" she asked.

Officer Lopez shook his head. "But she'll be on her way to the hospital soon," he answered. "And your father will soon be on his way to the police station."

"Oh my God."

Officer Lopez spoke to Alison with genuine concern. He was overweight, donning a salt-and-pepper handlebar mustache. He had a friendly smile for someone who looked like he was a part-time member of the Hell's Angels. He had become a friend to everyone in Alison's family except her father.

"She's going to make it, Alison. She always does. This time, your father needs to be put away. This has to end."

"Can I talk to her?" she asked.

Alison ran to her mother, who was being tended to by two paramedics on the front porch. One was a thin, angular, middle-aged white woman with a ponytail pulled tight; the other was a muscular college-aged Latin man with both forearms riddled with innocent tattoos, one of them professing his love for his grandmother, next to a rainbow full of unicorns.

"Mom! I love you!" Alison blurted out.

Susan Tradgett covered her bloodied face out of embarrassment to shield her daughter's eyes from the damage her husband had just inflicted on her with a few empty bottles of beer. The bottles had been violently smashed across her forehead and cheekbones.

"Sweetheart, please, don't look at me," Susan whimpered. "Please, look away. And, please, go away. You need to leave as soon as possible. You need to leave today. I'll be okay. Do not ever come back here."

Tears streamed freely down Alison's face as if a dam had burst. "Mom, I love you so much."

"You come to find me in a few years, Sweetheart. You won't be far away. USD isn't that far away at all. I'll come find you. How does that sound? You're the only one of us who has any chance to make it."

"Mom."

Her mother softly blew her a gentle kiss. "I'll be okay. I love you, Alison," she said. "Sweetheart, you make a nice life for yourself." That was the last time Alison ever saw her mother.

Just a few months before our wedding, Alison received word from her Aunt JoAnne that her mother had killed herself with an overdose of prescription sleeping pills and tranquilizers.

Before the unthinkable had happened, Alison decided to reunite with her mother and began writing her love letters, inviting her to our wedding. Alison told her how much she missed her.

By that time, though, Susan Tradgett had already taken her own life. None of the letters ever made it to her. And none of the letters ever came back. Alison had no idea.

"Grandmothers usually help their grandchildren. If mine was still alive, we'd be living with her," I said.

I felt like a desperate used-car salesperson, but we needed more money.

"Usually, they do, but mine won't."

"I think you have to ask," I said. "Maybe one of your aunts will help."

"Look, because of my father, my mother was disowned by them," she said. "He wasn't liked. He was divorced and had two children of his own. He was thirty, and my mother was still a senior in high school. He wasn't accepted."

"Yeah."

"I'm brushing my hair because I like having a weapon in my hand. In case I need to kill a freaking cockroach, Peter," she said with great sarcasm.

"I feel wonderful."

"You feel the way you're supposed to feel after what you did to me."

"Should we even try?"

"Try what?"

"Asking your family."

"They won't help us," she said. "It's wrong, but there's an ugly past. They hold it against all of us."

For example, on Thanksgiving Day in 1986, Ramona, the eldest of the Tradgett children born with Down syndrome, went berserk when the neighbor's cat ran through the living room where everyone was gathered for food. The cat had merely grazed her leg, but Ramona was unusually afraid of animals, even goldfish. Because of the cat, she threw herself on the ground and began moaning, screaming, and flailing about, as if the floor of the living room was part of the nearby Pacific Ocean and Ramona was a dying fish gasping for air.

Her maternal grandfather, Jose Ramos, took great exception to this display of unusual fright. "Please, get the creature from the black lagoon out of my house!" he yelled.

Thomas Tradgett genuinely felt Ramona was the only person on planet Earth who loved him unconditionally. He grabbed a handful of candied yams from his plate and smeared them all over the face of Grandpa Jose. He wrestled Grandpa Jose to the ground. There were now three people on the ground flailing about. Soon, there were five. Two uncles had to pull Thomas off, Grandpa Jose.

When the scuffling was over, and Ramona had calmed down, Thomas had these parting words for everyone who wasn't a Tradgett. "You are all such disgusting, heartless, cold souls," he said, "Last Christmas, you gave my children a cup of hard candy for Christmas? You know we're hurting. You know we need help. That's what you do to my children? You all disgust me. You'll never see any of us ever again."

"They never helped our family," Alison said. "I can't imagine them helping me now."

"At least call them and ask. We're desperate."

"Not this second, all right!? I just want to go back to sleep right now!" Alison snapped. "You know, I haven't slept since we got to this beautiful five-star hotel you booked for us. I'm about to die, Peter."

"All right, let's get some more sleep," I said. "I'm dead."

Alison closed the light. She made her way back to her mattress. She slowly sat down; the pain from her arthritis was obvious to anyone looking her way.

"This is all too much for me," she said. "On top of everything, I feel so awful."

"I know."

"Hey, Peter?" Alison asked.

"Yeah?"

"I figured you out, Peter. Yeah, I did," she said. "You're a self-indulgent, immature little boy intent on driving yourself crazy."

I did not want to debate my mental health. That was a debate I'd never win. "I think that's a perfect description," I said.

"You know, my mother wanted me to make a nice life for myself. Those were her last words to me."

"I know they were."

"You're my husband, Peter," she whispered with sadness. "It's you who's supposed to make a nice life for me. You're the one who's supposed to do that."

"Well, I'll keep trying to walk uphill naked in a sandstorm for you," I said. "That's all life has ever been for me."

"I know it is. I do. I just wish I would have known a lot sooner," she said.

| 6 |

In the morning, I decided it would be a good idea to invest a thousand dollars from the five-thousand-dollar Cashier's check in cocaine.

Eddie dealt powdered cocaine in small amounts to well-known friends, including his father and his father's fiancé.

"Look, you give me a thousand dollars," he said. "Within a week, five days or so, I give you back thirteen hundred dollars. It's guaranteed money, with zero risk." Eddie had spoken with the self-assurance of a successful hedge-fund manager.

"I'm in, Eddie," I answered. "I'll round up the cash in a couple of days."

"You are not in!" Alison said. "Are you out of your mind!?"

I positioned myself into a persuasive position, legs crossed Indian-style, upright torso. I was wearing grey boxer briefs and black socks, using my hands to punctuate my points. I should've created a PowerPoint on my laptop. Alison's a visual learner. Flow charts were her key to passing the California bar exam.

"Listen, you don't know much about this stuff," I said.

"And you do?" she asked, with raised, mocking eyebrows.

I threw an air of superiority back at her. "Yeah, I do. I dealt weed in college out of the Franklin House. All I did was sell to friends," I said. "And if a friend of a friend hit me up, I'd do my vetting to make sure they weren't narcs. It's one-hundred-per-cent safe. Plus, I'm not going to be interacting with anyone. I won't be selling it. I won't be face-to-face with anyone."

Alison was laying uncomfortably on her mattress, staring up at the ceiling, avoiding eye contact. "And if Eddie gets arrested, what do you think he'll do, say nothing about the two lawyers in the crack house who gave him money to fund his little side hustle?" she asked.

"That's not going to happen," I said.

"Everyone has a price, Peter. Don't be so naïve," she said. "Eddie will rat you out to save his ass, trust me. So will Heather. Jesus, Peter, use your brain."

I threw up my hands in surrender. "Hey, desperate times call for desperate measures," I said.

"This would be a one-time thing?"

"I don't know," I said. "Yeah, I guess. A one-time thing."

"You think it's safe?"

"As far as us ever getting arrested is concerned? Yeah, it's safe," I said.

"As long as Eddie's not a narc."

"He's not a narc, trust me. He smokes pot. I've heard him snorting coke in his bedroom," I said. "Probably off the small of Heather's back."

"You're sure about him?"

"Yeah," I said. "Why?"

"I don't know what to do. I don't know what we're supposed to do. I don't know what I'm supposed to do," she answered. "I don't know anything anymore, Peter. This is all madness. I'd better not be implicated in any way, shape, or form. You got that!? You tell Eddie you're doing this behind my back and that I don't know a thing about it! You got it?!"

I visualized us being dragged out of the crack house in handcuffs. "Yeah. I got it," I said.

Alison sat up and turned toward me. She moaned, not because of her pain but because of me. "No woman in her right mind would still be here with you," she said. "I'm going to the bathroom. I hope I don't catch any diseases along the way."

Inexplicably, my life started to flash before my eyes. I'm not somebody anybody should have in their life. All I do is create pain and chaos.

In Catholic school, I was constantly in trouble. I often had to stay late because of something I did that had riled the nuns. There was always some kind of non-compliance, either not doing homework or giving some cute girl unwanted attention by dropping a pencil at her feet and copping an accidental feel of her calf muscle as I retrieved the pencil from the floor. The girls didn't mind.

The trouble mostly came from not doing homework, though, or from turning in a blank piece of paper when time was called.

I told Sister Jacqueline in sixth grade, "I know what I know. I don't have to empty my brain onto a piece of paper to prove it." "Well, yes, you do," she said. "You're going be a hippie, young man." Even though I didn't know much about LSD back then, I wanted to be a hippie!

Things didn't change much in college. There, my transcripts were full of many incompletes and withdrawals. Even in law school, I just went through the motions.

During my first year, I figured out what the bar examiners wanted. There wasn't much energy used. My only goal was to get a J.D. degree, so I could sit for the bar exam. I'd sit in the back of class reading the Racing Form instead of listening and taking notes. Classmates called me "cavalier." Ultimately, I don't regret much academically. But I wish I had ended up with the type of pedigree that could have landed me a professorship at an Ivy League law school: "Full-time money for part-time work" is the word on the street about being a professor.

I do regret a lot when it comes to relationships. Nat had to endure the pain of a divorce when he was 5 years old.

I'd be helping him with his homework at Borders, he'd say, tears streaming down his cheeks, "Daddy, why did you have to get divorced? You need to put us all back together again. You can do it, Daddy. Please."

That's one of the reasons why he avoids me now. Childhood wounds run deep. Plus, his mother's propaganda doesn't help.

And I wasn't the best son, brother, brother-in-law, uncle, cousin, friend, or husband, either.

Alison certainly deserved better than me. With her looks, she could have mined North San Diego County for a kindhearted millionaire. All she would've had to do was become a regular at the bar inside the Addison at the Fairmont Grand Del Mar. Every man we've ever crossed paths with, no matter where we were or who they were, eyed her up and down. It was like I was with someone famous. All beautiful women are famous.

Anyway, whenever my life flashed before my very eyes, it was only the ugly parts. Self-pity is an opiate. Stronger than any developed by Big Pharma.

Alison returned from the bathroom and went back to her mattress. "Okay, where were we?" she said.

"Remember. Eddie. We don't have to do it if you don't want," I said.

"This place is disgusting, Peter," she said. "Cockroaches were crawling all over my feet. How do these people live here without complaining about it? This is just awful."

"I don't know. Eddie hasn't said a word about cockroaches to me."

"I'm breaking down, Peter," she said. "This crack house didn't help."

I rolled my eyes and shook my head. "I know," I said. "This just couldn't be a normal room in a normal house."

I could feel her energy disappear. Suddenly, there was a black hole in her part of the room. "When is something good going to happen for me?" she asked.

"We'll end up okay," I said.

"I need more than that, Peter."

"I know."

"I need a nap. Then we'll figure out if we're really going to do the Eddie thing or not," she said.

"All right," I said.

A couple of hours later, I had a meeting with Eddie in the living room. The furniture there consisted of two flimsy card tables and a couch without feet or cushions. There was a collection of cheap toys strewn about, with a play kitchenette full of real pots and pans. It was being used as a shelf by adults. Eddie and I sat at one of the card tables.

"Okay, Eddie," I said. "Alison has no idea I'm doing this. I have to go behind her back."

"I understand," he said. "I know."

"Yeah." I nodded. "I don't want to be ratted out if things go wrong, man."

"I'd never do that to anybody. Plus, I've been selling to the same people for five years. There have been zero problems."

"You're not wearing a wire, are you?" I asked, half-joking.

"Nah, man." Eddie smiled. "You watch too much TV."

I handed him fifty twenty-dollar bills.

"Here," I said. "It's all there."

He put it in his pocket. He didn't count it. "All set," he said.

Jerome walked into the living room and sat down on the cushion-less couch. Tall, about 40 years old, he was wearing only oversized black boxers that had pockets, a pair of blue slippers, and an ear-to-ear grin. Lean and muscular, with no excess fat. His daily routine was obvious.

"Good evening, Eddie," he said.

Then he looked at me. "Mr. Attorney," he said. "I'm Jerome, Teisha's husband."

"Yes, we've never met, but I know who you are," I said. "How are you?"

"I'm cool," he said.

"Jerome has an interesting story, man," Eddie said to me.

He smiled. "Too many stories," he said.

Eddie stood up. "I need to hit the sack, man," he said. "My alarm is set for 4:30."

"Is Mr. Attorney cool, Eddie?" Jerome asked.

"Absolutely," Eddie said. "One hundred percent."

"All right, good night, Eddie," Jerome said.

Eddie disappeared into his bedroom, where Heather was waiting.

"Mr. Attorney, you're part of a fucked-up system, man."

"I sure I am. Which one?"

Jerome ran his right hand through his short greying Afro. "Our legal system. It's fucked-up, man," he said. "You know that."

"It can be," I said.

"Especially for a Black man."

"Yes."

"I got fucked, man. Just last year, I finished a twenty-year stint at Chuckawalla for murder."

My muscles tightened. "What happened?" I asked.

Jerome sensed the tightening. "You sit tight, Mr. Attorney. We're cool," he said. "It's not what you think. It wasn't Murder One."

"What was it?"

"You tell me. I came home. My Black girlfriend was fucking a white guy. I thought he had a gun in his hand. I shot him three times in the chest, killing him instantly. I thought he had a gun in his hand, but it was a black dildo. As he fell back, the black dildo made it to the ground. It was still vibrating. I didn't run. I stuck around. I called the cops myself. I didn't touch the dildo. When the cops got there, the black dildo was still on the ground, vibrating."

I wanted to laugh. "Must have been an Eveready," I said.

His eyes were closed. He was reliving the moment. "I told the cops what happened," he said. "Of course, they didn't want to hear a word from me. I was cuffed and treated like a wild animal."

ADDICT'S WAY

"Sounds like voluntary manslaughter to me," I said. "Imperfect self-defense."

Jerome opened his eyes. "Wrong. I was hit with Murder 2."

"That's not Murder 2."

"Well, the Judge was white. So was the victim. What can I say?" Jerome said.

"Public defender?"

"Yeah. A white one," he said. "Two white prosecutors. I didn't stand a chance."

"You always need a private attorney."

Jerome scratched his chest. "I know that. I didn't have fifty-thousand dollars lying around back then. And I sure don't now, that's for sure. And neither do you, from what I've been told. At least not anymore, right?"

"Yeah, things went south," I said. "I'll pull out of it."

Jerome leaned his back against the wall and slowly surveyed the slum-like surroundings. There was dirty carpeting missing enormous patches. There were dirty white walls that hadn't been painted in years. There were torn curtains covered with layers of soot and broken windows that made the heating and air-conditioning work hard. There were cheap toys all over the place. You'd think you were at an indoor yard sale. All these eyesores were underneath a stucco ceiling caked with dust, cobwebs, and dead insects. It was a tenant's nightmare. A slumlord's dream.

"So, Mr. Attorney, what do you think about this place?" he asked me.

"It's like a slum."

"It *is* a slum," he said. "It's not *like* a slum."

"Yeah. It is."

"Teisha said she talked to your wife about something going on with the rent here."

"Yeah. We're thinking about what we should do about that," I said. "At the very least, this place needs to be turned into a place that's livable."

"Prison was better than this," Jerome said.

"What's that like?"

"Someone like you doesn't want to know," he said. "Let's just say that I'm happy with being a fry cook at IHOP. I'm happy to come home to Teisha, her kids, and our newborn. I'm a black ex-con, man. There's nothing more for me in life. I know that."

ADDICT'S WAY

"How much rent are you paying here?" I asked.

"Fifteen hundred for two bedrooms."

"For this? That's outrageous. That's borderline evil."

"It *is* evil!" he said. "We need to stop this!"

Before I said another word, Jerome gave me the Reader's Digest version of his life story. Compton. He had been born to a 15-year-old crack-addicted prostitute, Gwenda Jackson. His grandmother had raised him. Three days after his birth, his mother had been beaten to death by her pimp for refusing to get back to work. Gwenda took to the streets to sell her body when she was only 13 years old. It was done to escape sexual abuse from her father's brother, Dwight Jackson. Her uncle had bought her silence with a steady stream of weekly hundred-dollar bills. That's what she thought the world was – sex for money. She never fought her fate. That's just where the good Lord had put her, she thought.

Jerome, like me, had never met his biological father. His father happened to be Dwight Jackson, his great-uncle. When he was 12 years old, Jerome fled Dwight's sexual abuse. Dwight didn't rape Jerome, but he forced him to have sex with prostitutes while Dwight watched and masturbated. Throughout his teens and into his early twenties, Jerome financed his room-and-board by selling crack cocaine on various designated Compton street corners. He acted out with violence against anyone who crossed his path, whether they deserved it or not. In his early teens, he did a three-year stint in Juvey for robbing a streetwalker at gunpoint. The Judge had considered all this when sentencing him for the Murder-2 matter. Jerome's life was the stuff of movies.

"Not the best childhood," Jerome said. "I doubt I've had the worst. I've heard stories worse than mine. Anyway, mine isn't why I ended up in prison. I'm not playing that card."

"Man, I didn't have an uncle like that."

"Anyway, Mr. Attorney, can you help us?" Jerome asked. "Ann and Bill Trubble need to be called out for the slum they own. I think, maybe, God sent you and your wife here to help all of us."

"I can't imagine God sent me," I said. "Anyway, everyone living here has to be on board with the idea of going after Ann and Bill."

Jerome nodded. Then, he yawned loudly. It was the kind of yawn that signals the end of an evening. "Man, I need to hit the sack," he said. "I've got another twelve-hour shift tomorrow. I'll make sure everyone's on board, Mr. Attorney."

I stood up from the card table. "All right, Jerome," I said. "Talk soon."

"We will," he said. "I need to hear more about your story, man. Eddie told me a little bit."

Jerome slowly got off the couch. He looked depleted. It was as if he had just finished an exhausting set of squats and was too tired for the next phase of the workout. Everything was too much for everybody.

ADDICT'S WAY

I walked back into our bedroom. Alison was sitting on her mattress, cross-legged, with her tablet in her lap, even though it was midnight.

"What are you doing?" I asked.

"Looking for an apartment," she said.

"We can't afford an apartment right now," I said.

"I know that, but it calms me down," she said. "I won't stop dreaming. Someday, I will be living in a five-bedroom, three-bath home with a view of nature."

When Alison was growing up, her family was always renting because her father simply couldn't generate enough income for homeownership. In college, Alison finally understood and realized her father had done the best he could, with limited capability. This epiphany caused her great pain. All through childhood and teenagehood, Alison harbored deep resentment toward her father. She was ashamed. He didn't provide her with the finer things in life or even the average things in life. When young, she'd constantly ask her father, "Daddy, how come we're not rich?"

In high school, she understood procreation was a kind of lottery: some of us were born into poverty, some of us were born into wealth, and most of us were born in between. Still, she wondered why God had placed her in such a household. I felt bad for her: I was nothing more than an educated version of her father. All Alison desired was a

Home-Sweet-Home sign on a kitchen wall, sans bloodstains. But, now, she had to constantly flick cockroaches away. Even though she had married a lawyer.

"You'll get the big house," I said.

Alison looked up from the screen of her tablet. She shot me a disgusting glance. "When I remarry?" she asked.

"I gave Eddie the money. Teisha's husband wants us to sue the Trubbles."

"They'll be sued," she said. "Those people need to end up in jail."

"I'm sorry, Alison," I said.

"You really did a number on me, Peter. Look where we are?"

| 7 |

There was loud yelling, screaming, and cackling from children. From adults, there was a loud, controlled conversation that was trying to compete with the unruly, chaotic, joyful sounds of those younger than them.

I rubbed my eyes awake. There was a dull ache behind both. "Is that the fucking television on out there!?" I asked Alison.

Alison was face-down on her mattress. "Oh, I forgot," she moaned. "That's Teisha's sister's birthday party for her son. He just turned seven. We were invited. I forgot."

"Why are they having the party here?"

"I have no idea."

I grabbed my cell phone. "It's already 1:30, man."

"I've been up all night with pain all over my body," she said. "I need my Enbrel back, or, at least, my Celebrex."

Is there ever a break from fucking anything? I thought.

Alison faked a smile my way. "Well, I guess we should get dressed and join in on the fun," she said.

I had no interest in a birthday party. "Why am I alive? I should have been an abortion. Hey, suicide is just an after-the-fact abortion. It should be legal. I'll introduce a Senate Bill for that."

"There he goes again, the Hallmark Card writer," Alison said. "You need help, Peter."

Someone knocked rapidly on our door a few times. "Alison, it's Teisha. Come on out here and have some fun. You need to meet everybody who lives here. And some of my other friends. Okay?"

Alison cracked open the door. "Hi, Teisha. Okay. Sure. We just woke up. Can you believe that?"

"Well, that's what Sundays are for. And you guys have been through hell. Anyway, pizza and birthday cake," Teisha said. "Everyone wants to meet you. Jerome's here, Peter. He switched his days." Teisha was full of positive energy.

"I'll be there. I love pizza," I said.

Alison gently closed the door. "That's really a sweet person. Okay, I need to do what I need to do. You go on. Tell everyone I'll be right out."

I walked into a living room that was full of shiny, happy people. There was a small crowd of about twenty people, from babies to grandmas, laughing, talking, drinking sodas, and eating pizza. Children were running and crawling all over the place. All the children were laughing and screaming wildly. There was no adult interference at all. It was a kid's birthday party. Let kids be kids. Jackson 5 music was booming. There was dancing.

ADDICT'S WAY

A large cake on one of the flimsy card tables. It was surrounded by various snacks, mostly candy. It had eight candles waiting to be lit. Seven of the candles were standing straight up, while one of them, stuck at the north pole of a colorful globe, leaned toward the future. Underneath the globe, red icing proclaimed, in perfect cursive, "We Are the World, Happy Birthday, Baby Boy."

On the other card table, there were gifts and birthday cards for the Man of the Hour: 7-year-old Dwight Hamilton. He was the #1 Michael Jackson fan in attendance. He lived in nearby Riverside with his mother, Lucille Lopez. She was an overweight motel housekeeper. She looked like she had made some painful mistakes in life. Every adult in the room looked that way, me included. Most of the adult conversation centered on miserable bosses and how expensive it was to get through life with just the basic things. Like food that didn't make us sick and cars that started. Jerome talked about how he should have stuck with football. Eddie wished he had gone to college. Heather should have become a nurse. Teisha should be teaching kindergarten. Lucille should have married her high school sweetheart, who was a dentist now. I should have been an abortion.

Lucille handed me a paper plate with some pepperoni slices on it. "Three pieces. You're a skinny guy."

I smiled. "Thank you," I said.

"Can I talk to you about something in private?" she asked.

I took a quick bite of pizza. "Sure," I said. "What's going on?"

We ended up in a nearby hallway, on the other side of the mold-and-mildew-infested kitchen, not to mention the cockroaches.

"Dwight's father rapes me," she said. "I can't live this way anymore."

"Are you married to him?"

Lucille shook her head. "We never married," she said.

"Have you told the police?"

Lucille shook her head again. "He says he'll kill Dwight. I believe him. He's not right. He'll kill me, too."

"What can I do?" I asked her.

"You're a lawyer."

I wondered how it felt to be Lucille Lopez. Like a goddamned prisoner with nowhere to run. I stomped on a cockroach that had darted out of the bathroom. "You need to get a new life," I said. "You need to get you and your son out of this mess."

"How?"

"There's no one who can help you? Family?"

"Dwight and I have nobody," she said. "Just Teisha and Jerome. And Jerome doesn't want to kill anybody again."

"You know, if not the police, we need to get the courts involved," I said. "Maybe we can figure out a way for you to get into a shelter. I'm just thinking out loud."

"Whatever you think," Lucille said. "I just don't want to be killed."

I nodded. "Neither do I," I said. "I think we should get Child Protective Services involved. Yeah, that needs to be done. If anyone catches wind that you're doing nothing to protect Dwight, he'll be taken away from you. Yeah, let's get CPS involved. That's the best thing to do. You'll be put into a protective shelter."

"It'll be safe?"

"It'll be safe enough. I mean, the safest option. There's really no other option."

"Will you be my lawyer?" Lucille asked.

"CPS will give you a free lawyer," I said.

"I don't want one of those free lawyers. They don't give a shit about nobody," she said. "They're not going to fight."

She was right. I had a case a few years back where the assigned social worker had done her best to kidnap two blonde-haired, blue-eyed boys from their parents. At first, I couldn't believe my ears what the parents of the twin boys were telling me about their case. All involved social workers were doing their best to kidnap their sons from them by outright lying, fantastic fabrication, all under oath.

Nick and Gabrielle Wasserman had come to my Pasadena law office. "What is the purpose behind all this?" I asked them. "I mean, what's the point?"

Nick Wasserman was an unattractive, balding man with thick-lensed glasses perched atop a large, bulbous nose. "Blonde and blue-eyed boys sell for the most money on the black market," he answered matter-of-factly.

I nodded. I didn't believe a word of what he had just said. "Hmm. Okay." Sure.

Gabrielle Wasserman was the exact opposite of her husband. Long, light-brown hair cascaded softly down to the middle of her back. Angular facial features and a lithe, dancer-like frame were her hallmarks. "I know you don't believe us," she said. Her sultry voice sounded like she could easily gain employment as a telephonic sex worker. She and Nick didn't go together. At least not based on looks. Soon, I learned Nick was an actual member of Mensa who worked for NASA. Gabrielle had to have been attracted to his mind. Sometimes, that's how it goes.

"I don't know what to believe," I said. "Lawyers are always the last to know the truth. Clients lie."

"Look, we're not lying," Nick said.

ADDICT'S WAY

"How'd you guys meet?" I asked.

"I used to be a dominatrix," Gabrielle said. "Nick was a client."

My mind summoned a visual of Gabrielle dressed for work, involving red stilettos and a black whip.

"It's not what you think," Nick said.

"It rarely is," I said. "Anyway."

"I'm surprised you don't know about any of this," Nick said. "It's all over the place, Mr. Panelli. It's very prevalent. You can Google it."

"You'll be amazed," Gabrielle said. "It'll blow your mind. I can't believe it myself."

"Yes, I know social workers can get a bit overzealous at times," I said. "I just don't know if it's to sell children on the black market."

Nick looked at Gabrielle. "He's not going to help us if he doesn't believe us."

"I'm listening, Nick," I said.

"Do you know the societal role Planned Parenthood plays?" Nick asked.

"Abortions."

"And much more," he said.

"Okay," I said.

"They have agents who kidnap newborns so they can be ground up into mulch and eaten with tortilla chips by Satanic cults," Nick answered.

"Kind of like a human hummus," Gabrielle said.

I gazed out the window. My office had a pleasant view of the Pasadena foothills. On a clear day, I could see both Catalina and the Rose Bowl from my window, depending on which way I looked. Those were the days, eating lunch, having drinks in Old Town, and stealing off to Santa Anita Racetrack whenever I wanted. The money was flowing back then, and so was the scotch. Those were the days, my friend, we thought they'd never end.

Nick and Gabrielle's story was too fantastic to understand sober. Magic mushrooms should be sold in vending machines. I wanted to jump out the window or disappear. The mentally ill frighten me. You never know if you're going to be their next bloodletting. I had no idea what these two had on their mind. They both seemed way off.

"That's not what they want to do with our sons," Gabrielle explained. "Our sons, they want to sell them on the illegal market to pedophiles. That's what this is all about, Mr. Panelli."

"Peter," I said. "You can both call me Peter."

"Will you help us?" Nick asked. "We have money, Peter."

Among lawyers, money is a 4-letter word because it often makes lawyers take cases they shouldn't take.

"What would be your retainer, Peter?" Gabrielle asked.

"Do you have the case file with you?" I asked.

"We can get it to you, no problem," Nick said.

"There's no problem with me handing you sixty thousand dollars cash right now, is there?" Gabrielle said. "I want a lawyer on the case."

Nick and Gabrielle became clients on the spot. I was able to keep their family intact. I learned along the way that Child Protective Services could be a corrupt, destructive machine without any real oversight in place. Even some of the judges seemed to be out of touch with what was really in the best interests of the children. Some of them were on the take, I sensed.

I told Lucille Lopez, "I'm just not in a position to take on a case for free. I mean, I need money right now. I didn't walk into this place with wads of cash in my pockets."

"Do you like orgasms?" Lucille asked me.

"I like double-bacon cheeseburgers," I said. "I don't know how to answer such a question, Lucille."

"I'm serious," Lucille said. "I have a niece who's a stripper. She turns tricks when she's not at the club. She's twenty-one and gorgeous. She dabbled with porn for a little bit, but there was too much cocaine on the set. Tall, thin, big tits, and shaved pussy. You'll like her."

"Are you wearing a wire, Lucille?" I said.

"I'm serious as a heart attack, Mr. Attorney," she said. "That's how I can pay you, for real."

"No," I said. "I'll at least help you get the case started."

"You're a good man, Mr. Attorney. Your wife is lucky," Lucille said.

"No."

"I'm just desperate, you know," Lucille said. "I don't know what to do. I'm sorry if I freaked you out. I'm not myself right now."

"It never happened," I said. "I'll help you as much as I can."

"I'm an awful person," Lucille said.

"You're not awful."

"Do I need to sign anything?" Lucille asked.

"Lucille!" Teisha screamed out from the living room. "Time to sing Happy Birthday!"

We walked back into the living room.

"Before we sing Happy Birthday, Dwight is going to lip-sync his favorite song for us," Lucille announced.

Everyone gathered around Dwight. Children made an inside circle. Adults made an outside circle. Lucille walked over to the nearby boombox underneath the card table with the cake on it. Play was pressed, and Dwight, in the middle of both circles, started lip-syncing and happily dancing. 'We Are the World' reverberated through the house. Dwight was dressed in Michael Jackson garb, even wearing the signature silver glove on his right hand. He was all smiles, nothing but joy and happiness. Everybody joined hands. Alison was MIA.

Dwight bowed like a Broadway star. Everybody clapped. He had put on a good show. He had practiced. Art takes discipline.

"Everybody, I have an announcement to make!" Jerome shouted.

Everyone looked his way: "Attorney Peter and his lovely wife, Attorney Alison, they're going to stand up to the Trubbles for us. Be right here tomorrow night at eight o'clock. They're going to explain the entire process to us. There's nothing to be afraid of anymore. We now have some firepower on our side."

Everybody clapped. We sang Happy Birthday to Dwight. He was given the first piece of cake. "Ooh, this tastes yucky, Mommy."

Lucille grabbed Dwight's plate and took a forkful. "This cake is as stale as a breadcrumb. This tastes like frosting on cardboard," she said. "This was done on purpose. This should have been thrown away, but that Trump-loving cracker sold it to a Black person instead. I'm going to get that kid fired. This is unacceptable."

"Yeah, this is unacceptable, Mommy," Dwight mimicked.

"See you tomorrow night at eight o'clock!" Jerome yelled my way as I was disappearing into our bedroom.

| 8 |

At the eight o'clock meeting, Jerome suddenly announced to everyone he was going to get his shotgun from the trunk of his car.

"Jerome, settle down," Teisha pleaded.

Jerome was not going to be easily persuaded by Teisha: "Have some self-respect, woman!!" he snapped. "That crackhead nigger isn't getting away with this!!"

Alison had just told everyone their rent had been getting paid by grant money since the first day they had moved in. John Trubble had been illegally pocketing their cash payments every single month for years. Alison had made all this unbearably clear. Legal pad on her lap, a pen in her hand, she was sitting next to me on the broken couch.

"Did John ever give any of you receipts for the rent money you gave him?" she asked the slumlord tenants.

Jerome violently shook his head. "No, man. Some bullshit about the IRS. John said something about not wanting to pay taxes."

"That's why some months when we don't have the money to pay, he'll just let it slide," Teisha said. "That's why he doesn't ever push it."

"Because the grant money pours in every month!!" Jerome snapped. "I'm grabbing my fucking shotgun!! John Trubble is a dead man!!"

"Not yet, Jerome," Teisha said. "You, of all people, don't need any police."

"I just don't want any of this to backfire on us. I don't want any of us out on the streets with nowhere to live," Eddie said. "That's all I'm saying tonight."

"Nobody will be out on the streets," Alison said.

Jerome stood up and began moving around like a preacher intent on swaying the congregation to his point of view: "I'm sorry I got heated, everybody. But I'd rather be out on the streets than pay money to live in filth like this," he said. "We need to draw a line in the sand. Are we animals or human beings? I need to see hands."

Everyone raised their hands. Then Alison sprang into action. "I need to meet with all of you, separately and privately," she said. "How about we use the den on the other side of the house? I'll start with Heather and Eddie."

"How are we going to pay for this?" Eddie asked.

"It's not that kind of case," Alison said. "You don't have to worry about money, Eddie."

Alison went to grab her portable printer from our bedroom. Jerome and I walked outside into the backyard. You could hear the hum of the city, but you couldn't hear the real city. You couldn't hear the knifings, the rapes, the murders, the prayers being said in vain – but you could hear a constant, dull, sad hum. Sadness infiltrated the white noise the way it does a funeral for a toddler.

In the backyard, Jerome and I were standing in a certifiable junkyard. There were old cars and several mounds of decade-old trash. It was an amusement park for various rodents and oversized rats. There was a landfill-like stench. Like rotting eggs and rotting apples.

"Man, Mr. Attorney, I don't know," Jerome said. "I think I dug myself another grave a few weeks ago."

"What's going on?" I asked him.

"You don't want to know, but you need to know," he said.

"Okay, what's happening?"

"I was at this party in Granada Hills," Jerome began. "There was an amazing-looking woman from Guatemala there. I'm talking about Victoria's Secret-type beauty. Kind of like your wife."

"Yeah," I said.

"I'll get straight to it," he continued. "She drank so much that she ended up being carried off by three people into one of the bedrooms. I saw them take her there. She was basically under anesthesia, out-cold."

I already knew what had happened. "And what happened?"

"I walked into the room and had sex with her."

"You mean you raped her."

"Yeah, man, she didn't move," Jerome said. "I used to do that to my college girlfriend, who was an alcoholic. But she was cool with it. She knew. But this woman, she didn't know."

"Did anyone see you go into the room?"

"I'm not sure," Jerome said. "But someone walked in on us. I didn't see them. The door immediately slammed shut after they said, 'Beautiful.' A man's voice."

"He doesn't know what he saw," I offered. "He saw two people making love."

"That's right."

"When did this happen?"

"About three weeks ago," Jerome said. "Should I just sit tight?"

"Yeah," I said. "Just hope it goes away. Do not do anything. Wait it out."

"Not a word to Teisha," Jerome said.

"I can't. I won't. I wouldn't."

"What the fuck is wrong with me?"

Off in the distance, a police siren chirped loudly, crazily. Like a rabbit being eaten by a pack of coyotes. That's what went through my mind.

Jerome pulled out a crack pipe and took a hit. He blew out the white smoke very slowly so that most of it made its way up to his brain. I knew the drill. I remember those days. Psychotic paranoia eventually stopped them for me.

"Now, Mr. Attorney, what is going on with you?" Jerome asked. "You pull up to a crack house in a brand-new Lincoln Navigator with a dime for a wife."

"I fucked-up my entire life with a gambling addiction. That's what's going on with me," I said.

I tried to find some comfort in the humming sound of the City. I couldn't find any. Somewhere on planet Earth, someone was committing suicide this very second. Also, someone had just climaxed. So there.

"I know a lot about prison," Jerome said. "You're in the worst kind. You can't escape your mind. It's solitary confinement 24/7. That's the worst."

A rat scurried from one mound of trash to the next. I'm sure it was happier than I was.

"I have zero peace of mind," I said. "I've never had any real self-confidence. I never thought I was going to achieve very much.

That's how I've been living my life. When I turned 30, I said to myself, 'This is the decade to get your shit together.' I said the same thing when I turned 40. Then when I turned 50. I didn't say shit this year when I turned 60."

Jerome took another hit. "You mean, you never realized you were white, and the world was your oyster?"

"How come you don't get paranoid?"

"I just don't," he said. "I guess I'm blessed."

"The paranoia became psychotic for me," I said.

He nodded. "You can't smoke crack and do life. It's not like pot. You can't smoke a bunch of crack and then pour out pancake batter onto the grill at IHOP. That's why I don't do it very often." Jerome quickly looked down at the concrete slab we were standing on. He began furiously stomping on something with both his shoes. It was as if his life depended on killing it, whatever it was. "Oh, shit, look at that!" Jerome said. "Fucking son-of-a-bitch!"

"What the hell!?"

"A goddamned scorpion!" Jerome had stomped it into something that now looked like an alien jellyfish. "If my baby dies from a scorpion sting, it'll be game over, man," he said calmly. "I'll kill Ann, Bill, and John Trubble with my own fucking bare hands."

ADDICT'S WAY

Suddenly, I thought about an era from my teenage years. Sometimes, we'd all drive through Beverly Hills together. We'd get high on weed and look at all the mansions and proclaim our dreams to one other, to the world.

I was going to be a famous writer, a combination of John Updike, Charles Bukowski, and John Fante. Jeff Stakee, may he rest in peace, was going to own a restaurant franchise. Steve Kahn was going to be a famous artist. Mike Cabraloff was going to own liquor stores. Jeff Mook was going to inherit millions from his parents. All of us had grown up in prosperity, but all of us had ended up with nothing. Except for Phil Italiano. He ended up with a pension from the Riverside Sheriff's Department. The only one of us who wasn't a tortured soul.

Alison stuck her head outside the sliding-glass door: "How's it going, guys?"

"Fine," I said. "Jerome just killed a scorpion."

"Sometimes, they make their way inside the house," Jerome said. "Be careful."

Alison was in lawyer mode and wasn't fazed by the scorpion, even though insects usually frightened her beyond belief. "I need the password to your laptop to prepare some retainers," she said.

"The year you were born followed by the year Nat was born," I said.

Before I finished telling her, she had already walked back inside.

"She's a certifiable beauty, Mr. Attorney," Jerome said. "Thousands of people would switch places with you. You just need to figure a few things out."

"Yeah," I said.

"Fear is your driving force," he said. "If I may be honest, you are a frightened man."

I nodded. "Of everything."

"You fear everything is bullshit."

I shrugged. "It is, isn't it?"

Jerome stared off into the distance at the slow-moving lights on the freeway.

"You know, when I was in prison," he said. "I met some incredibly wise people, believe it or not. I'll never forget one of them. Robert Johnson. He was a wise, old Black man doing time for a series of armed robberies. He knew why life was a broken mess for a lot of people."

"I'm sure you did."

"To him, the world was a stage. There were too many actors playing the wrong parts, though. Accountants who should be poets.

Lawyers who should be playwrights. Factory workers who should be philosophers. You need to find your right place, he'd tell me."

I nodded. "Yeah, a while ago, a therapist told me it's wounded-childhood stuff. She said I'm having trouble forgetting things I can't remember."

He nodded knowingly. "You just described every Black person in America. You know that?"

I knew what he meant. "Yeah."

"I learned more about life in twenty years of prison than I would have learned from any university," Jerome announced. "Mr. Attorney, it's time for you to revolt against yourself. You need to rise up against all your demons and become the person you can still become. Your life matters."

Alison stuck her head outside again. "What do you think about Intentional Infliction of Emotional Distress?" she asked me.

"At least. There's a few more," I said.

"This is exciting," she said. "Bye."

"She's a special person, isn't she?"

"Yes," I answered.

"Then give her the life she deserves," Jerome instructed. "Only massive action is going to get you out of this mess. Thinking and over-analyzing lead to psychiatric care. That's what happens in solitary confinement."

Alison stuck her head outside one last time. "All the retainers have been signed," she said. "Jerome, Teisha signed for the both of you."

Jerome nodded. Alison slid shut the sliding-glass door.

"I can't wait to see the looks on their faces," I said to Jerome.

"Stopping crack is on my to-do list," Jerome said.

"I know it is," I said. "You have a baby boy."

"You're right," he said. "I need to shatter this crack pipe before it shatters my life."

"When?"

"Before it's too late," Jerome answered.

"I quit cold turkey," I offered.

Eddie walked outside. "Hey, Jerome, do you have a few rocks you can front me until I get myself to an ATM? The powder's not working tonight."

A shooting star disintegrated in the night sky like a lazy, beautiful firework. A rat jumped up like a flying fish. Jerome handed Eddie a few rocks of crack.

| 9 |

"I don't want to get out of bed today," I told Alison.

"All right, let me just get some stuff organized," she said. "I'm going over the slumlord case."

"I need therapy. I need meds. I'm not well."

Alison looked up from her papers. She nodded. "Yeah, you need help. The car crash made you different. You're struggling."

"Yeah, I called my mother yesterday. All she had to say was Steve Harvey was living in his car, and he made it. Was Steve Harvey living in his car with a fucking brain injury, you fucking idiot!?! My family's so fucking stupid!"

"I'll make you an appointment with Scripps," she said. "Who are these people? I've never seen people like your family. 'Hello, your son is really struggling. His forehead cracked a windshield. Hello.'"

"It's all because I'm adopted. Do you think my fucking sister would be treated this way if the circumstances were the same? Fuck that. Fuck them."

We went back to sleep. We didn't wake up until early evening.

I saw that an envelope had been slipped under the door. I picked it up. There were three hundred-dollar bills inside. And there was a yellow Post-It note stuck on the top bill: "Like I promised you, Eddie."

I held the bills up for Alison to see. "Food money," I announced. "It's from Eddie. This week's profit. I told you."

"All right," Alison said. "Hand it over."

I put the money back inside the envelope. I reluctantly handed it over because I needed some walking-around money.

"Okay. I'm hungry. Where should we eat?" I asked.

We decided on the El Mexicali Café, just a few miles away. When we were waiting for our food, Hurricane Alison was in full force: "You're a frightened 9-year-old little boy," she started in on me.

"Yeah, that's what you said. Can't we just have a nice dinner?"

"I agree with what your therapist told you. We all stop growing emotionally at the point of the spiritual wound."

"Okay."

"You need to turn the 9-year-old boy into a man."

"Fish can't climb trees," I said.

Our food came.

"I want a margarita," I announced.

"Of course, you do."

"I'm an awful person because I want a margarita?" I said.

Alison took a bite of her taco that she had smothered with green sauce. "I didn't say that," she said. "The sauce isn't too hot. I think it'll be okay for you."

I ordered a pitcher of strawberry margaritas.

"You'd better help me draft the complaint," she commanded.

"I said I'll help you. Can I just eat?"

Alison was relentless. "No," she said indignantly. "What are you going to do about all your messes?"

No, dinner had not been served with a side of peace of mind. Yes, she had the right to be angry. Life for me has always been one big knotted, tangled ball of yarn, which I've always been unable to untangle. Life is calculus. I barely know arithmetic. I'm a lawyer, which is a laughable camouflage for one's mediocrity. I never know what I'm doing.

"I need to get enough money together for bail," I said.

"You need to clear that up, A-SAP."

"I will."

"That's what you've been saying."

"Can I just eat and drink a few margaritas?" I asked. "Can you take a break from being yourself?"

"It's been knocked down to a misdemeanor by the judge herself," she continued. "But you still need to appear and deal with it."

"How do you know?"

"I ordered the case file."

"Is anything private?"

"No, you're married," she said.

I sighed. "To you."

I wrecked my car seven more times after the May 2016 car crash, with the seventh time resulting in a hit-and-run charge. Six of the seven crashes did not involve other cars. One time, in a Costco parking lot, I backed up into a fire hydrant that was 50 yards behind me. The misdemeanor matter happened on the drive back from the Las Vegas film festival. The night before, I had been drugged by a group of unsavory people. I woke up the next day at almost midnight after having slept over 24 hours. All my cash and my cell phone had been stolen. I had no idea how out of my mind I was on the drive back home. Allegedly, I caused a car crash and took off. I remember little. My family laughably assumed I had become a hopeless drug addict, suddenly slamming into cars, and fleeing accident scenes.

Alison wouldn't let up on me. "We need to get to the Victorville Courthouse sooner than later," she said.

I said nothing. I was enjoying the food. It was good, with a homemade taste. Our server was friendly and always smiling. There was catchy background music. It was soothing and rhythmic. I felt comfortable and safe, trying to forget my current fortunes. I was enjoying the brief break from the crack house. I poured myself some more margarita.

I stared out the window, looking at the boulevard. It was full of several homeless people, the kind with their life's belongings in a stolen shopping cart. I wondered if it would ever get that bad for me.

Alison's cell phone beeped. She grabbed it out of her purse. "Great," she said, looking down at it.

"What?" I asked.

"I got a referral for a psychiatrist for you. I put in the request this morning. That was so quick. Great."

"Scripps?"

"Yes."

"Who?"

"Dr. Guessner."

"Where? Del Mar?"

Alison shook her head. "No, right here, in Indio."

I gulped some margarita. "Indio? Who in their right mind sets up any kind of practice in Indio?" I asked. "Yeah, I'll be sitting in the waiting room with street whores, meth heads, and emotionally-troubled gang members?"

"And you'll be the emotionally-troubled lawyer," Alison said.

"All right, fine."

"How about some flan?"

"When?"

"Right now. I'm craving it."

"No, the appointment."

Alison gulped some water. "Thursday," she answered. "That hot sauce is hot all of a sudden."

"Yeah, it's called hot sauce."

Soon, a plate of flan was in front of her.

"I'm not giving up the dream," I said.

"Yeah, the dream," she said. "Why can't I walk into a bookstore and buy one of your novels right now?"

"Go to hell," I said.

"All right. I'm sorry I said that," she said. "But why, all of a sudden, this renewed passion for writing? You need to start practicing law and bringing in some money for the household."

"The renewed passion is because I'm going to die soon," I said. "You're just like my parents. Fuck my dreams."

During my senior year in high school, my three short stories earned second place, third place, and an honorable mention in the school's creative writing contest. My story, The Darkside of the Earth, placed second. It was a story about a man whose car had broken down on the side of the road, and no one would stop to help him. Winners were announced at a banquet. My parents were there. My father announced on the drive home that it had been the saddest night of his life: "Ray Dominguez is going off to Harvard to study medicine. What are you going to do, order Chinese take-out and walk around with ink-stained fingers in some flea-bag apartment with greasy hair?" Even though my life's purpose had just been confirmed, I felt like a complete failure that night. Fuck you, Dad.

Two years later, I announced to my family that I was no longer interested in becoming a novelist. I became a closet writer. I'd share no dreams with my family ever again. They'd only mock them. "Get a real job, Peter," my sister said about my wanting to become a writer. Forty-two years later, it was now time to skate on the rings of Saturn. Fuck everybody.

"You're so mid-life, Peter," Alison said.

"Yeah. Fuck chasing whatever it is that feeds our souls."

"Do you want some flan?" Alison asked. "It'll make you feel good. You need to eat more carbs."

"Yeah. Carbs. Carbs are the secret to happiness."

When we got back to the crack house, there was a ruckus out in the hallway after Alison had left our bedroom to throw away some trash. I was still in the bedroom when it began. I darted out into the hallway. Heather was wearing only the top part of a karate outfit. All her legs and most of her ass were visible to anyone whose eyes ventured that way. "You're a stupid bitch," she said to Alison. "Didn't you see my signs in the refrigerator?"

"I saw your signs," Alison said. "I moved some of your stuff to make room for some of ours."

"You ask permission."

"No."

"You'd better!" Heather snapped.

"You're a gang-banging lowlife!" Alison snapped back.

"Eddie!" Heather yelled.

Soon, all four of us were out in the hallway.

"What the hell's happening?" Eddie asked.

"You couldn't hear?" Heather asked him.

"I had my headphones on," he answered.

"This bitch moved our food to make room for hers," Heather said.

"Jesus, Heather," Eddie said.

"I see the way you look at her. Do you want to fuck her, Eddie?"

Heather took off the karate outfit top. Now she was completely naked. "Isn't this good enough for you, Eddie? Don't you like my shaved pussy?"

Heather's young body looked like smooth rubber, not a wrinkle anywhere, and symmetrical.

"Have you been drinking?" Eddie asked her.

"Tell her she needs to ask for my permission before she moves anything in the refrigerator," Heather said. "Stand up for me, Eddie."

Eddie rolled his eyes. He shook his head. He looked down at the ground. He slowly blew out some air. He looked at Heather. "Come on," he said.

"I'm not asking you for permission to do anything," Alison said. "This isn't Cellblock 32."

"Can't we all just get along?" I said. Long live Rodney King.

"What the hell, Heather?" Eddie said. He just stood there. He slowly shook his head some more. Heather quickly disappeared into their bedroom. The karate outfit top was on the hallway floor. Eddie picked it up.

"We're cool?" I said to him.

"Yeah," he said.

Back in our room, I asked Alison why she had been so brave. "I knew you were standing there with your knife in your pocket," she said.

"I think I'll only use it on myself," I said.

"Are you in a sexual mood?" Alison asked.

"Not in this slum," I said. "Are you kidding?"

"Good."

A little later, there was a meek knock on our door.

"Yes?" I asked. I didn't open the door.

"It's me, Eddie. Peter, can you meet me out in the living room?"

"Okay. I'll be right there."

Eddie was sitting at one of the flimsy card tables. I sat down across from him.

"She goes crazy a couple of days before her period," he said.

"It's demoralizing, isn't it?" I asked.

"It steals your spirit," he said. "Anyway, I want to end up handing you five hundred dollars instead of three hundred dollars."

"All right. How?"

"I need you to come with me to meet my new source."

"Eddie, I don't know you from Adam."

"I get it, man," Eddie said. "I'm not a narc, man. That's not my style, man."

"All right. Okay." I was satisfied. I believed Eddie. I made it back to our bedroom.

Alison asked, "What was that all about?"

"Hormones," I said.

"I'll use your knife on her myself."

"I'm afraid you'll use it on me."

"Yeah," she said. "You were a complete mess at the restaurant tonight."

"Yes, it was such a relaxing dinner," I said. "Where are my leftovers?"

"In the refrigerator," she said. "That's what caused all the mayhem. I had to make room."

"All right," I said. "I'll get some later."

I curled up on my mattress. I could hear the crickets outside our window. I held my arms tight against my chest. I closed my eyes. Fuck.

| 10 |

There was a maniacal look in his eyes. John Trubble had pointed a shotgun directly at my face.

"What the fuck, John!!" I yelled at the top of my lungs. I wanted to send up a flare: I hoped Eddie or Jerome would hear the chaos.

I kept yelling: "What the fuck is wrong with you, John!?! What the fuck are you pointing a shotgun at my face!?!"

Alison was playing dead on her mattress, not moving. I could hear her breathing. It was the restricted breathing of a frightened person.

I wanted to lunge at John and wrestle the gun away from him. Then I wanted to shove the end of it up his anus. Then I wanted to pull the trigger. Then I wanted to see his insides, feces splattering everywhere. Then I wanted to piss a stream of urine into his mouth. Of course, I did nothing like that. No director was yelling, "Action!"

"You and Alison need to get the fuck out of here!!" John screamed at me. "You need to go back to living in your fancy car!!"

"Fuck you, John!! Kill me!! I don't care!! Put me out of my misery!!" I screamed.

John's eyes widened. All the features on his face slowly fell, like a clump of wet clay sliding down a wet wall. "What the hell is wrong with you?" he said, as if asking himself

Jerome calmly walked into the room with his shotgun. He loudly pumped it. John's eyes, still looking at mine, widened.

"Don't move a muscle, John," Jerome said. He pressed the shotgun's barrel at the base of John's skull. "Nobody is going anywhere, John," he said. "Slowly give your gun to Mr. Attorney. You're dead if you try anything stupid, John."

All the rageful enthusiasm had left John's face. "All right," he said. "All right."

John slowly handed me the shotgun. Then he raised his hands in the air. I put the gun in the space between my mattress and the wall.

"Turn around, John," Jerome said.

John turned around. Alison still hadn't moved a muscle. I was hoping I'd get to see John's death. I didn't like him from day one. If Jerome did pull the trigger, I sensed he'd be saving John the effort of suicide. When I met him in the church, something seemed wrong with him. John handed me the shotgun. "I'm sorry, Mr. Attorney," he said.

Jerome kept his shotgun poised for action. "Out in the living room, John," he said. "You, too, Mr. Attorney. We need to get to the bottom of a few things, don't we, John?"

"Okay," he said. "Yes."

ADDICT'S WAY

We sat at one of the flimsy card tables. Jerome held his shotgun across his lap, the barrel pointing toward the backyard. John appeared nervous and sweaty.

"What the fuck is going on, John!?" Jerome barked. "Are you high!? Are you out of your mind!?"

John exhaled heavily. He slowly shook his head. "There's a lot of shit," he said.

"What's with the shotgun, John!?" Jerome said sternly.

"Everything's a shit fest," John said.

"What have you been doing with all the cash you've been stealing?" Jerome asked. "There was no need for you to collect rent from any of us."

"I need a lawyer," John said.

"We're not the police, John," Jerome said. "This isn't 48 Hours."

"Are you just taking the money for yourself?" I asked.

John looked at me. His eyes were twitching about frantically. He nodded. "Yeah," he said. "My mother's going to kill me. Bill will go ballistic. So will Pastor Ricky. I'm dead."

Jerome looked my way. I could tell he eventually wanted my assessment and involvement. "Is it drugs or gambling, John?" I said.

John's breathing was suddenly labored. "It's crack and meth," he said. "I've gone off the rails of a crazy train."

"Ozzie Osborn. You fucking junkie," Jerome said.

"I need help, man," John said.

"You're not going to collect another penny of rent from anyone," Jerome said. "And you're going to pay back every single penny."

"I need help," John whimpered.

"I've seen your memorabilia collection," Jerome said.

"Take all of it," John said. "I can't go back to jail."

"We'll figure something out, John," I said.

"Get out, John. Go home, John," Jerome said. "I'll keep your shotgun safe for you."

Later in the afternoon, Alison announced she wanted to adopt three children. "I just don't think it's going to happen naturally," she said.

"I thought we were going to do the procedure."

"The Catholic church says no," she said.

"A procedure that can bring life into the world. The Pope's against that?" I said. "I understand abortion, but why in-vitro?"

"We just need to adopt," she said.

"Okay," I said.

"Well, wait, we can't," she said.

"Why not?"

"You have a warrant out for your arrest," she said. "It'll surface in the background check. Peter Panelli, fugitive."

"All you want to do is abuse and belittle," I said. "I'm hungry. I'll be out in the living room eating the leftovers. 'Table for one, please.'"

"Hey, maybe, Heather will let you use the microwave," she said. "But you'd better ask her first."

When evening finally rolled around, I went for a walk. Poverty and graffiti were apparent. I started kicking a Red Bull can down Monroe Street, one of the main drags. All I wanted to do was write. I wanted to write ten thousand pages a day to make up for lost time.

I wondered if piping loud classical music into all cities across America could help us be better people. Could you kill someone, or beat your wife, if Louis Armstrong's What a Wonderful World was blasting in the background? Could you cheat to Ed Sheeran's Perfect or Andrea Bocelli's More? Indio could use some piped-in Mozart. The world could.

I made my way to a Circle K. I gave a bare-footed homeless man by the gas pump two dollars. I wondered if his mother had ever kissed his toes. I felt a long night ahead. I wanted a bottle of scotch. Circle K didn't sell scotch. I ended up with a bottle of red wine.

The cashier was a cheap-looking, dirty-blonde thirty-something who looked like she did nails on the side. You could tell she thought she was better-looking than she was. God's gift to below-average men. "Sir, please, don't give money to the homeless that litter our property," she said.

"I'll do what I want," I said.

"You don't know what they cause," she said.

"They aren't pieces of litter," I said. "They're not trash."

I had lost my patience. There's Ann, Bill, John Trubble, people like my sister, and now, this Circle-K malcontent. I wanted to slug her in the mouth.

Out by the gas pumps, a girl about 15 years old with short brown hair, and freckles, came up to me. This is how she had left her house today: tight-fitting white blouse, tight-fitting blue shorts, brown sandals. The length of her legs, the wealth of her breasts, and her camel toe were quite evident. Showing braces, she smiled. "Mister, can you buy something for me?" she asked.

"Beer?"

"Condoms."

I tried not to sound too surprised. I smiled. "To make water balloons?" I said.

She laughed. "You're silly. What do you think?"

"Why can't you just buy them yourself?"

She smacked some bubblegum. "That lady inside said she wouldn't sell them to me," she said.

I shook my head. "Nah."

"We could use one together."

Somewhere in some luxury hotel, someone was listening to classical music with their teenage daughter, but not in Indio.

"You should get yourself a better job," I said. "You're too cute and innocent for this."

She licked her lips provocatively. "I'm not innocent, Mister," she said. "I've been doing this for three years now. Since I was twelve."

I shook my head again. "Your parents must be proud," I said.

"I have no idea who they are," she said. "I live with my grandmother. All she does is drink. You're missing out on some great pussy, Mister. It's shaved."

I had no more energy for this poor soul. I made it back out toward the boulevard. A homeless man with one leg was crawling on the sidewalk. His hair was greasy, and his skin was dirt-caked. His clothes were tattered and soiled. Our eyes met. His were sad. The eyes of a wounded animal caught in a trap.

"Where are you heading?" I asked him.

He pointed up the street with his head. "Subway," he said.

"You need some crutches."

"I had a wheelchair, but I had to pawn it for food."

"Is there still time to get it back?"

He wiped some sweat from his forehead. "Yeah, I've got time still," he said. "But I don't have the money."

"Can you meet me here at the Circle K tomorrow morning?" I asked him.

"You'll help me?"

"I'll help you get your wheelchair back."

"It'll be almost two hundred bucks."

I handed him a twenty-dollar bill. "Take this for now. We'll go to the pawnshop together. I'll see you tomorrow at noon."

He was touched and wanted to cry. "Nobody gives a shit," he said. "You don't know how it feels."

"Yeah, I do," I said. "A lot of people know how it feels."

I kept walking. I had no interest in getting back to the crack house anytime soon.

ADDICT'S WAY

I made my way to a dive bar called Your Uncle. It opened at 6 a.m. It closed at 2 a.m. It was decorated in an awful red-white-and-blue motif like every day was the 4th of July.

I ordered a house scotch on the rocks. The bartender was a tall, pale, ugly, skinny guy with tattoos and piercings. I'm sure he had to pay for sex. He put the scotch down on the counter. I looked around the place. It was full of attractive Latino women. They were all provocatively dressed. All seemed intent on looking slutty. It was obvious they were working in this place instead of the streets. One of them smiled. I smiled back. Then she opened her legs to give me a look at her black lace panties. Then she licked her lips and stared at me with inviting eyes.

I laughed. I turned back to my scotch.

"All of them are working," the bartender said.

"Yeah."

"My uncle's the owner. I think he pays vice," he said. "This place seems off-limits to the cops. They're never here. Not even when we need them."

"What's with the red, white, and blue?"

He shrugged. "My uncle served in Vietnam," he said. "I think that's what it's about." He grabbed a red-white-and-blue towel and started wiping the insides of glasses with it. "Yes, very patriotic. So, what brings you in here?"

"It's a long story."

"I've heard a lot of those. You live around here?"

"No, just passing through. I'm staying at a crack house right now for just a little while."

"Yeah," he said. He laughed. "I've done that before."

I splashed the last of the scotch down my throat. It felt nice and warm. I felt good in this place full of whores, dope fiends, and alcoholics. I needed another drink. I didn't want to go back yet. "One more," I said. "Make it a double."

"Do you want some coke?" he asked.

"Nah, crack brought me to the point-of-no-return years ago."

"That's too bad. It's Peruvian pink, man."

"I wish."

"Are you sure?" he asked again.

"I'll take a rain check."

"You're not really living in a crack house, are you?"

Throughout three more doubles, I gave him the awful highlights of my life story, from my horrible time in the amniotic fluid to now. "My son's written me off, man," I said. "But I don't blame him. He has a multi-millionaire stepfather. I've been a do-nothing, go-nowhere loser my entire life. I guess it was just my fate. I'll die a loser."

He was wiping down the entire length of the counter now with wide swirls. "Hey, don't say that about yourself, man," he said.

"I was supposed to be a writer," I told him. "I drink instead."

"It's not too late."

"It is too late," I said.

He held out a pen for me to take. "There's plenty of napkins," he said.

I took the pen from him. I began writing on a napkin. I spoke what I was writing: "The early waters must have been polluted, tainted, for I have been drowning ever since. What did these early waters hear or see that made them swirl so aimlessly? With destruction as their only star, these waters slithered near and far."

"That's amazing," he said.

I shrugged. "I don't know," I said.

I could feel the goodness of the scotch dissolve all feelings of failure and insignificance. It's no wonder A.A. was formed. There's no paranoia with alcohol. Alcohol is liquid silk that coats your brain with impossible pleasure.

"Can I keep the napkin, man? You might be famous someday."

"Yeah, sure," I said. I laughed. I handed him the napkin. "You can put it inside my coffin."

I slowly walked back to the crack house, paranoid. I knew the streets of Indio weren't safe for a white man.

Alison could tell I was drunk as soon as I walked into our bedroom. "You smell like a brewery," she said.

I fell onto my mattress. "Actually, I smell like a distillery," I said.

| 11 |

I woke up later than had I wanted.

"You're a complete mess, Peter," Alison said.

After being awake for less than three minutes, I already wanted to be non-existent. Eric Clapton said that alcohol was more dangerous than heroin. He's probably right. I wanted to pour some scotch over some Cheerios. Alison was not so marvelous anymore. I no longer saw a future in her eyes. I knew I couldn't make her happy, not after everything I had done. I wanted to be a god that was worshipped by homemakers and bums. All the mediocrity and madness could be traced back to the womb in which I floated, but that didn't matter -- everything was my fault.

"I hate this place with all my heart," Alison said. Never, "Good morning, Peter. How are you?"

We could never even be just mildly content. There was always something wrong, something to complain about. Refrigerators hummed too loudly. Birds chirped too noisily. Freeways could be heard miles away.

"Yeah, this time, I agree with you," I said. "It's disgusting. Finally, we really are living in a disgusting place."

"No, this is just the most disgusting," she shot back.

"I'm still waiting to die in my sleep," I said.

"Today's your appointment with Dr. Guessner."

"I hope he specializes in assisted suicide."

"Yeah, that's the first question you should ask him," she said. "That'll set the tone; it'll let him know what you're all about."

Dr. Guessner's office was on the top floor of a 4-story non-descript business center. It was a clean, well-kept building, but nothing fancy. I imagined the rents were reasonable, like most in Indio. Dr. Guessner himself fits the description of the building. He was an unassuming man who seemed to purposely underdress. He wore a white button-down shirt and black slacks. There was a small, gold yarmulke on top of his balding scalp. He was about forty pounds overweight, all of it in his stomach. He had a round face and a friendly smile that made me feel like he would be on my side. Some shrinks seem intent on wanting to kill you.

Dr. Guessner called me into his office. Alison had handled all the paperwork for me online, so we were able to get right into it. "Describe yourself in one word," he said.

I barely had the chance to sink into the soft, black leather couch. I glanced around a bit before answering. Office walls were a soothing cobalt-blue wall; no pictures or degrees were anywhere. I liked him already.

"Cursed."

"Cursed?"

"No. Compromised."

"All right."

"Actually, possessed."

He nodded. "Go on."

"You want the Reader's Digest version?"

"Any version."

I told him everything. Turned out all the gory details of my pathetic life could be told to a psychiatrist in just under 40 minutes. "We can only keep our insanity a secret for so long," I ended. "Now, everybody knows."

"Everybody knows what?"

"That I'm incapable."

"Of what?"

"Of living life. Of thriving. Of succeeding. Of chasing dreams. Of doing the basics just to get by."

He scribbled. He looked down at his notepad. A yellow legal pad inside a black leather folder. His pen was gold, matching his yarmulke. He glanced at his watch. "I'll see you in three days," he said.

"I don't think we should wait a week." He scribbled some more. His brow was furrowed. He handed me an appointment slip. I'd probably make him write a prescription for himself. "Okay. I'll see you soon," he said. "We might have to become virtual because of COVID-19. I'll let you know. We can set up Zoom."

I took a cab back. Lucille Lopez, and her son, Dwight, were waiting for me in the living room. "He raped me twice since the party," she announced.

We all got inside her car and headed over to Child Protective Services. Dwight was dropped off at the courthouse's daycare center. Juvenile dependency courts are sad places. Sadder than adult bookstores that are being mopped down at 2 a.m. Every parent in such a courthouse is either abusing drugs or their child, or both. Sadness hangs in the air. The only good things that happen in dependency courthouses are adoptions. However, many of those are often the result of the biological parent losing their child to the system because of a heroin or crack addiction. Many times, the child was lost to other parents during the pregnancy.

Lucille's matter had been assigned to an older social worker. Hilda Gomez. In her early 70s, she had a perpetual scowl and a just-going-through-the-motions attitude about her. I didn't like her. I wished we had been assigned a caseworker in her early twenties because the younger ones wanted to save the world and wanted to help. Jaded and bitter, the older ones wanted to destroy the world.

Lucille's office was one of those full-of-shit offices, with plagues and degrees hanging on the walls.

I handed her my card. "I'm Lucille's attorney," I said.

Hilda wanted nothing to do with me. "You know, Ms. Lopez, you are entitled to a free attorney if you qualify," she said.

"I don't want a free lawyer. They care less about me and my son," Lucille said matter-of-factly.

I shot a disgusted glance at Hilda. "Yeah, that's why I'm here," I said. "I'm here to make sure she's not screwed."

Hilda ignored me. "Ms. Lopez, what brings you to my office this afternoon?"

Lucille looked at me. I nodded. "You can tell her," I said.

"I'm being raped by my son's father."

"Have you called the police?" Hilda asked.

"I'd be dead if I did."

"Have you told anybody about this?" Hilda asked.

Lucille nodded. "Just a few."

"They did nothing to help you?" Hilda said.

"Does Teisha know?" I asked Lucille.

"Yeah," she answered.

I remembered what the Wassermans had told me about the mulch made from aborted fetuses. Nobody gets out alive, even if you've never really been alive. Everything about this was wrong.

"Look, cut the condescending crap," I said. "You need to find safe housing for Lucille and her son. You're not going to make her life worse. You don't care about people anymore. You're just waiting for your pension to hit."

Hilda tried to feign competence and empathy. "A lawyer has never spoken to me like this," she said. "I will have you know I take my job very seriously."

"Prove it," I said.

In the parking lot, Lucille said, "You're a good lawyer, Mr. Panelli."

"No," I said. "I've just had it with everything."

Out in the car, Lucille caressed Dwight's cheek. "Mr. Panelli's a lawyer, Dwight. He's going to help you and Mommy," she said.

Dwight looked at me and smiled. The poor kid didn't have a chance. The moment a kid walks through the metal detector of a juvenile dependency courthouse, it's the beginning of the end. It doesn't matter how old they are. Not even the ones in strollers escape the madness. As soon as they make it through the metal detectors, it's game over.

Twenty minutes of bumper-to-bumper traffic had drained me. I struggled to get out of Lucille's car. I had her drop me off just down the road from Your Uncle. I was meeting Eddie there for drinks. It was time to take the cocaine dealing to the next level.

"Keep me posted, Lucille. Bye, Dwight," I said.

I sat at the bar. I ordered a scotch from the same bartender as last time.

"How's it going today?" he asked.

"Shitty," I said. "I was in court. Kind of."

All the workers from last night were here. Most of them tried to catch my eye, but I kept looking away. A man among prostitutes feels like he's famous.

"A lot of people would like to be a lawyer, man."

I poured all the scotch down the back of my throat. An instant coolness settled in on my skin. I could feel goosebumps all over. "Yeah, everyone wants to become a lawyer until they become one," I said.

"You know what I'm saying," he said.

"Yeah, I know."

He poured me another scotch. Evan Williams. A bourbon scotch. I was quickly becoming a fan. "Hey, we might need your help," he said.

"Okay."

"My uncle blew a point one seven the other night."

"That's high," I said. "He's all right?"

"Yeah. He just didn't feel like waiting for the light to turn green," he said.

"We've all done that."

"As soon as he busted through the red, flashing lights and sirens," he finished.

I handed him my business card. "Have him call me," I said.

He looked at my card. "He's a cheap motherfucker, Peter. I just want to be straight with you."

I took a sip. "They're all cheap," I said. "It's not like on television."

Eddie sat down next to me at the bar. He was wearing a white button-down with faded jeans. He took off his Prada sunglasses. He put them on the bar. "I'm sorry I'm a little late," he said. "Heather stuff."

"What do you want?" the bartender asked him.

"I got it, Eddie," I said.

"Just a beer," Eddie said. "I don't care what kind."

The bartender handed Eddie a bottle of Bud Light.

"So, what's up with Heather today?" I asked.

"She's pissed again," Eddie said.

"There's always something," the bartender said.

One of the Latino workers, sitting by herself, started laughing so hard she fell off her seat. "Before careful, Lilly!" the bartender shouted at her.

Lilly was mildly sexy. It was obvious she wore no bra, no panties. Sprawled across the floor, the lips of her shaved pussy glistened in the dim lighting.

"The world is crazy! Especially you!" she yelled at the bartender.

"Lilly looks out of her mind," I whispered.

"Every night," Peter said. "She'll just burst into a fit of hysterical laughter for no reason."

"I admire that," I said.

Eddie's cell phone made a ping sound. He looked at the screen. "We need to head out pretty soon," he said to me. "That was Julio."

Driving to Julio's, Eddie announced, "I can't get it up, man. It happened again."

"Oh," I said.

"Yeah, it's been going on a good three weeks now."

I laughed. "I don't think Heather thinks it's been a good three weeks," I said.

"Ha, Peter."

Eddie stopped at a red light.

"The crack house isn't a very romantic place," I said.

He accelerated through the intersection. "Nah, that's not it," he said.

"Then what?"

"Can I tell you something crazy?"

"Yeah."

"In confidence?"

"Yeah, man. Of course."

Eddie sighed heavily. "A few weeks ago, me and a couple of buddies headed out to the desert to do some mescaline," he said. "We hung out in one of those abandoned shacks in Twenty-Nine Palms."

"Yeah."

"Have you ever done mescaline?"

I shrugged. "Maybe. Probably. I don't know."

"Anyway, on the drive home," he said, "I stopped off at one of those jerk-off parlors and watched some transsexual porn. I said to myself, 'That is my sexual preference.'"

"That's what you said?"

"Yeah," he said. "You should see some of those ladyboys."

"I'll take your word."

"Some of them are prettier than women," he said.

"Well, there's a lot of ugly women," I said.

Eddie took both his hands off the steering wheel. He slammed them back down on it. "Fuck, what is wrong with me?" he said. "Jesus Christ, I'm a mess."

"You're not on Death Row. Take it easy on yourself, man."

"Yeah," he said. "I just thought I might be going crazy or something."

"We're all doing that," I said.

"I don't find men attractive. I want to make that straight."

"I know. No pun intended, right?" I smiled.

Eddie laughed. "I knew you wouldn't trip. I just needed to tell somebody," he said.

"I understand," I said. "I'm not fazed. Maybe you just need to find some Viagra to get back in the groove with Heather."

Julio lived in an upscale trailer park on a golf course. The inside of his trailer looked like a mansion. Elegant décor and furnishings. There was a big-screen television in every room. There were even a couple of chandeliers. Instead of the artwork you'd see in most homes, Julio had pictures of high-definition Goth pornography hanging on the walls. Julio himself looked like a Goth porn star. He was skinny and pale, with tattoos and piercings everywhere. His black hair sported a Catholic schoolboy haircut. The three of us were in the living room, which had ten empty goldfish bowls scattered about. "Thank you for coming, Attorney," he said. "I have friends in the porn industry."

"I see," I said.

"If you want to fuck any of the Goth stars, you just let me know," he said.

"His wife is a dime," Eddie said.

"Still, you let me know," he said to me.

Julio disappeared. He came back with a mound of cocaine on a black plate. He nonchalantly drew out some lines. Like he was getting some chips and salsa ready. He snorted them all very quickly. "Anyone else?" he asked.

"Not right now," I answered.

"Maybe later," Eddie answered. "Beer?"

Julio nodded. "Refrigerator," he said.

Eddie left. He came back with a six-pack of Heineken.

"Do you have any scotch?" I asked.

Julio slowly swung his head toward the room behind him. "There's some in the chest at the foot of the bed," he said. "Eddie, would you?"

Eddie came back with a bottle of Jack Daniels and a short, wide, square glass. He handed both to me. I poured some scotch into the square glass. "Thanks," I said.

Julio took another quick snort of a line. "Attorney, I need you to act as my legal counsel," he said.

"Peter," I said.

"Peter, I need you to be on my payroll."

Eddie twisted open a beer. He took a swig. "So, what's the plan?" Eddie asked.

"We'll get to that," Julio said.

"Okay," Eddie said.

"What do you need me to do?" I asked Julio.

"I usually need help with a lot of stuff from time to time. Drug dealing, drug possession, prostitution, solicitation of prostitution, driving under the influence, and hit-and-run. You name it," Julio said. "Every now and then, some statutory rape."

"You sound like a busy man," I said.

"You'll mostly be helping my friends."

Eddie took a line. He asked me if I wanted one. I quickly shook my head.

"I can bring you a lot of business, Peter," Julio said. "Right now, my best friend is dealing with a solicitation charge. The massage parlor was wired. Sheriffs stormed in as soon as he nodded yes to paying sixty bucks for a blow job."

"All he did was nod?" I asked.

Julio shrugged. "That's what he says."

"Do they have a video?"

He nodded. "Yes. That's what I've been told."

ADDICT'S WAY

I took a gulp of scotch. I winced as I swallowed it down. I handed Julio a business card. "I'll look at the tape and see what the D.A. has in mind," I said.

Julio examined my card. "Bring me a stack of these," he said.

I nodded. I took another gulp of scotch.

"So, Julio?" Eddie said.

"In a minute," Julio said. "I'll be right back."

Julio walked to the far end of the trailer. Then he came back with a ceramic urn in his hand. It was grey. "My grandfather's ashes," he said. "He killed himself."

"Sorry," I said.

"Damn," Eddie said.

"No, my grandmother was a bitch," Julio said. "One day, I think he had had enough. It was either kill her or kill himself. He shot himself watching a Seinfeld rerun during a commercial break. He used to joke that he never bought in bulk because he was suicidal. That's why he'd never go to Costco."

I poured myself another scotch. The liquid was working its magic. It was keeping the awfulness away. I'd make it through another day. Unless I was killed instantly in a car crash on the way home. What if Eddie snapped on the way back to the crack house and wanted to plow into a telephone pole at full speed because he now liked transsexual porn? I doubt I'd be that lucky. "Suicide is painless; it brings on many changes," I said out loud.

"Aren't those some weird lyrics?" Julio said.

Eddie snorted another line. "Maybe the devil gets inside you, man," he said.

Julio took a pinch of his grandfather's ashes from the urn. He put it on the plate. He mixed the ashes with some of the cocaine. He took a deep snort of the grey mixture. "I love you, Grandpa!" he yelled.

I poured myself some more scotch. I couldn't believe where I was.

"Here's what I'm thinking," Julio said. "Peter, I give you twenty-five hundred cash every month to be on call for any of the matters I might have. That'll be just to have you answer the phone."

"That'll be fine," I said.

"I'll give you twenty-five hundred tonight."

"Okay."

"Eddie, you need to be compensated for bringing Mr. Attorney my way," Julio said.

"All right," Eddie said.

"You only have to give me seven-hundred-fifty cash, Eddie, instead of a thousand cash from now on. And I'll give you the same amount of material."

"Thanks," Eddie said. "I can give you seven-fifty right now."

Julio nodded. "All right, let's get the cash stuff taken care of right now."

Julio liked the word cash. Everybody did. Except for the IRS.

On the way back from Julio's, I asked Eddie, "Are there any casinos close by?"

"Yeah, Fantasy Springs," he said. "You want to go?"

"Yeah. Fuck it. Maybe just get a drink."

I bet the entire twenty-five hundred dollars on a single hand of blackjack. I was dealt two jacks. The dealer busted. We left. We headed straight to Eddie's car.

"Let's get the hell out of here, Eddie," I said. "When you win big, bad things can happen in parking lots."

We made it safely to the car without having been confronted by a knife, gun, or prostitute. "I can't believe you're up twenty-five hundred bucks just like that!" Eddie said.

"Actually, I'm down about four million," I said.

| 12 |

I wasted my entire life chasing the impossible dream of becoming a millionaire by betting on horse races. I would have been better off becoming a slave in a cubicle. Ironically, in avoiding paycheck-to-paycheck misery, I became miserable anyway.

I needed to stop thinking. The Goddess of Depression had sent all her demons to me during the night. I needed to skip breakfast, find a liquor store, and get out of the bedroom before Alison started in on me. And that's what I did.

I ended up at a park not too far away, with a bottle of scotch and a paper cup. The liquor-store owner nonchalantly put the paper cup inside the bag. It was done out of habit. He knew why we were buying scotch before noon. It wasn't because our throats were dry.

I sat at one of the park benches, drinking. Soon, an elderly man came up to me. He was dressed in modern skid-row attire. He had a wrinkled face that looked like a gigantic pink prune, from years of sun and alcohol abuse. He looked old and harmless, a shadow of whom he used to be. "You need to get out of this park right now," he said.

"Why? What's going on?"

"This is my turf."

"What does that mean?" I asked.

"It means I'll stab you with a knife if you don't leave right now."

"Thanks," I said. "That'll save me a whole lot of trouble."

"What?" he asked.

I ignored the threat. I filled the plastic cup halfway with scotch. I drank it all down with a single gulp. I could feel the instant relaxation. The old man knew his gig was up. "I won't stab you if you give me three dollars," he said.

I gave him all the change from the liquor store. "Sounds like a deal," I said.

He counted it quickly. He said, "This is six dollars. Do you want some back?"

"No, you can keep it for next time."

"Okay, you're paid in full for next time," he said. "God bless you, soldier."

I smiled. "So, a three-dollar cover fee every time I come to this park?" I said.

He started walking away. "If you'd be so kind to oblige," he said.

"Hey, why are you out here, buddy?"

He shook his head. "I don't talk about that," he said. "See you next time, soldier."

I just sat there, trying not to think. I just listened to the stillness of the early morning, the chirping birds, and the distant traffic. Too much thinking always causes problems. It makes me depressed. I haven't yet mastered the art of controlling my thoughts. They've always controlled me like an abusive cellmate.

Behind me, a sultry female voice softly called out to me: "Hey, Mister."

I turned around. It was a short, thick Native American girl with red hair, wearing nothing but a black bikini. Her left arm was covered in tattoos. So was her right leg. If she had been a flashing-neon sign, "SEX FOR SALE!" would be the words flashing.

"Hi," I said. "What's up?"

"You want a date?"

"No."

"Are you sure?"

"Yeah."

"You would have been number eight-hundred-and-two," she said.

"What do you mean?"

She laughed. "I keep track of all the times I've been paid for sex."

"I'm sure the IRS appreciates that."

"You're funny," she said. "I'd bet you be a good fuck."

"Same to you."

"So, you want to?"

"No," I said. "I meant you're funny, too."

She left. She walked aimlessly toward a school bus that had just pulled into the park's parking lot. Three female teachers and dozens of children got off the bus. The children were laughing and screaming. They were full of sheer joy. They were about 7 years old. They quickly made their way to the sandy playground. It had a swing set, slide, carousel, and monkey bars. Their gleeful laughter made me sad.

I poured some more scotch. A police car sped down the street, sirens blaring. I still took a sip. You could hear a helicopter chopping in the air. The wail of a fire engine was getting closer. Somebody must have let their insanity get the better of them. I pictured police tape, a body bag, and a coroner's van. Yelling, screaming, fighting, crying, madness. Home sweet home. A restraining order would be filed in the afternoon if nobody had been killed.

I poured some more scotch. I remembered I had to be back in a couple of hours to go over the lawsuit against the Trubbles. Alison had set up an early-afternoon meeting with everyone. All the tenants would be there, wanting to know the next move. Eddie and I were supposed to pick up some pizzas. Alison didn't trust pizza delivery. It's a long story.

I still had some time. I poured another scotch. How else could I get through a meeting like that? Alison and I were always butting heads about law as a career and a profession. Alison thought it was noble and wanted to dedicate her life to it. I thought it sucked, and I wanted to surrender my license.

During the two-and-a-half years I couldn't get out of bed after the car crash, I abandoned every case I had been working on. I did not abandon them on purpose. I simply was not of sound mind. I was like a frightened teenage girl who had left her newborn in a trash dumpster. She knew better than to do that but was incapable of doing anything else.

I was unable to answer e-mails, return phone calls, pick up mail, or go to court when we were living in our car in various Walmart parking lots. I couldn't do anything. I felt like I was trapped underwater, and I couldn't swim to the surface. I felt like I was living in a haunted house but too afraid to go outside. Nobody got it.

A friendly German shepherd found me. His tail was wagging. He wanted to play. I didn't have any energy to offer. He reminded me of Nat's dog, Reggie. Nat had to part ways with Reggie when his mother divorced her second husband, the one after me. There was no longer a backyard for Reggie. Nat was devastated. It broke my heart to see his crying face. Nobody understands the relationship between a boy and his dog. It runs deep. If you lose a dog, you'll cry harder than you'll cry for a dead person. People aren't worth tears. Save them for dead pets.

The shepherd held his paw out for me to shake. I shook it. I petted him. I held my face against his. He was a kind soul with kind eyes. He knew who I was. He knew what I was feeling. I shook his paw again. He curled up at my feet for a bit. Then, a cat caught his eye, and he took off running. He disappeared into the distance. I should have run with him. The life of a dog appealed to me.

I slowly walked through the park. Past the other benches, the trashcans, the litter, the dog shit, the empty heroin balloons, the meth needles, the diapers, the condoms, the graffiti, the sleeping bums, the dandelions trying to escape the constant winds tearing them apart. I made it back to the bench. I poured more scotch. I took a sip. I hadn't been in a park by myself in over thirty years. Parks are made for homemakers, bums, English majors, graffiti artists, petty criminals hiding in plain sight, and people who have nothing to do and nowhere to go. Parks were safe havens for misfits. There were no long corridors that led to nowhere.

A shadow poured onto the bench. A pretty high school student took off her backpack and sat down. She was dressed in black denim. She was mostly plain-looking, without any noticeable features. She wore no makeup. Her round eyes were two black saucers. Her ancestry spoke of Native Americans. "You don't mind if I sit here, do you?" she asked.

"No, it's okay."

"I'm glad someone's here today. I never feel safe by myself."

"Yeah."

"I come here to do my homework," she said. "I can't do it at home. It's awful there. My sister's evil."

I took a sip of scotch and pulled it through my teeth.

"Why are you drinking out here?" she asked.

I laughed. "I can't do it at home. My wife's evil," I said.

She smiled. "I'm serious. Why?"

"What are you studying?"

"Just high school stuff. There are no majors in high school, you know."

I smiled. "Yeah, I know."

"You're a good person, aren't you?"

I shrugged. "I don't know," I said. "Dogs and little kids like me, I guess."

"You are."

"How do you know I'm not a serial killer?"

"I can talk to anybody," she said. "All my friends are shy types. They're always telling me to shut up."

"Maybe you should become a talk-show host."

She laughed. "I should."

"Where do you see yourself in five years?"

"My last year of college."

"What major?"

"Undecided."

"That's a major? I wish I would've known that."

She frowned. "Right now, I'm undecided."

"I'm just joking," I said. "I'm still undecided, and I graduated from law school."

"You're funny."

"Sad people are funny," I said.

"I want to be happy."

I took a sip of scotch. "I'll drink to that," I said.

"You're not from around here, are you?"

"No."

"People will bother you. Be careful."

"That happens everywhere," I said. "I will."

"I'd like to become a journalist," she said.

"Then read the New Yorker as much as possible," I advised. "Find your voice. Writing is all about voice. Don't let anybody tell you anything else. It's not about sentences, grammar, and punctuation. It's about voice. It's about staining the pages red with your blood."

Her eyes widened. "You're a writer?"

"Kind of. Not yet."

"What advice would you give? I'm a junior."

"The same thing I told my son," I said. "Happiness doesn't come from mansions and fancy cars. Happiness comes from having the courage to chase your dreams. I wish I had done that. And I had known better."

I sensed her parents had already disappointed her. Teachers and television were raising her intellect without much nutrition. She was hungry for something that might make sense.

"Live with courage," I continued. "Chase your dreams. If you listen hard enough, the gods will tell you your life's purpose. If you ignore the gods, your life will be miserable."

I took a gulp.

"And if you have the soul of a poet, realize happiness will be exceedingly difficult to find. You'll probably live a life of misery if you don't become a poet – if you have that kind of soul."

I took another gulp.

"A poet doesn't mean an actual poet. A poet is someone who feels their pain and everyone else's. A poet is someone who gives a shit about other people. A poet is someone who realizes life is a piece of shit, but they keep trying, they keep loving, they keep thinking, and they keep creating anyway. There are poets, and there is everyone else."

Her eyes widened again. Her features tightened. "Amazing. Okay. I'm Spring."

"Peter," I said. "I hope I'm not bringing you down, Spring."

"Not at all," she said. "No one talks like this to me."

I nodded. I took a sip. I wasn't in the mood for a gulp. Suddenly, things had grown heavy and weary.

"I did not come from a family of poets," I said. "What about you, Spring?"

"My parents work the swing shift at a factory. The same factory. That's where they met," she said. "No one's ever home. There's no one around. The only advice I get is to make sure I don't get pregnant."

"I'm sorry," I said.

Spring looked at her cell phone. "I need to get back in time for sixth period. Maybe I'll see you again."

I threw what remained of the bottle of scotch into a nearby trash can. I called Eddie. It went straight to voice mail.

Then, I called my parents.

"Mom, it's me," I said.

"Hi, Peter. How are you?"

"Okay. I'm not great."

"How's Alison."

"She's okay."

"When are we going to see you guys?"

"I don't know, Mom."

"Please, Peter."

"I don't think you understand, Mom."

"I know."

"You don't know, Mom," I said. "I don't think you know what happened. When I got in that car crash, I was really hurt. Nobody gets it.

The day after the accident, I became impotent for several months. Alison and I were trying to have a baby. How do you think that felt?"

"I know."

"Three days after the accident, we tried to have sex. I fell off the bed right when I was about to climax. Unbearable pain shot through my head. I fell off the bed. Are you listening, Mom?"

"Yes."

"My pituitary axis had been damaged," I said. "Three days after that, I couldn't move. I was paralyzed in bed for two straight days. But all you can talk about is Steve Harvey."

"Okay."

"I went out of my way to tell everybody how bad off I was. I sent Internet links to Dad, Amanda, and Jay. I tried to tell everybody how horrible I was doing. Nobody gave a shit about me and Alison."

"I'm sorry."

"I couldn't get out of bed. I wasn't being lazy. I wasn't being a bum. I had a brain injury."

"I know."

"They just didn't give a shit. Amanda just wants to punish me and Alison. That's all. It's all bullshit."

"I don't know what to do."

"We ended up living in our car for three months!!" I screamed. "Then it was flea-bag hotels!! Now it's a crack house!!"

"I'm praying."

"I'm done," I said. "I'm barely surviving out here. This is a nightmare life."

"I'm sorry. We just didn't know."

"Nobody wanted to know," I said. "I told them everything they needed to know."

"What can be done now to make things right?"

"Some things are unforgivable. I have no family."

"Peter!"

"Goodbye, Mom."

I swiped to the right. I ended the call. I ended everything. Nat would be next.

Suddenly, the children started screaming hysterically. The screams were coming from the playground.

"SOMEONE CALL 9-1-1!!!" a woman screamed. "9-1-1!!! 9-1-1!!!"

I ran to the playground. All the children were screaming. Some of them were bleeding badly on their lower legs and feet. Two of the teachers were tending to them. Another was on her cellphone, screaming: "I DON'T KNOW THE NAME OF THE PARK!!! JUST GET THE PARAMEDICS HERE AS SOON AS POSSIBLE!!! HURRY UP!!! NOW!!! THEY'RE BLEEDING!!!"

I darted to the teachers who were tending to the bleeding children. "What happened!?" I asked.

"SOME SICKO PUT RAZOR BLADES AND NAILS IN THE SAND!!!" one of them screamed.

"HELP US, JESUS!!!" the other one screamed.

Soon, the paramedics and the police came. They eventually got everything under control. Nobody was going to die. But someone would be going to Hell.

Eddie parked in the driveway. "You go on in, Eddie," I said. "I might just sit in the car for a little while if that's cool."

"All right, man."

I handed him all the pizzas.

"Yeah. I'm not going to make it to the meeting. Tell Alison for me."

"What if she wants to know where you are?"

"You can tell her. That's fine."

"Man, what happened today? What's going on with you?"

"I just need to be by myself," I said.

| 13 |

I spent the night in Eddie's car. I was curled up on my mattress now. "I don't know what to tell you," I said.

"I don't know what's going on with you," she said.

Alison was pacing around like a lion, ready to pounce.

"I don't either."

"You know what's going on, Peter. You just don't want to say it. Your male ego."

I sat up. I leaned my back and head against the wall. I exhaled. "I have a brain with two broken legs, two broken arms, and a broken neck."

"What about Dr. Guessner?"

"What about him?" I said. "He's a Jew, but he's not Jesus."

"Did you talk about your brain injury?"

"A little."

"Why not tell him everything?"

"We'll get around to it," I said. "There's other shit going on, Alison."

She slowly sat down on her mattress. Her pain was obvious. "Well, I got everyone to sign the fee waivers last night," she said. "Hey, let's go to the courthouse today. Let's get everything filed. The window closes at four-thirty."

"I have no energy."

"Take a little nap."

"I just woke up."

I forgot my wallet. I had to stand in the public entrance line to get inside the courthouse, which meant I had to empty my pockets, take off my shoes, and take off my belt. I had to hide my pocket knife outside somewhere because it was not allowed inside the courthouse. Anyway, we got the lawsuit filed. Then, we went to a Mexican place in a nearby strip mall with authentic food. Alison was hungry, craving enchiladas.

Our food quickly made its way to our table. I wanted a drink, but the place didn't sell margaritas. Still, it drew a sizable crowd.

"We're all alone," she said.

I mixed my rice and beans and salted them. "I know. Fuck everybody," I said.

She scooped up some salsa with a tortilla chip. "They just don't care," she said.

"Yeah. I mean, who doesn't help someone with a brain injury?"

She looked at all the food. "Everything looks and smells so good."

"This is a lot of food," I said.

"Remember, we can take it home if we don't eat it all."

"And I'm the villain," I said.

"They're narcissists. That's all it is. A lot of people need help for whatever reason. They just didn't want to help us. Oh well. That's them. It's sad, though."

We sat in the restaurant for two hours. We wondered what the future held for two homeless lawyers. One with a brain injury, one with full-body arthritis, and both with no family. "I'm just going to keep praying," Alison said.

Later that night, I talked with Eddie at one of the flimsy card tables. "I've been thinking about you, man. Xanax," he said. "Xanax is the answer. There's no more paranoia with Xanax."

I shook my head. "I can't go there, man. Nah."

Eddie's pupils were dilated. You couldn't tell the color of his eyes. "Just so you know, I have a buddy who can get us any prescription without a prescription," he said. "But yeah, I can have someone serve the lawsuit for us. It's a done deal. Just get me the papers."

I went to our bedroom. I came back with three conformed copies of the lawsuit. I put them on the card table one at a time. "One for Ann. One for Bill. One for John," I said. "They all have to be served individually."

Eddie took all three copies with him. "I'll be right back," he said. He came out of his bedroom with a small stack of different papers stapled together. He handed them to me. "I got these today, man. I need help."

I looked over the papers. They were court papers. I read every word worth reading. I knew the parts that didn't matter. The mother of his daughter wanted full custody, with Eddie having supervised visitation only. And she wanted child support raised. Typical stuff.

I pushed the papers into the middle of the card table. "Did anything happen between you two recently?" I asked.

"I told her that I couldn't handle the drive out to Los Angeles," he said. "I said meeting halfway was only fair. And I told her I couldn't afford much child support on a busboy's salary."

"Anything else?"

"No."

"What did she say to you?"

"She said she understood," he said. "She said she understood that I was a loser. She said she understood that I was a horrible father."

"She just got a new boyfriend, didn't she?"

"How did you know?" he said.

"There's always some bullshit in the background."

"I don't know what to do," he said. "Now she wants me to take a drug test."

"She wants you to disappear, man. She wants to raise your daughter with her new boyfriend, with you completely out of the picture."

Eddie looked worried. "Can that happen?"

"No."

"Can you help me?"

"We'll work something out," I said. "I can't commit myself to a custody battle all the way out in Los Angeles. I'd need to be paid, Eddie. I wish I could help you for free."

Custody battles are rich work. They get in the way of your sleep patterns. All the negative energy hides inside the pages of the case file and oozes into your heart and soul. I'd rather clean sewers.

"I'll take care of you, man," he said. "I'm a nervous wreck, man. I can't believe she wants to take my daughter away from me."

"That's what she wants to do," I said. "She even got herself a Century City law firm."

"Her family is loaded."

"I call them custody wars because they're not merely battles."

Eddie needed to relax. We ended up at a bowling alley. We went to the bar. It was dark and empty. I drank scotch. Eddie drank beer. I told him about all the knifings, murders, and rapes I had seen in family law court through the years.

I shook my head. "It's always the women causing the problems," I said. "Only mothers know how to be good parents, not fathers. According to mothers anyway."

Eddie gulped down the last of his beer. "I'm ready for war," he said. "I'll borrow money, man. Julio will help out. All right, back to the penthouse."

I could tell Eddie was feeling the beers, but we made it back safely without any police contact. We sat back down at the card table for a little bit, mostly talking about nothing. Eddie stared up at the ceiling: "God, with your help, I, Eddie Rodriguez, will become a father my daughter can be proud of. Amen."

I got up from the table. "Amen," I said. "I need to get back to Alison. I wish I could help you for free, man."

Eddie smiled. "So do I," he said.

I fell asleep. I had vivid dreams about horse races, cocaine, and my dead grandmother – until I was woken up by somebody knocking on our door. Who was at the door? Alison left me a note that she had taken a drive to our P.O. Box in Del Mar. I didn't move from my mattress. "Who is it?" I asked.

"Beatrice."

"I don't know anyone named Beatrice," I said. "I'm sorry."

I heard Eddie's door open.

"Beatrice, what's up?" Eddie said.

"Where's Ernesto?"

"In jail."

"I looked through his window. He's here."

"His stuff is, but he's not," Eddie said.

"What happened?"

"He got popped for the reason you came here."

"Oh," she said. "Do you have any?"

"I don't. You know that."

"All right. The powder does nothing for me, Eddie. All right."

"Take care of yourself, Beatrice."

"What about Jamaal?"

"He moved back up to Oakland about two weeks ago. He doesn't live here anymore."

"All right. Bye, Eddie. Tell Heather I might need her to babysit for me next weekend."

I heard Eddie's door close. I heard Beatrice slam the front door on her way out. I shouted to Eddie, "This really is a crack house." He shouted back, "Not at the moment." We both laughed.

An hour later, Alison came home with the mail. Almost immediately, she began pacing back and forth, holding and looking at a legal pad. That was never a good sign. Usually, she used legal pads to compile lists of everything I was doing wrong.

"Well, Mr. Peter Joseph Panelli, the State Bar of California is about to disbar you," she began.

I sat up on my mattress. I wanted to snap my fingers and disappear. "I know."

"You failed to give Richard Stearns a refund."

"Yeah, that asshole. Richard Stearns," I said. After the brain injury kicked in, I abandoned more than a few of my cases. I was out of touch with most of my clients when I was living in Walmart parking lots. Who wouldn't be? I couldn't do much of anything back then. The State Bar can go fuck itself. Like, I'm Michael Avanetti, taking millions from a paraplegic client. Like I'm that crook, Tom Girardi, husband of that fake bitch, Erika Jayne, who stole millions from burn victims. "Fuck everybody! It's such bullshit!" I snapped.

"You still have time to fight this."

"I can't fight it," I said. "I can't do it."

"Why not?"

"I don't have the capability right now," I said. "My brain doesn't work like it used to work. It just doesn't. I can't battle with State Bar prosecutors. I just can't do it. I can only do mindless stuff now."

"Then let's hire a lawyer."

"Those guys charge a minimum of twenty-five thousand dollars. You're about to lose your license. They know that. They take advantage of that."

"How do you know it's twenty-five thousand dollars?"

"I know."

"This is sad," she said.

Alison had fallen asleep. I wanted to do the same, but I remembered I had forgotten about the one-legged homeless man.

He needed to get his wheelchair back. I needed to find him. Right now. I knocked on Eddie's door. "All right. I know where to go," he said. "I know where he'll probably be. I've seen the guy. There's a little ravine behind Circle K."

We parked the car on a dark side street. Then we walked down an easy embankment into the ravine. Thirty yards later, we came upon a makeshift homeless camp. There were at least sixty pop tents and well over one-hundred people, including about thirty children. People were talking, laughing, screaming, sleeping, and shooting up. Lanterns and a few campfires were used for light. Several women were prancing around half-naked, doing what needed to be done to survive. This was not a city-sanctioned gathering. There was not a good vibe to the place. I sensed predators and fugitives. Mania and madness swirled about like a toxic mist. Nonetheless, I followed Eddie right into the middle of things. I felt like a third-party observer who somehow belonged here.

"I think his name is Brian," I said.

Eddie was looking around, taking in everything. He didn't seem to share my uneasiness. Indio was his hometown. He was okay with everything.

"I know who he is," he said. "We could sell a lot of blow here, man."

"It doesn't seem safe," I said.

"Just follow my lead," he said. "I know all the chiefs."

"All right."

A gangbanger-type, in his forties, with the physique of a sumo wrestler and a face covered with jail tattoos, suddenly came upon us. "What's up, Eddie?" he said in a gentle voice.

"Hey, Armando. How are you?"

"Living the dream, my man," he said.

"All right. This is my friend, Peter."

I nodded. "Hi, Armando."

"I've got some pizza back at the tent if you guys want any," Armando said.

"I'm okay," Eddie said.

"I'm good," I said.

"We're trying to track down Brian, the guy with one leg," Eddie said.

Armando slowly shook his head. "Man. Yeah, he was taken in, man," he said. "He got popped for trying to buy some meth from an undercover."

"They're the worst," I said. "A guy with one fucking leg?"

"They don't give a shit," Armando said. "At least he's had a bed for the past few days. That's how I'm looking at it."

"Still, that's cold," Eddie said. "That's who they fuck with?"

An emaciated naked woman walked our way. She was wearing only a pair of Crocs and a smile. Once, she was pretty, but meth or crack, or something, had taken her down. Her long blonde hair was lifeless, cascading down her back like a stiff, frozen, dirty waterfall. "Hi, Armando," she said. "Who are your friends?"

"Doris, please, go back to your tent," he said. "You're going to be voted out of here if you don't start wearing clothes."

"I can't afford any," she said.

I pulled some money out of my wallet. Armando waved me off. "No, man, she'll put that money straight into a pipe," he said.

"I'll buy clothes, Armando," Doris said with obviously-fake sincerity. "You know I will."

"Doris," Armando pleaded, "there's no reason for you to be standing here."

"You never know," she said.

"I know," Armando said.

Doris skipped away, laughing. There wasn't a single ounce of fat on her body. There were no bouncing breasts or jiggling ass cheeks. Doris was nothing but skin and bones. I wondered what her story was from the beginning.

ADDICT'S WAY

"Man, that's mostly what's in this place," Armando said. "They've all reached a dead-end. Usually, it's drugs. Sometimes, it's an incident they just couldn't cope with, and they're shattered now. A lot of them get comfortable with this life. I'm here because of alcohol, but I'll make it out of here, man."

"You need anything?" Eddie asked him.

The flames from one of the campfires danced in Armando's eyes. "Nah, I'm cool, man," he said. "I'm forty-five days into A.A., man. This has to be the last rodeo for me, or I'm dead. Everyone in my family had already given up on me. You know what I'm saying?"

"Yeah," I said. "For me, it was gambling, mostly."

"You do the meetings?" he asked.

"Not really," I said. "I'm just doing my best."

A young child started screaming at the top of its lungs for several seconds, then suddenly stopped. "Damn, the noises here drive me crazy," Armando said. "It's not just the babies. Nobody's courteous."

"I get it," I said.

"I think you need the meetings, man," he said. "We all need them."

"Do you think I could move stuff through here, Armando?" Eddie asked.

Armando shook his head. "Eddie, these people are hurting, man. If you're coming down here, you should be bringing boxes of diapers and bags of groceries. Don't add to the misery, man."

"I can help with that," I said. "I'll bring food and whatever else I can."

"That would be wonderful," Armando said. "These people need help, man."

"All right, let's head out," Eddie said.

"What did you want with Brian?" Armando asked.

"I just wanted to help him get his wheelchair out of hock," I said.

"That's cool, but don't hand him any money," Armando said. "He puts it straight into the pipe, just like Doris."

"Everybody's here because of drugs?" I asked.

He shook his head. He nodded. "There's a few hard-luck stories," he said. "You know, health problems, not enough money to pay the medical bills, or pay any bills, period. Some people lost their jobs and couldn't find another one. But, yeah, mostly, drugs and alcohol."

"People are living like this?" Eddie said. "We live in a country full of millionaires and billionaires."

"That's why we have people living like this," I said.

We walked up the embankment. We got inside Eddie's car. We clicked our seatbelts on. Eddie started the engine. "Armando's right," he said. "I can't be selling to people like Doris."

"You can't," I said.

We heard yelling close by. Eddie turned on his headlights. Two twenty-somethings, an opposite-sex couple, were in a scuffle of sorts in the middle of the street. The man was tall and thin. The woman was short and petite. We couldn't make out their features, but the woman had an attractive silhouette. It was a lover's quarrel based on jealousy. Not satisfied with simply screaming vulgarities at her, the man pushed her to the ground and then began kicking her in the head. Eddie rolled down his window. "Hey, you fucking piece of shit! Leave her alone!" he yelled out.

"This isn't your business, bitch!" the man yelled back.

"FUCK YOU!!!" Eddie screamed.

There was one last solid kick to the woman's head. I could see blood and/or teeth fly from her face. The man started running away. Eddie turned his headlights off. He accelerated toward the man. He ran him over on purpose. The car jolted a bit from the impact. He sped away. "Holy shit," I whispered.

We made it back to the driveway of the crack house. We drove there with no headlights on. Eddie knew what to do. Indio was his hometown.

"We'll figure it out tomorrow," Eddie said.

"I hope you didn't kill the guy."

Adrenaline was still pulsing through Eddie. "I hope I did kill him," he said.

| 14 |

The morning sun was unbearable. Eddie didn't want to talk inside the crack house, so we were at the far end of the backyard. Everything stunk like a bloated landfill, but the Trubbles didn't care.

"What the hell?!" I asked him.

"I freaked out," he said.

"Now what?"

"You don't get what happened."

"Tell me," I said.

"I grew up seeing my father beat the shit out of my mother all the time," he said. "When I saw that guy kicking that woman in the face, I ran over my father."

"Okay. I understand," I said.

He wanted to cry. "Fuck," he muttered.

"I wouldn't tell anyone about last night," I said. "Alison knows nothing. Neither should Heather."

He started crying. "I won't tell anyone," he said. "What if I killed somebody?"

"Hey, if it plays out in court, I'll help you figure it out," I said. "You have some good facts on your side. All right?"

"I can't believe this life," he said. "I don't even know what I'm doing anymore."

"We'll get it figured out, Eddie. Do not say a word to anybody," I said. "If the cops make their way to you, do not say a single word to them."

I was in the car with Eddie last night. If I had any sense at all, I'd go straight to the police department and come clean with everything.

He stopped crying. "You think they will?"

"I don't know," I said. "I'd get myself a good carwash."

He nodded. "Yes. Good idea," he said. "I'll go right now."

I walked back into our bedroom and sprawled across my mattress. I wanted some wine, but I didn't have any. Still, it felt good being back inside. At least the crack house had air conditioning that kind of worked. Alison was still under the covers, gently breathing. I realized I'd never be a happy person. So, I made the trek to Dr. Guessner's office in 117-degree heat. I have no idea how or why people lived in Indio. "So, where were we?" he asked.

"You were scribbling on a notepad," I said.

"Based on everything you said to me last time, we're dealing with implicit memories and some explicit memories. Explicit memories can be dealt with. Implicit memories, not really at all. At least not very well."

"That was mentioned to me once before," I said. "I never made it to the next session."

Dr. Guessner provided me with a brief lecture on implicit and explicit memory in the context of my life. Of course, a baby given up for adoption cannot remember the time in its mother's womb or the adoption process itself. But the baby emotionally remembers virtually everything about that time, even during the last trimester. This implicit memory results in adopted people going through life fearing abandonment and rejection. Implicit memory works on a subconscious level. The effects of it cannot be managed or solved by cognitive insight. Reading books, watching videos, and listening to various uninformed commentaries (i.e., verbal therapeutic intervention or the insights of well-meaning family members) do not help at all. These embedded memories invariably cause behavioral problems that usually begin at age 5. When I was 6 years old, the death of a goldfish triggered a prolonged sadness in me. Typically, these behavioral problems persist long into adulthood. The manifestations are various, including addiction, low self-worth, anger, anxiety, stress, and deep depression. Ultimately, implicit memories cause psychological problems that are virtually incurable. On the other hand, explicit memories are clinically easier to deal with. An example of such a memory would be the Saturday morning I was told I was adopted. That morning can be recalled as an actual episode in my life. The effects of that morning's memory can be profoundly lessened into a benign state, unlike the adoption itself, of which I have no explicit memory.

Done, Dr. Guessner furrowed his brow. "There's no conscious retrieval of implicit memory. It's emotionally based," he said. "It's like a computer program always invisibly running in the background. It's always impacting our behavior on a subconscious level. We don't know how to eradicate its impact. You'll find some who talk about rewiring the subconscious, but there's no evidence that that is possible. It's a bunch of Law-of-Attraction hogwash: 'Just say this every day for thirty days, and your life will miraculously change.' We just don't know how to do that. At least not yet. Positive thinking is no match. It's much easier to deal with explicit memories. With those, you can have some kind of impact."

"No matter how hard I tried, I was always on some kind of autopilot. I just couldn't fight."

"Your life has been a textbook example of Adopted Child Syndrome," he said matter-of-factly. "This should have been tended to years ago when you were a small child. Then there might have been a chance to at least minimize the effects." He carefully moved around his chair to get comfortable, as if he had ended up on the floor during a past attempt. "Now, it would be like a mechanic taking apart the car's entire engine and then putting it all back together with new parts. During such a process on your psyche, you'd be rendered completely debilitated. You don't have the time for that. There are other things we can do."

"Maybe, I can have some peace the rest of the way."

His pen hovered over his notepad, ready for action. "Tell me about some of your explicit memories."

"Next time. I've completely shut down. I feel drained."

He grabbed his prescription pad. "I want to put you on Wellbutrin," he said. "It'll help with energy and depression."

"I took Prozac a long time ago."

"I find this to be more effective," he said. "It does an excellent job of treating symptoms, but it doesn't initiate any organic change."

"All Prozac did was get me out of bed. I was still insane."

He glanced at his watch. "We've got a few more minutes," he said. "None of this is your fault. I don't want you to let anyone tell you otherwise. Early-childhood trauma changes the brain itself. You didn't have a chance. Not without the proper help at a very young age. Implicit memory is like a bottle of wine spilling all over a white silk tablecloth. You can never really get the stain out. All we can do now is deal with all of the aftermath – the stress, the anxiety, the depression, and all the anger."

"Yeah, but I've still wasted my entire life," I said. "It's not like my family will want to understand any of this."

Before I filled the prescription, I went to Julio's to talk to his friend, who had been charged with solicitation. We all watched the discovery video of the incident.

"It doesn't look too good," I said. "The context of everything that was said is too easy to figure out."

"I know. Hey, I was caught. What can I do?"

His name was Watson. He poured himself some scotch. I wasn't in the mood to drink right now. He shot the scotch to the back of his throat. He gargled with it for a bit, like it was mouthwash. He didn't wince. He was a massive man, almost 7 feet tall. His head seemed the size of a basketball. His arms hung low, like a gorilla's. He looked like a peach-colored gorilla with almost orange-colored eyes. When he smiled, you could see that he had lost a lot of his teeth along the way. A jury wouldn't like him.

I was in the mood for some scotch after all. "I'll have some," I said.

Watson handed me the bottle. "There's no need to take this before a jury," I said. "I'll talk to the D.A. I think we can get it over with quickly."

"What'll happen?" he asked.

"Were you ever convicted of this before?" I answered.

"This very thing?"

"Yeah, this very thing."

"No."

"That's good."

"So, what do you think?"

I took a splash of scotch. "You won't do any jail time," I said. "You'll pay a fine. You'll have to attend a few sex-education classes. You might have to do some community service. After a year or so, we'll be able to get it off your record. You'll have to stay out of trouble for three years."

"Sex education classes?"

"About STDs."

"Oh. All right. I see."

"Where's Julio?" I asked.

"He's running some errands," he answered. "He'll be back soon."

I gulped the last of the scotch and stood up. "I can't wait around," I said. "I have too much stuff to do right now. All right, it was nice meeting you, Watson."

I took the prescription to a nearby CVS. There'd be an hour-long wait. I said I'd come back: "Maybe this evening or tomorrow morning."

When I walked back inside the crack house, I could hear sexual sounds. I followed the sounds to the room just off the living room, which had a big-screen television, a sofa, and three oversized chairs. Teisha's 12-year-old son, Dante, was watching porn and masturbating on the couch.

"What's going on, Dante?" I said.

He put a blanket over his stomach and lap and pointed the remote at the television to turn it off. "Nothing's going on," he said.

"Yeah, I can see that."

"Are you going to tell?!"

"Dude, what's going through your mind?" I said. "Where's your mother?"

"In the shower."

"Where are your brothers?"

"Taking a nap."

"You're not afraid of anyone seeing you?"

"They won't," he said. "Just don't tell."

"This is not a good thing, man," I said. "You're messing around with the insides of your brain."

"Just don't tell. I'll stop. I just don't want to be killed. Jerome will kill me. He beats me every time I wet my bed. He's a mean dude."

The shower turned off. Dante quickly disappeared into his bedroom. Teisha appeared. Her hair was wet. There was a towel wrapped around her torso. "Oh, hi, Peter," she said. "What are you doing in here?"

"Oh, I'm just wondering if Jerome's around," I said.

"His shift ends about now," she said. "He'll be here pretty soon. He needs to talk to you, he said."

"Okay."

She nervously adjusted her towel. "Yeah, his brother-in-law was in a horrible accident today."

"What happened?"

"Motorcycle accident. I'll let him tell you about it," she said. "He was airlifted to Martin Luther King in Los Angeles this afternoon. He's in a coma. It's not good."

"Okay," I said. "He can knock on my door. I'll be up. I'm sorry to hear this."

I walked to CVS to pick up the prescription. A couple of hours later, Jerome and I were sitting at one of the flimsy card tables. We talked about his brother-in-law's accident. "I saw the police report," Jerome said. "All the fault was placed on FedEx."

"I'll need a copy of that."

Jerome was still wearing his IHOP garb. "I'll get it for you. I have a copy in my room. Can you drive out with me to Compton tomorrow?"

"Compton?"

"I told my sister that you'll be handling the case."

"Okay. Thanks," I said. "All right."

"My sister listens to me," he said. "I want her to sign all the paperwork. We need to get this done. Can you kick a little my way?"

"Yeah. Okay."

Jerome smiled. "A FedEx truck ran into him, man."

I smiled. "That's beautiful," I said.

I told Alison about the case before we went to bed. "Now that's a good case," she said. "It's not like all those other stupid cases you used to take."

"I took those cases, so we'd have cash flow."

"You took those cases because we were always dead-broke because of your gambling. Suing FedEx, maybe we'll finally get something that'll help us."

"We will," I said. "The guy's in a coma."

I took the Wellbutrin. I went to sleep. An hour later, I woke up. I looked around the room. I knew the lights were off, but it was as if I had x-ray vision. I could see through the darkness as if the lights were on. Alison had a blanket wrapped around her. I could see her nakedness through the blanket, through her pajamas. I felt like I was in the middle of an acid trip. I took my phone out to the living room to call my cousin Victor. He was a pharmacist who lived in Brooklyn. Years ago, he graduated from Columbia University School of Pharmacy. I told him what was going on. "Well, I'm not a doctor," he said. "From what I do know about all this, you could be a little bipolar."

"Really?"

"Yeah, maybe," he answered. "Call your doctor. Wellbutrin might not be a good fit for you."

"Plus, I feel wired," I said. "I won't be able to go back to sleep now."

"Yeah," he said. "You need to take it in the morning. It keeps most people awake. It's a stimulant for a lot of people."

"All right, I'm sorry I bothered you."

"How is everything else going?" he asked.

"Well, overall, it's some kind of awful," I said. "There's no help."

"Yeah," he said. "Rite-Aid wants to fire me. I have diabetes. It's hard for me to stand an entire shift anymore."

"That's awful," I said. "The ADA's on your side."

"Still, the stress is unreal being treated this way. I've been with them for over 40 years."

"Companies don't give a shit."

"That's a fact. Call your doctor tomorrow," he said. "Elisa told me what's going on with you and Alison. I'm sorry I can't help out with any money, Peter. I wish I could. I should have gone to med school. I'm barely making it myself." Whenever the cry for help crosses over into a cry for money, everybody is broke.

| 15 |

We were on the swooping 10-and-the-110 merge, just below Downtown Los Angeles. Jerome said, "Thanks for everything you're doing for everybody."

"I don't mind," I said. "So, where are we headed?"

"What are you worried about?"

"The last time I was in the area, it didn't go that well."

"Yeah, what happened?"

"I was chased out of Watts," I said, remembering.

"What the hell were you doing in Watts?"

"That's exactly what my father said."

"So, what happened?"

"I was selling insurance to members of the Retail Clerks Union."

"Yeah."

"I had an appointment with a Ralphs checker in a project in Watts," I said. "I never made it to the guy's front door."

"I don't even go into Watts," he said. "Anyway, my sister lives in some projects on Imperial. We're not going to Watts."

"On the way to where Hollywood Park used to be," I said.

"Yeah, you've seen them," he answered. "You'll be safe with me."

"We'll see. 'White Lawyer on Way to Help Black Family With Lawsuit Shot Dead by Crack Dealer in Projects.'" I laughed.

Jerome smiled. "I got your back."

His sister was pretty, with radiant green eyes. Her hair was straightened. Her make-up was lightly applied to smooth features and perfect skin. A Black Lives Matter t-shirt hung loosely over her thin frame. There was nothing friendly about her. "Hello. I'm Angela," she said matter-of-factly, like someone who had been reluctantly pulled into a Zoom meeting.

We all sat down at the kitchen table. The apartment was plain and drab. There was no attempt at style at all. It was as if she knew this was just a stop on the way to somewhere else, somewhere better. It was a tribute to Target and Walmart. "Hello, Angela," I said. "How's your husband doing?"

"Leroy hasn't moved a muscle since the accident," she said. "The doctors have told me he'll pull out of it, though."

"I promise FedEx will pay," I said.

"Would you like anything to drink? We don't have much."

"I'm fine," I said. "No, thank you."

"So, what do you think is going to happen?" Jerome asked me.

"It'll settle before trial," I answered. "That's what happens when fault doesn't have to be litigated. The police report says FedEx is one-hundred-percent at fault. We just need to know how much medical help your husband will need moving forward. There's a lot of things to sort out."

"How much is this all worth?" Jerome asked.

"I don't know yet," I said. "Without really knowing what the doctors have said, I'd say, at least five-hundred-thousand dollars. It could be more."

"That's like winning the lottery," Jerome said.

"My husband is in a coma, Jerome," Angela said. "How is that like winning the lottery?"

"All right," Jerome said.

"All right, let's handle the paperwork," I said.

"Let's do it," Angela said.

As we merged onto the 110 South, Jerome said, "Hey, do you mind if we visit my boyhood church?"

"Sure. Okay. All right."

"It's in Inglewood," he said. "It's not too far away. That's why I went south."

I looked to my right. We were passing USC. Most of my memories had been born at UCLA, Westwood Village. I'm sure some of them still linger there in some form or another. Everything is energy.

I had never seen a bigger church in my life. It was the kind they don't make anymore. The façade was 19th-century architecture, with an attention to detail that demanded your admiration and respect. Inside, there was no sign of modern-day life. It's as if nothing had ever been renovated or remodeled in well over a century. Jerome sat down in one of the middle pews. I sat down next to him. He pointed up at the choir loft. "I used to sing up there with my grandmother when I was a little boy," he said.

"You can sing?"

"Not good enough."

"I was an altar boy," I offered.

"I heard some almighty stuff in here when I was a kid," he said. "There were some almighty preachers that walked across that altar."

"I only remember Father Krekelberg in Sierra Madre."

Jerome's eye moved about the church. "It all began and ended in this church, man."

There was a bit of a poet trapped inside Jerome's soul. It takes one to know one. "I understand," I said.

"I never thought I'd end up doing time for murder."

"I never thought I'd end up where I am."

Jerome slowly shook his head. "I'll never forget one sermon," he said. "It was about deception, distraction, division, and discouragement. I'll never forget the message."

I nodded. "Satan's all over the place."

"In the Garden of Eden," Jerome said, "Eve was deceived by the devil, with the promise that the apple would make her and Adam as smart as God. This promise distracted them from seeking God's knowledge. Then, Adam and Eve were divided, their bond to and with each other having been broken by not obeying God's simple instructions. Also, their bond with God had been broken. When we're lost and lonely, we get discouraged."

"I remember this from Catholic school."

"If you went to Catholic school, I'm sure you've heard it," he said. "There's a lot of knowledge in the Bible."

"Alison reads it."

"You need to read it with her, Peter. It's a book that'll keep you grounded, man. We need to always be moving away from evil," he said.

I looked up at the crucifix. The sad eyes of a man who was just trying to help. "Yes," I said.

"I'm not trying to make you upset. But you're empty inside, man," he said. "How do I know? I used to have a heart like yours. I thought I was the only master of my destiny. But when you think like that, you become a slave to the wrong things. Like self-pity. '*Peace* I leave with you, my *peace* I give unto you: not as the world giveth, give I unto you. Let not your heart be *troubled,* neither let it be afraid.' I know you've heard that before. I still have the words in my mind."

"Did you plan this detour?" I asked.

He pointed at the man with sad eyes. "No, but He did. I just wanted to visit my roots at the last minute. '*Pray* unto the Father with all the energy of heart, that ye may be filled with this love, that ye may become the sons and daughters of God; that when He shall appear, we shall *be* like Him.'"

"You sure read it," I said.

"I do," he said. "I led the Bible study in prison. You find God in prison. Prison is the rock-bottom of rock-bottom. You can't go any lower."

"Thanks, Jerome," I said.

"I think we should check in on my brother-in-law," he said.

ADDICT'S WAY

At the hospital, we weren't allowed inside the room because the doctors were performing a procedure that would take a few hours. So, out in the hallway, Jerome said a short prayer and quickly made the sign of the cross. "Amen," he said.

Stuck on the 60 East, Jerome shared a biblical story where a man was possessed by the devil and shackled inside a cave. The man hadn't seen his family for several years, but Jesus finally found the man and set him free. Immediately, the man asked if he could follow Jesus, but Jesus said, "No." "Why do you think Jesus said no to the man?" Jerome asked me. "The answer is in one of the Ds."

"Division," I answered. "Jesus wanted the man to reunite with his family."

Jerome grinned as if proud of me. "That's right," he said. "You're a smart fuck."

I laughed. "But as dumb as smart can be."

"I know Whittier is just off this freeway," he said.

"I don't know. My sister did some awful stuff."

"Should your parents suffer because of what she did?"

"No," I answered. "I just need to get stuff sorted out. Exit Hacienda. It's just up a few miles ahead."

"I wish I still had my parents."

After a few miles of bumper-to-bumper silence, I said, "I don't know what to do."

"About what?" Jerome asked.

We had just entered the part of the freeway where all you could smell was the nearby landfill's methane fermentation. There was nothing about the odor that made you think of the fragrance counter at Nordstrom. I was always reminded of my grandparents whenever passing through this part of the freeway. The scent always made its way to their resting place, just across the freeway. Hundreds of years from now, I couldn't imagine archeologists discovering anything flattering about us.

I said it quickly: "I caught Dante watching porn and masturbating on the couch."

"When?"

"Yesterday. Teisha was taking a shower, and you were at work."

"Man, that's some brazen shit. What'd you say to him?"

"I told him he was messing with his brain. That's about it," I said. "He didn't say much. He said you beat him because he wets the bed. He's afraid you'll kill him now because of this."

Jerome took his right hand off the steering wheel, then put it back down. "Man, I'll tell you. This kid has some problems. I don't beat him. I just get madder than I should. I know that. It's a tool of Satan."

"It's the lowest form of human expression," I said.

"Poor kid. His bio father's a trailer-park meth head. Lives in Bakersfield."

"He's pretty rude to Alison, by the way," I added.

"I'm sorry about that. This isn't good," Jerome whispered. He exhaled loudly. His shoulders dropped. His jaw tightened. He didn't say a word the rest of the way to Indio. Neither did I.

| 16 |

I missed it all. I had incorporated the loud police sirens, the banging on Eddie and Heather's bedroom door, all the noisy scuffling, and Heather's screaming into my dream. The police had been here to serve a murder warrant on Eddie.

Without knocking, Heather busted into our bedroom. Her face was painted with panic and fear.

"Peter, the cops said Eddie killed somebody!!" she screamed. "What did he do, Peter!!?"

I quickly sat up on my mattress. Alison shot me a glance full of daggers.

"What did they say to you?" I asked.

"Not much, really," she said. "They just wanted to know if I knew where he was."

"What did you say to them?"

"I said I didn't know."

"All right," I said. "Where is he?"

"On the way to work"

Alison's face was tired. Her eyes were grey. Her body was lifeless. Everything bad in the world was my fault. "What's happening?" she asked.

"He didn't kill anybody, I know that," Heather said. "He's not a killer. Eddie doesn't kill people, Peter."

I told them what happened on the way back from the homeless camp.

Heather was inconsolable. Her body was in fits. "Oh my god, Eddie, what were you thinking!?"

"He wasn't thinking," I said.

"You were in fucking the car, Peter!" Alison barked.

"What do you think we need to do, Peter?" Heather asked.

Alison was at a breaking point. "Unbelievable!"

"I've never handled a murder trial," I said.

"That's not the question," Alison said. "Heather, Eddie needs to come forward and tell the police what was going through his mind when he did what he did. He either does that, or he flees to Mexico and never comes back."

Heather was crying. Her shoulders were heaving out of control. "Oh my god, I can't believe this," she said. "What is going to happen?"

"Another thing I'm dragged into," Alison said.

"You're a lawyer, Peter," Heather said. "You can tell them what was going through Eddie's mind, right? You can help him, can't you?"

"Maybe this can be your swansong," Alison said. "Maybe you can pull off a Jose Baez."

"This is a lot different," I said.

"Heather, call Eddie and tell him to turn himself in," Alison said.

"No," I said. "Tell him to meet me at Julio's. Tell him to not go to work."

Julio wasn't pleased. He hastily drew out some lines of coke that had been laced with a "safe mixture" of fentanyl. "You're a goddamned liability, Eddie!" he shouted.

"I know," Eddie said.

He quickly snapped a line up into his left nostril. "Look at the situation you put Attorney Peter in," Julio said.

"I know," Eddie said.

Julio forcefully shook his head. There was a small clump of cocaine hanging on his upper lip. It fell off. "This is some real fucked-up shit, Eddie. Somebody is dead, man!"

"I know. man," Eddie said.

Julio turned his attention from a photograph of a blowjob to me. His pupils were immensely dilated. "Right now, what should be done, Counselor?"

"Turn yourself in, Eddie," I said. "Bail yourself out."

"With what money?" Eddie asked.

"That's not a concern of yours," Julio said. "What else, Peter?"

"For now, that's it. Nothing else."

"You'll do some time. You won't end up on Death Row," Julio offered Eddie.

"We'll talk more about everything later on," I said.

Someone banged loudly on the front door. Julio pulled a gun from his jacket pocket. He slowly walked toward the door. He was ready to use the gun. "Who is it?" he asked.

"It's Etiwanda."

"Are you alone?"

"I'm alone."

Julio put the gun back in his jacket. He cracked open the door a little way. "What's going on?" he asked.

"Can I come in?"

Julio opened the door. "Of course," he said.

Etiwanda looked like she had just walked into a strip club for her next shift. She was wearing an orange bikini and purple stilettos. Her body was the body of a personal trainer. It was all cut up. It spoke of a certain routine – either time in the gym or daily meth use. "Hey, Julio," she said.

Julio smiled. "I see you're dressed for work."

"And I ain't working for that punk-ass bitch anymore, Julio," she said. "You need to help me break that contract."

"I am not getting involved with that guy," Julio said. "An LAPD gang-banger? No, thank you, Etiwanda."

"What am I going to do with my life, Julio!?!" Etiwanda shrieked.

Julio laughed. "Porn," he said.

"Hey, Eddie, let's get going," I said. "Nice to meet you Etiwanda."

"You want a date, handsome?" she asked me.

"It'll be on me," Julio offered.

"No, I'm good," I answered. "Take care, Julio. Eddie and I will head to the police station tomorrow. Then, we can make bail arrangements. I'll call you."

ADDICT'S WAY

Walking out to his car, Eddie said, "Suddenly, I'm in the mood for a lap dance."

"Gee, I wonder why," I said.

On the drive back, I thought, You know, maybe, I'm just on a natural path of self-destruction. Like a moth intent on burning its wings on a hot porch light. It's just what moths do to themselves.

| 17 |

"I'd sit at the top of the street, drinking beers," I told Dr. Guessner. His office had a new addition today. A glorious tropical fish tank, where fish swam back and forth, going nowhere. "Sometimes, six beers. Sometimes, it was twelve," I said. "I'd sit there waiting for that snap to happen. The snap never happened."

He scribbled some on his notepad. "What's the 'snap'?" he asked.

"You know, snapping out of sadness, snapping out of confusion," I answered. "You know, snapping into happiness and joy."

"This was in high school?"

"Yes. When I was a teenager. Late high school. Early college. It's all about the same time."

He scribbled some more. This time, with great enthusiasm. Like a journalist interviewing an alien from another solar system.

"So, you felt sad and confused back then?" he asked.

I nodded. "Yes. And dull," I said.

"You were dull?"

"No. Life was dull," I answered. "There was no excitement. I didn't feel anything special was going on with me or the world. I was just going through the motions. I felt like an empty shell. I had no idea why I was alive. I still don't. It's always been like an out-of-body experience for me."

"The last time we met, I told you that I knew what was wrong with you."

"Yes."

"Adoptive Child Syndrome, an anxiety disorder, severe A.D.D. That's my official assessment, not to mention all the subconscious wounds. And depression."

"Now what?"

"Compulsive gambling had a soothing effect on you. It's one of the reasons why you couldn't stop. A.D.D. – it's like throwing a bunch of confetti up into the air. Every piece of confetti is one of your thoughts."

"All this stuff sounds incurable."

"Look, it would be like taking apart a car's engine and putting it back together – this time, with premium parts. It would be very difficult for you. You'd be institutionalized during the process," he explained. "All we should focus on now is peace of mind and a sense of purpose for you the rest of the way. There's no undoing of anything."

I felt sadness and disappointment invade my features. "Yeah," I said.

"Hey, you caught a bad break," Dr. Guessner said. "These people were supposed to help you, no matter what, but they didn't help you. Someone with a brain injury shouldn't be living in their car."

"That's the way it went."

"You're waiting for your biological mother to come to rescue you," he continued. "You're hoping she finds you and helps you. You're waiting for her to make things right. Your life has been one big cry for help."

"Yeah ..."

"You get very angry at people when they don't do what they're supposed to do. Parents are supposed to have a child, keep it, and raise it. Yours didn't do that. Now, when people don't do what they're supposed to do, you go ballistic. That's why you have such a hatred for your sister. After the car crash, she didn't do what she was supposed to do. She was supposed to help you. That's what family does."

On the way to the Indio police station, Eddie said, "It might be best if we just head down to Tijuana, or up to Canada."

"Eddie, a murder warrant is sent out as an all-points bulletin, man," I said. "We need to just get this over with. We'd never get passed the border."

He screeched the tires to an abrupt halt for a red light. "Maybe I should just kill myself," he said. I wondered if he might decide to run the next red. A Mack truck t-boning the passenger side, killing me, would be a mercy killing.

"You're talking to the wrong person if you want me to talk you out of suicide," I said. "I'm pro-suicide."

"Hey, man, you seem off today."

"Look at my life. Fuck everything."

Eddie smiled. "Damn, you're dark today."

We were led into the interrogation room by a female detective. She was a throwback to a 1950s librarian. Horn-rimmed glasses, hair up in a bun, a drab, grey dress that fell to her feet like a set of curtains, a nondescript face that you'd never remember. She instructed us to take a seat. She was all business. This would not be like having a drink with a friend. There's a certain type drawn to police work. It's a type I don't care for. "I'm Detective Lock. I understand one of you is here because of an outstanding warrant." Her dull tone and forgettable face seemed like a surefire cure for insomnia. I yawned. "Is that correct?" she asked.

"Yes," I answered.

"What did you do?"

"My client is here on a murder warrant," I offered. "I'm here as his attorney and a percipient witness."

"Explain that to me."

"I was in the car when the person was run over, in the passenger seat."

"I gathered that much," she said.

"You're a detective, I hope you did," I said. "Anyway, tell her what happened, Eddie."

Eddie's face looked like the face of a ghost who had just walked out of a sauna. Pale, dripping wet, empty eyes. He explained everything in vivid detail, including all the nuances of his then-mental state. "I saw my father punching the teeth out of my mother's face when I saw that man beating that girl. I just lost it. I'm sorry. I ran over my father."

Detective Lock itched the left side of her face. She stood up. She hovered over Eddie. "Mr. Rodriguez, bail has been set at one million dollars. You'll be taken into custody shortly. If you can make bail, you'll be released as soon as you can. Your attorney can explain everything else to you, I'm sure." She left the room. There was no eye contact with either of us.

Eddie's wet ghost face was now caked with worry. "A million dollars, man!?" Eddie said. "What the fuck!?"

"Hey, we don't need a million dollars."

I had no idea what the outcome of Eddie's case would be. It depended on the personality of the prosecutor. If we ran into an unemotional type, without the ability for cerebral thought, we'd be screwed. We needed someone who understood the vagaries of humanity. Yeah, good luck finding someone like that in the D.A.'s office. Poor Eddie. All I'd be able to do is lessen the length of his sentence. He'd be dressed in orange sooner or later. The law doesn't allow for emotional excuses. No one cares if you were sodomized in the basement by your uncle or your father.

I walked through Indio to get to Julio's. If Indio were emotions, they'd be sad, angry, or in need of an anti-depressant or psychotropic. Everyone is just going through the motions, without any sense of joy or wonderment. There's no happiness here. Except, maybe, from an occasional fast-food binge or happy-ending massage. The people here walk past graffiti-riddled walls, vacant lots full of smoking bums, thrown-away appliances, and stray dogs. They walk with empty, lifeless eyes. The unbearable heat doesn't help any. The hum of the nearby freeway is constant, a reminder that not everybody lives in Indio. People are driving to better places to live and die.

As I made my way through the heat, my cell phone vibrated. It was a text message from my brother-in-law, Jay: "Turns out Tom Girardi had an insider at the State Bar that protected him from all the corrupt bullshit he was doing during his entire career. It's in the L.A. Times."

I texted him back: "Fuck that. I have a brain injury and can't get out of bed to respond to a bar inquiry because I was living in my car and couldn't. I collapsed into a wide-awake coma after Richard Stearns, that litigious lowlife, had given me seventeen-hundred-and-fifty dollars of filing fees. Fuck! 'Behind every great fortune there lies a crime.' – Balzac."

I needed a beer now. I needed to feel that snap. Plus, I was thirsty. I made my way into one of those liquor stores you know are only in business because of the neighborhood alcoholics. There's just no interest in making the store look the least bit desirable. The owners are aware of their limited clientele. The addicts will shop there no matter what the place looks like. Crooked signs, dirty floors. There's no care about breaking the retail cycle of mediocrity. I guzzled down a twenty-five-ounce Michelob Ultra in about two minutes. A peaceful calm poured over me like a blanket taken from a freezer. The world's a ghetto, I thought. Even Beverly Hills. Alcohol didn't have a chance against my worldview. It could only sometimes help with the moods, barely.

I told Julio Eddie's bail had been set at one million dollars. "All right, let's head out to my bail-bonds guy," he said. "He'll do it for one percent."

I was moving slowly. The beer and sun had dulled me, and everything else: "All right."

"You love this guy we're going to meet. He'll throw cases your way, as long as you throw him a bone."

Julio was wearing a black bathrobe, sipping the scotch as he drove us to the bail-bonds connection. He had done this before. The level of the scotch never slanted. "You know, I've known this guy forever. He always takes care of me. I mean, putting up ten thousand for a million is unheard of."

"You're driving through Indio with ten thousand on you?"

"Yeah, it's in the glove box."

"Must be nice," I said. I wanted Julio's life. It was better than mine. Life with Alison had become unbearable. Mostly, she was like a gorilla in a cage at the zoo hurling feces, through the bars, at everyone eating popcorn and cotton candy, erasing all smiles. She was like that even before the car crash, even before our tax problems. It was too hard.

Julio took a swig as he made a one-handed left turn into a parking lot. He sloppily parked the car in front of the bail bonds. It was in a cheap strip mall, stuck between a massage parlor and a strip club, which made a lot of sense. Location, location, location. Glowing neon light from the massage parlor made the parking lot look like a giant cherry snow cone had been spilled across it by a dump truck. The moons of my fingernails shined pink. Julio grabbed the stack of money from the glove box. He held it in his right hand, like a letter being taken to the post office. He disappeared inside the bail bonds. Two minutes later, he was back in the car. "The cage will soon be opened for our Mr. Eddie."

Alison and I were deep asleep. It was a couple of hours past midnight. Suddenly, someone violently busted through our bedroom door. Alison shrieked, "Peter!" I quickly sat up. I immediately sensed evil. I was right. John Trubble flicked on the light. He angrily waved a silver handgun at me and Alison. He was drooling from both corners of his mouth. The whites of his eyes were a deep blood-red. "You two are getting the fuck out of here right now!!" he yelled.

"Hey, settle down, John," I said. I spoke calmly. He wasn't going to shoot us. This was just another trip-out for him. "What's going on with you, man?" I asked.

Alison screamed at the top of her lungs: "THIS IS AGAINST THE LAW, YOU MOTHERFUCKER!!!"

John matched Alison's fury: "GET THE FUCK OUT OF THIS HOUSE!!!"

I remained calm. "Hey, John, what's going on? This is madness, man."

Alison had a death wish: "ARE YOU ON DRUGS, YOU MOTHERFUCKER!?!"

John screamed like a diabolical maniac: "GET THE FUCK OUT OF THIS HOUSE!!! YOU GUYS FUCKED ME IN THE ASS!!!"

"Hey, Alison," I said. "We need to just get our stuff. We need to get the hell out of here. John's having a bad night. I think he's teething."

Alison screamed: "JEROME!!!"

John was suddenly calm as if he had just been shot by a tranquilizer gun. His eyes were now white as if the Visine had finally kicked in. "Jerome's making pancakes at I.H.O.P.," he said. "He's not around to come to your rescue. Nobody is coming."

"Okay, okay. I understand, John," I said. "We're leaving. You let your own people live like this?"

We had taken little stuff inside the room, so we were out in just a few minutes. "I'm sorry it had to end like this," John said.

Alison pushed the ignition button. The Navigator was at risk of being repossessed at any moment. All the dealership needed to do was activate the LoJack system. Alison looked over her shoulder to back out of the driveway. Tears filled her eyes. "Now what? Now what, Peter!?"

I couldn't leave her worse off than when I had met her. I owed that much to Father Ranieiri. Everything is always complicated beyond a solution. Probably because feeling, experiencing, and remembering are all I've ever done.

ADDICT'S WAY

Part TWO

| 1 |

Alison was so rattled by John's violence, that she drove in the wrong direction for over two hours, through 29 Palms. We had to backtrack. Of course, it had been my fault for not noticing her error. I had been in a trance-like state taking in the unusual scenery of the desert city known mostly for a Marine Corps training base and over several hundred abandoned homes, leftover from a period when the federal government was almost giving away land so people could have their piece of desert paradise. Now, the abandoned homes are shacks, tarnished through the years by elements and vandals, uninhabitable. Impossible to be thrown in the trash, they just sit there like monuments of forgotten mediocrity, telling from an anthropological standpoint, many of them lacking even roofs now. Still, I wondered if you could make do in one of them with a sleeping bag, space heater, and dorm refrigerator. The weather would never be your ally, but you could just disappear. That was an undeniable amenity for the transient-minded like me.

We ended up at a Marriott Residence Inn in downtown San Diego, just a couple of blocks from San Diego Bay, a tourist destination because of the many sightseeing boats and whale-watching tours, among other nautical attractions. Alison negotiated a long-term rate for us with the money from Julio's advanced legal fees, the cocaine-dealing profit, and the fortunate blackjack hand.

From our top-floor room, you could see the sun kiss the harbor in the near distance, just beyond the historic County Recorder's Office, where small-boat sailing is popular. Nearby Seaport Village is home to many popular, crowded restaurants. There was a lively feel to the Harbor View area, which is what the locals call it.

San Diego was voted the number one city in the world for an older man to find romance with a younger woman, or vice-versa. This was not a surprising statistic given the number of neighboring colleges, universities, and bars. Here, I felt like I was on some weird vacation, with no end date or place to return.

Still unpacking, already Alison had nothing but complaints about the place. I was fine with the 2-bedroom: there was a full kitchen and a living room with a comfortable couch and big-screen television, not to mention a view of ocean water not too far off. The queen beds were inviting. There was even strategically-placed artwork on the walls, with the color coordination painstakingly considered.

I had no complaints, but I rarely complained about my physical surroundings. I didn't need much, even though I had grown up in prosperity. And that's why I didn't need much by way of materialism, either.

Alison, on the other hand, grew up in poverty, and that's why she left home as a chronic complainer. There was a complaint about everything from her: from the stores we shopped at, to the restaurants we ate at, to the cars we drove, and everything else in between. She was a living, breathing Yelp! review, giving everyone and everything one star. An infuriating personality, even when not hormonal. I wanted to be anywhere but here. Often, just the essence of her is demeaning and belittling.

We had finished transferring all our stuff out of the Lincoln, which hardly had the pleasant feel of a vacation-like activity. I felt like I was helping an enemy move furniture, the way she barked and snarled.

"Hey, I'm going to walk over to Little Italy," I said. "Maybe I'll grab some wine and spaghetti. You want to come?"

"Be careful out there," she answered. "This place isn't safe."

"It's just streets full of tourists."

"A lot of crazy homeless around here."

"There's no need to mention the nice view of the harbor, is there?"

"I'm still angry that you didn't tell me about all the money you were hiding," she said. "I hate you and your secrets."

"I wasn't hiding anything," I said.

I slammed the door and ended up at Filippe's, an old-school Italian place, with red-and-white checkered tablecloths, which served wine in short, stubby glasses, without thin stems, like they do in Italy. It's where I proposed to Alison, but that's not why I ended up here.

I ended up here to drink wine and fool myself into feeling good. I ordered half a carafe of chianti. I poured myself a full glass and drank it down in a matter of seconds. I quickly poured myself another glass and drank down that one just as fast.

The feeling of calm quickly arrived. It kept me from thinking about how awful things were. Yes, there was a much livelier vibe here than in Indio. There were things to do, places to go, and people to see!

A plate with a single meatball was soon in front of me. The meatball was the size of a baseball and covered in marinara sauce. I sprinkled parmesan cheese on it and cut into it with my fork. I loved the way it tasted. It made me think of my dear grandmother Dina, born in Sicily, who was always cooking up wonderful Italian meals.

I longed for the days when I was a young boy, sitting at my grandparents' breakfast table and drinking coffee that was mostly milk. There was always a feeling of calm in their house, which is the calm I'm always trying to revisit. Just up the street, in my parents' house, my father was always screaming and yelling, angry at anything and everything back then.

I liked how I was feeling. I felt like a changed man. I felt like I was on vacation, almost joyous. Italian food and wine always calmed me. Being only two blocks from the ocean, also, helped soothe my nerves. Little Italy was nothing like Indio.

Indio. I vowed to not simply abandon, Eddie, Julio, Jerome, and everyone else I was helping in the crack house. Even if I lost my law license because I was simply physically and emotionally unable to respond to the pending complaint, I'd still find a way to follow through for them. They weren't like most clients I had known through the years: they were appreciative of me, and they valued my time and expertise.

Law is a thankless profession, full of crookery and adversarial posturing just for the sake of adversarial posturing. I never liked it. Teaching it was much more rewarding: teaching students to think like a lawyer, I liked that.

I swallowed a spoonful of the marinara sauce that sat on the meatball like a shiny red blanket sprawled across a rock at the beach. The only thing missing right now was money. That, and a way for me to earn some consistently.

Thankfully, Alison had a law license, and she was willing to put it to use now. Recently, she had gotten herself on the list of some insurance-company legal plans; so, hopefully, the phone would start ringing, so we could feel like there was a potential end to all this madness.

I looked around the restaurant: there was a mixture of locals and tourists, and the tourists made you feel like you might be on vacation even if you were a local. I considered myself a local, as I figured my stay here would be an extended one.

Overall, Little Italy had me hopeful, but I still felt a little uncertain. There was still the constant headache at the point of impact from the car crash, and my severe fatigue was evolving to disabling again. Every day, I was getting weaker and closer to giving up. I had been running on fumes and adrenaline for too long: I felt drained now, but the wine was helping; and so were the new surroundings. Our room was conveniently located just a short walk from the courthouse.

I poured myself another glass of wine. Again, I drank it quickly, as if I thought it might be weakened by even brief exposure to air as it sat in my glass. I was not a connoisseur; sipping didn't interest me: I wanted to feel the snap in my brain from the sudden flow of alcohol.

Feeling the snap, I surveyed the room, which was not well-lit. There was a bar off to the side used only by the servers, where carafes and glasses of mostly red wine sat, ready to be served. At the back of the bar, there was a huge plastic tub with rubber spickets, where the wine was sourced from. The ambiance was not fancy, but it was comfortable and not distracting. The carpeting was hard to see because of the poor lighting, but it looked to be a mixture of red and black, or red carpeting that had simply been blackened by years of use.

Only the girl working the cash register was young; all the other employees were either middle-aged or older. My server was in her seventies. She was fit, tan, and well-kept, and her short hair dyed blonde.

"Can I get you anything else, honey?" she asked with a smile, her brown eyes widening.

"I'm fine," I answered.

"You can just bring me the check."

"No dessert?"

"No, that was enough."

I waited for the check. I was glad there was still some wine left in the carafe. It was something to look forward to. A call from Alison right now was not: I wanted to feel the wine swirling through me. I answered because I didn't want to deal with an argument about why I didn't answer.

"Yeah," I said. I didn't hide my annoyance.

"What's wrong with you?"

"I'm just trying to take a break."

"There's no breaks, Peter," she said. "We need to get out of this hole. We need to spring into action. Things aren't going to get better without movement."

"All right," I said. "So, what's up?"

She was upbeat: "I already got us a case from the lead service I signed up for. The clients are coming in tomorrow at 1 p.m."

"Coming in where?"

"I signed us up with an executive-suite service," she said. "We pay for conference rooms as we use them. It's in a nice building."

"All right."

"I don't mess around, Peter," she said. "We need to get moving. I don't deserve this, Peter. I deserve a home. I want a five-bedroom-and-three bath as far away from downtown San Diego as possible. It's what I deserve."

"All right."

"Where are you?"

"Felipe's."

"Hurry back," she said. "It's a probate case, by the way."

"Okay, sounds good," I lied.

When I got back to the room, Alison wasn't through with me. She was sitting bare-footed on the couch across from the large-screen television, wearing pajamas: a pink bottom and a grey top.

"You have quite a to-do list in front of you," she said.

"Yeah?"

"Do I have to tell you?"

"I'm sure you will." I was glad the wine was still active.

"Contact the State Bar, get a valid driver's license, and clear up the court matter," she said, looking at the television screen even though it wasn't on. "It's hard to respect you, Peter. This stuff should have been done two years ago. Keep seeing Dr. Guessner. You can use Zoom to do that."

"All right," I said. "I'm doing the best I can. I'm a train wreck from the car wreck."

There was no repentance in her voice. "I know. Tell me about it, Peter. What are we going to do?" she asked the cosmos. "There's no help coming."

"Yeah. I know. Though love on someone with a brain injury."

"If they cared about you, they'd educate themselves and try to understand what you're going through. I saw it and I see it firsthand. You're just not right," she said. "The same thing happened to my father. A steel beam fell on his head at a construction site, and he was done."

"They don't give a shit."

"They're just mean people," she said.

"They're dysfunctional. A lot of unspoken hatred building up through the years."

"I've never seen people like them," she said. "Would you go get me a brownie from Starbucks? I need chocolate."

"Anything that'll raise your serotonin, I'll do it. Yes."

"No more crack house. Yay."

| 2 |

I couldn't wake up. I felt like I was made of concrete, sunken deep inside the mattress itself. I didn't want to wake up, but that was not an option. I had to drag myself to the consultation.

"I'm taking a shower now, Peter," she yelled out from her bedroom. "Let's get going!"

"All right!" I yelled back. Fuck! I thought.

All three of the potential new clients were absolute white-trash lowlifes trying to trick the probate court.

There was Lula Mae Taylor, an 80-year-old winner of a recent poker tournament, who, despite her age and wrinkled skin, wore provocative clothing as if she still stripped part-time. It was obvious she was at best decent-looking in her prime, never even pretty. Lula was the kind of woman who would need perfectly-coifed hair and the right amount of costume jewelry to be barely classified as a six on the "toxic masculinity" scale of 1 to 10. She radiated whoreness. She'd engage in sexual acts to further her cause.

She came with her son, Nick Zambito, a Vietnam vet who looked like his life's purpose was to manage a trailer park. Muscular, though fat, he sported a thick mustache and many tattoos over his forearms. He'd never get through the first interview if he were trying to find a job with a Fortune 500 company. He was not the least bit handsome.

Lula also came with her boyfriend, a 60-something, non-descript, multiple-bar-exam failure, Bill Tedzak. I knew he was bad news when he asked us if we'd file suit against a judge if the judge had ended up violating their constitutional rights. Because he wasn't intelligent enough to pass the bar exam, he hated the entire system and everyone in it. People who are vexatious litigants usually suffer from a personality disorder.

"So, Lula, you're trying to take from the Estate of Nick Martino, but there's a divorce on record that you divorced Nick Martino over thirty years ago?" I said.

"Yes, but that divorce was a fraud perpetrated on the court," Lula said.

"All right, let me search for that on my laptop," I said. "That sounds very odd."

"Well, there was an elaborate plan perpetrated by Nick Martino's mother to ensure Lula would not take from his estate," the multiple-bar-exam failure said.

I found the divorce judgment on my laptop. "Really?" I said, looking at the screen.

"Yes," Lula answered.

"Okay. So, you're saying the entire proceeding set forth in the divorce judgment, which indicates several hearings, as well as your signatures, is a complete fiction," I said. "I mean, you were never there? You never stepped foot inside a courtroom for this divorce? You never signed documents or spoke to a judge?"

"Yes. That is what I'm saying," she answered.

"So, the attorney listed as your attorney of record, never stepped foot in a courtroom, either?" I asked. "You never met him?"

"Yes."

Alison was seated at the far end of the large oblong conference table, writing on a legal pad. She was wearing all black – black blazer, black blouse, black pants, black shoes – mourning her life. Even her pen was black. So was the ink.

"Are you getting all this, Alison?" I asked her.

"Yes, I am," she said. "Well, Lula, you will have to get that supposedly-fraudulent divorce judgment, from twenty years ago, set aside. You can't just walk into probate court and tell the judge the divorce isn't real."

"It sounds like you don't believe what I'm saying," Lula said.

"I'm just saying, it'll be very difficult to find a judge who believes it," Alison said. "It's very difficult to believe you were never mailed a copy of the divorce judgment from the court clerk."

"I wasn't."

"Right now, you have no standing to walk into a probate hearing claiming you have an interest in Nick Martino's estate," I stated. "As far as the court is concerned, you'd be a woman – a divorced woman – trying to take from the estate of an ex-husband. You'd be laughably thrown out of the courtroom."

"I went to law school," Bill Tedzak offered.

"All right. Are you a lawyer?" I asked.

He shook his head. "I could never finish on time. I took it six times, then stopped."

"Anyway," I said. "What's on your mind?"

"Well, I can help out as a law clerk," he said. "You know, maybe, to help keep costs down for Lula and Nick."

I shook my head. "No. That's okay," I said. "Now, Nick – Mr. Zambito – why are you here?"

"I'm Lula's son," he answered. "I think I qualify as a stepson heir of Nick Martino?"

"I think he does, too," Bill chimed in.

"Bill. Please. You can't pass the bar exam," I snapped. "Tell me why you think you're a stepson heir, Nick."

"Nick Martino loved me," he answered. "I've known him since I was six years old. We always had a father-son relationship."

"Did he ever try to adopt you when you were under eighteen?" I asked him.

"Yes, but his biological father wouldn't allow it," Lula offered.

"That's why he qualifies," Bill said.

I rolled my eyes at Bill. "Did Nick Martino adopt you after you had turned eighteen?"

"No," Nick answered.

"Why not?" I asked.

"I don't know."

"Well, because he didn't adopt you after you had turned eighteen, you're not a stepchild heir," I explained. "After you had turned eighteen, your biological father could not get in the way of Nick Martino adopting you. Because of that key fact, you are not a stepchild heir."

"What about a de facto adoptee?" Bill asked.

"Not likely," Alison offered.

"Correct," I said. "Bill, I get that you know how to use Google. That doesn't mean you're a lawyer. A de facto adoptee is a longshot argument, likely to not prevail."

"Can we at least try?" Nick asked.

"Can we at least try to set aside my divorce?" Lula asked.

"Do you mind if I and Alison have a quick meet-in-confer in our office?"

Lula, Nick, and Bill nodded in unison.

"About ten minutes," Alison said to them.

We walked down the hall to our new office, which had the vibe of a jail-holding cell. Four white walls, no pictures on them, a desk, a few chairs not worthy of description, and a fake plant. It was just a boring workplace without any distractions: we'd never use it to meet clients.

"These people are out of their minds," Alison said. "These are bad people."

"No way," I said. "These people are a bar complaint waiting to happen. They're snakes. They'll end up biting you."

We sent Lula, Nick, and Bill on their way: Alison was friendly; I was sarcastic and condescending, and they left knowing what I had thought of them.

Then, Alison and I went down to the restaurant in the lobby of the high-rise, for a late lunch, where masks were mandatory.

We sat at the bar, which had an impressive wall of bottles behind it, sitting in front of a large mirror, and four big-screen televisions: two played sports and two played news. Bright light behind all the different bottles cast a multi-colored light across the granite-top bar and the hands and arms of everyone seated there.

I ordered a scotch and felt comfortable in the surroundings, but I wished I had been in bed instead: I barely had the energy to keep my eyes open. The scotch would help. It always did.

I could tell Alison was concerned about me, wondering if my days of being an able-bodied person were over with. So, we talked about my after-the-car-crash health before we ordered entrees.

"I don't know. All of a sudden, I feel worse. I dropped low," I said. "I started feeling shitty the last few months, but I didn't want to say anything, because of all the bullshit going on. I'm not doing well. I'm struggling. There's always a weird feeling throughout my forehead and behind my eyes. There's always some kind of crackling happening. It's like a lightning storm all over my head." Alison shook hers. "And the fatigue is out of this world," I continued. "It's more than just being really tired. This sucks. Drinking lifts me. At least for a little while. It makes the forehead stuff disappear."

A guacamole-and-chips appetizer was placed in front of Alison by a smiling Mexican man with jet-black hair and pink chubby cheeks. They're always happier than I am. "This is all too much," she said. "How am I going to do everything myself?"

| 3 |

I was on my cell phone with Dr. Guessner. I wasn't a fan of Zoom: I didn't want to take the effort to look presentable. I was sitting in bed in my underwear.

"I couldn't remember what to do," I told Dr. Guessner. "I had to pay for a consultation with a law firm, so they could walk me through the process. I said, 'I'm a lawyer and I have a brain injury from a car crash recently and I just don't remember what to do with a situation like this.' It was an easy thing to handle. I just couldn't remember."

"That's common after an accident like that."

"I was bedridden. Unable to think or handle anything that dealt with life. I was a mess. I was yelling at judges, yelling at clients, yelling at Alison, yelling at the moon," I explained. "My family's reaction didn't help. We needed an entire loaf of bread. We needed more than just a slice."

"Your family's reaction. I don't think it's a healthy topic for you anymore."

I exhaled heavily. "I agree. I need to switch my focus."

"I wouldn't waste my time waiting for them to apologize to you and your wife. We need to focus on your recovery. We need to deal with the anxiety and the depression."

Before Alison woke up, I decided to walk to the nearby Ralphs to get a couple of 24-ounce beers.

As soon as I walked outside, I was confronted with a beautiful view. The sky was sunny and cloudless and the water in the bay, just two blocks away, was shimmering from the sun's constant abuse: during the day, the poor ocean had nowhere to hide.

I could hear the foghorn of a nearby ship, which I think was blown simply to appease the tourists. Waterfront Park, just across the street from our hotel, was a tourist magnet with high-end seafood restaurants in between the permanently-docked ships, which were attractions you had to buy a ticket to experience. There was the Star of India and the USS Midway, which had been turned into a nautical museum, in between a few other interesting ships. Down by the Seafood Market, there was a large statue of the famous picture of the sailor who had kissed the girl after WWII had ended.

There was nothing wrong with the surroundings, and it felt good to be among them. It felt much safer here to walk for a beer as you felt all the happy tourists had your back. In Indio, I worried about being killed just because I was white.

Anyway, walking down Pacific Highway, I spotted a homeless man holed up behind one of those large green metal boxes used by the phone company. He had two purple pillows and a red sleeping bag. He looked like he hadn't showered in weeks; his skin, like his clothes, was soiled. He was a down-on-his-luck white guy with a beard and wearing a knitted beanie cap. He looked about forty with smooth features and a sense of happy confusion.

I gave him a smile and a thumbs-up sign. He smiled back at me.

"Hello, sir," he said. "Isn't it an absolutely gorgeous day? Isn't the weather awesome? We're all blessed by God. We all have our own little piece of heaven."

"Absolutely, brother," I said.

The homeless were plentiful downtown: you'd see several on any given day. Most of them seemed to be in their forties or fifties. All of them had the undeniable look of being homeless. I wondered if people could tell I was homeless. Sometimes, even though I didn't look like I was, I felt it was easy to tell I was homeless.

I kept walking. Past the locals, the tourists, and the other homeless. To my left, I could see the Santa Fe Depot, which had been built in 1887; and when you looked at it, it took you back in time. I'm glad some idiot hadn't yet lobbied for its modernization. And I could also see all the marvelous high-rises with their angular architecture and interesting use of windows and neon. The neon was in place for any low-flying planes.

Instead of making it to Ralphs, I ended up at a bar in the Gaslamp Quarter, which was the home of vibrant nightlife. Deemed a historical neighborhood, it's a place full of people who want to eat, drink and smile. Full of people who wanted to have a little fun on this planet.

Inside the bar, I don't think I had ever seen a more beautiful bartender in my life. Nowhere near as beautiful as Alison when I had first laid eyes on her, but an eye-catcher, for sure. I'm sure she made a killing in tips. Smooth, attractive features met in the middle of her liquid brown eyes, which sat underneath long, straight brown hair, which softly fell on an orange blouse that revealed a flat, sexy midriff above a pair of tight jeans. Her smile was inviting, and she moved behind the bar with an elegant grace: smooth and fluid like she was swimming in slow-motion. In my mind, she was swimming nude.

"What can I get you?" she asked me with a smile.

"I'll have a Long Island iced tea. Actually, three of them. But don't bring them all at once."

"That's old school," she said.

"Then cut me off," I said.

I surveyed the crowd. I wondered how many strangers would end up in bed with each other tonight. I knew I wouldn't be so lucky because the anti-depressant cocktail I had been taking had completely dropped my libido. I hadn't touched Alison in over three years, anyway – I had been placed in solitary confinement by Warden Alison for all my misdeeds – and had welcomed Prozac's side effect. Interestingly, my sexual appetite had disappeared, but it had been replaced with a deep appreciation for the visual aspects of a woman's beauty. "Wow, she's very, very pretty," I'd think to myself with no sensuality siding up to the thought at all.

I drank the first Long Island iced tea in less than a minute, sucking it swiftly through the straw as if it were fast-acting hemlock, but no such luck. "I'll have one more," I said.

I was handed another. "This one's on me," she said.

"Really? Thanks. Cool."

She turned away and then started to pour a beer from the tap. "Yeah, I have a certain amount I can comp every night."

I felt flattered but did not let my mind imagine anything impossible. Plus, I had nothing to offer her, and secretly meeting her for food and drinks would be impossible, and nothing I could afford. And meeting her for sex? Well, no interest in that. Plus, I could never do that to Alison. It wasn't in my D.N.A.

"Thanks," I said.

This exchange was noticed by a blonde-haired college kid/surfer-type, sitting next to me, wearing a Quicksilver hat: "It's the grey hair, man," he commented.

"Yeah. They think I have money."

"It's all good," he said. "Whatever it takes. Cheers."

Close by, a man in a suit started coughing and hacking as if he was choking on a broken beer bottle. When he stopped, he said, "Don't worry, I didn't just get back from China."

I had two more drinks before I left, thinking I'd come back just to see her gracefully moving behind the bar and have the mere sight of her increase my loneliness like it had this evening.

When I got back to the hotel room, Hurricane Alison was in Category-5 mode. She was sitting on the couch, wearing a pink bathrobe. The vibe was not welcoming.

"The frolicker is back. How nice. Is the leading-us-nowhere frolicker drunk?" she said nastily.

"What's your problem?"

"You."

"Why can't you just be a nice person?"

"What is there to be nice about? I should kill you."

"Can't you ever just enjoy the moment? Why are your moods always linked to external things? You're not going to be happy until you live in a house."

"That we own!" she snapped.

"That's sad."

She lunged at me like a wild bird. She began flailing her arms, wildly, at me, like they were a set of dangerous wings. Her fists were making solid contact with my face and chest. I didn't fight back.

She screamed loud enough for someone to call 911: "WHAT KIND OF SIXTY-YEAR-OLD MAN DOESN'T HAVE A DIME TO HIS NAME!?! YOU LOSER!!! I HATE YOU, PETER!!! I REALLY, REALLY HATE YOU!!!"

I took a few steps backward, out of her range, but still aware she might lunge at me again, so I stood on the balls of my feet.

"So do I," I said. "I wish you had never met me."

I escaped into my bedroom and took my daily 80 milligrams of Prozac, the highest legal dose allowed.

I lay on the bed, my mind racing. I held my pillow, tightly, like it was a flotation device that would keep me from drowning; but I was well aware of the 40-pound anchors tied to each of my ankles. There was no way to swim to the safety of the shore.

| 4 |

Sometimes, I wish I had opted for a life of crime, the kind of crime Bernie Madoff and Jordan Belfort, The Wolf of Wall Street, had gotten themselves into. At least there would have been an excess of money, and Alison would have been happy because we were living in a mansion and never had to worry about money.

As the years passed, I realized she just wasn't capable of love for love's sake. To her, a husband had to be a provider of comfort and wealth. I never felt like we had been a team bonded by love. We could never just be happy. There was always some kind of complaint stewing in her, some kind of disappointment at the forefront of everything.

Alison married me to escape the poverty of her Chula Vista childhood, but she did not choose wisely. But how could she know an attorney with a professional level of legal knowledge, and skilled at teaching people how to pass the California bar exam, would turn out to be such a hopeful loser?

Ever since I was a young boy, I had always felt something about myself that just wasn't right. There was always a kind of wrestling match with the momentum of destiny, which I always knew I was losing; it was easy for life to pin me whenever it wanted.

Poor Alison: I knew I had ruined her life. Still, I resented her lack of capacity for true intimacy; I resented how limited in scope she was when it came to connecting on an emotional level, with unconditional love. Even though it was all my fault, I wanted to somehow blame her. That's how addicts do life: fate is never on their side; fate is always the enemy.

If I had been a GPS gadget, there would have always been some glitch that had gotten in the way of where you wanted to go, of where you needed to go. Yeah, I should have become Jordan Belfort. At least, then, I would have been able to snort cocaine off the flat stomachs of young starlets, never having to worry about how a bill might get paid. Excess financial security was an aphrodisiac that automatically raised your testosterone levels. It was a world where hundred-dollar bills worked better than Viagra.

Hurricane Alison was still blowing with great intensity: I could hear her in the kitchen talking to herself (i.e., complaining to the world), and making coffee. "Peter, you stupid dumbbell. You stupid asshole. You're a loser. You're a leech. You provide nothing. You ruined my life." Her mantra had been perfected over time.

Yeah, listening to that, was just how I wanted to start my day. I did my life hack to drown her out: I'd always wet two small pieces of toilet paper under the bathroom faucet and then stick them deep into my ear holes.

I curled up into the fetal position. There's no way out of this, I thought. I'm going to have to kill myself. There's no genuine exit other than jumping off a building. But I don't want to kill my mother in the process.

I closed my eyes and tried to force myself back to sleep. There'd be no use in getting into an argument with Alison, not when it was that time of the month; and, lately, it had always seemed like that time of the month.

Looking back, I don't think she was ever emotionally stable. There was always some hormonal imbalance or rage ready to hatch. I can't live this way anymore, I whispered to myself. She kills me. All she does is break my spirit.

"What?!" she yelled out.

"Nothing."

"I heard something."

"I was talking to myself."

"No television, no computer, no laptop! I don't want to hear any sounds right now! Let me wake up, Peter!" she barked.

I pulled the covers over my head. "Another wonderful morning with Alison Tradgett!" I barked back. "Fuck this!"

"Go to hell, Peter!"

I waited for the sound of her turning on and getting into the shower, and then I put on some jeans, a black Nike pullover, and a blue Rusty's baseball hat, and left the hotel in search of beer.

ADDICT'S WAY

I headed to Karl Strauss on Columbia Street, which, thankfully, opened before noon. "I'll have a pint of Follow the Sun," I said.

The bartender was twenty-something wearing a bright tie-dyed t-shirt: oranges and yellows. "Sounds great!" he answered with youthful enthusiasm, the kind we all have before we figure it all out. It was obvious he hadn't yet figured it all out. He was free of stress and anxiety, nothing but a walking smile, the poor kid.

I couldn't wait to feel the beer splash down the back of my throat.

"Here you go, my friend," he said. "Any food for you?" I shook my head.

"Not right now," I said.

I held up my glass: "I'll stick with the liquid bread."

"Ha! I like that!" he said.

He floated down to the other end of the bar, near the entrance, where daylight was slowly pouring in through an overcast sky.

I poured the beer down my throat. The beer had become my Xanax, but the reprieves were only short-lived. There had to have been a better way: I should have switched to quaaludes and cocaine. Like Jordan Belfort.

I felt my cell phone vibrate. It was my homeless friend, Robert Trevino. He didn't live on the streets per se: usually, it was in his car; sometimes, it was in cheap hotels when he could scrape enough money together.

Robert looked like a Mexican gang elder, the kind you'd see in the movies: he had dark skin like a Native American, a thick black mustache, messy salt-and-pepper hair, and a mouth that was missing ninety percent of its teeth due to a years-ago battle with gum cancer.

He didn't have much, but his attitude was always positive and uplifting; it was as if he knew the key to happiness was to lower your expectations. He lived with his dog, Guitar, a handsome German Shepard whose tail was always wagging. There were times when I'd envy Robert. He was a single man, and it never seemed like he ever had anywhere to be. He could always join you at a moment's notice. There was never any calendar for him to check.

"Hello, Roberto," I said. "What's up?"

"Hello, Professor. How are you today? What's the plan?"

"I'm drinking beer right now."

"Where are you? I'll be right there."

Thirty minutes later, Robert and Guitar sat at my table; the former in a chair, the latter on the floor.

ADDICT'S WAY

Our table was across from the bar. There was an interesting view of all the silver brewing equipment, which was visible through a large pane of clear glass behind the bar. It looked like it had all been haplessly thrown inside a big see-through closet just to get it out of the way, the way tennis racquets, golf clubs, and skis are tossed inside nearby cubbyholes whenever people are coming to visit. There was no care for symmetry, but it was interesting to look at.

"Hello, Professor," Robert said with a smile.

Guitar yawned and wagged his tail.

"Hey, brother. Hey, Guitar." I softly patted the top of Guitar's head. "What kind of beer do you want, Robert?"

"I'll take a Modelo. Guitar will have a Corona."

"It's not that kind of place."

"What kind of place is it?"

"You've never been here?"

"Never," he answered.

"They make their beer. There's no brand names."

"Oh. Whatever you're having."

After a few gulps, Robert said, "My brother needs your help, counselor."

"What happened?"

"Twenty kilos."

"Of what?"

"What do you think?"

"What happened?"

"Before I get into that, I've got some Peruvian pink with me. You can be awake on this, you can sleep on this, you can fuck on this. It's a wonderful batch. Would you like to try a taste?"

"I wish I could, but it just doesn't go with my brain anymore. I'll do a line, and then I'll think everyone in here is a serial killer. That stuff hits my brain the wrong way, man. Thanks, though."

"If you don't mind, I'm going to head off to the restroom, if you know what I mean," he said. "Watch Guitar."

A few minutes later, Robert sat down looking like he had just eaten a powdered doughnut. "Your mustache has dandruff, man."

He wiped it clean. "Shit, thanks."

"Anyway."

He gulped some beer. "Yeah, twenty kilos."

"What happened?"

"Quickly. He knew undercover was on his ass, so he sped up and dumped the stuff in a trash bin behind a gas station. Some homeless guy saw him do it and told the cops. He even gave the cops my brother's license plate number, which I think is complete bullshit. I think they're doing whatever they can to take him down."

"Why?"

"Because of me. They know he's my brother. These same fuckers put me away for ten years for the same thing." There was more than a trace of anger in his voice, but he made sure to keep the conversation within our table. "Don't these fuckers have anything better to do with their time than fuck with people barely making it? He's just a mule. He's not making millions like I was."

"Millions?"

"Dude, millions. I had a mansion in Rancho Santa Fe. I was moving a lot of product," he said, obviously remembering. "Good days. I only got caught because a friend turned on me."

"What happened?"

"I did ten years."

"Shit."

"Awful," he said. "Ever since, it's been impossible to get a job or rent a place. That's why."

"What did the friend do?"

"Wore a wire and ruined my life."

"Why?"

"I started dating his ex."

I shook my head. "Fuck. Movie-stuff."

"It's not a world that lasts very long."

"But you tasted the high life."

"There are better ways to taste the high life."

Given the career choice, I was certain Robert had tasted a bit of hedonism on par with Jordan Belfort. I envied that.

"What do you need?" I asked.

"My brother needs a lawyer."

"It's federal stuff. What was he charged with?"

"I don't know exactly, but I'm sure it's possession with intent to distribute," he said. "We need to kill that homeless guy."

"If he even exists."

"That's right."

I laughed. "You're on your own with that."

"Kidding, counselor. You know I couldn't hurt a fly."

"I know. Where's your brother?"

"North County."

"Have you seen him yet?"

"No, but maybe we can both get there this week."

I quickly drank the last of my beer, then I motioned to the bartender to bring more.

I took a gulp of my new beer. "I mean, I'll talk to him, Robert, but I can't guarantee I'll take the case. I've got a murder case up in Indio to handle for a friend."

Robert nodded. "Understood. Maybe you know someone."

I nodded back. "I do. Either way, somebody will be on it for your brother. What's his cash situation like?"

"There's money. Don't worry about that."

"All right. Let's eat something."

"I'm a little light right now."

"I got it."

After we had given most of the cheeseburgers and fries to Guitar, Robert said, "I, myself, need a favor, counselor,"

Now and then we helped each other with money. "You need some cake?" I asked.

He nodded. "Yeah, but not for fun."

"I don't care what you need it for. I've got cake for you."

He leaned in closer. "I know you don't care but let me tell you what's going on."

"All right."

"I'm behind on my storage."

"Okay."

"It's more than that."

"What?"

"I'm three months behind and there's a kilo inside the unit."

"Shit."

"Right. I have to act fast. Do you think we can go there and square it up today? It's close by. It's not far."

"How much?"

"The bill's eight hundred, and I have half of it."

"You need the other half?"

He nodded. "Maybe an extra hundred if you can spare it."

"All right. Alison will kill me, but all right," I said. It wasn't about the money: Alison hated the friendship I had with Robert. "He looks scary," she'd say. Her intuition told her he was a bad influence. But Robert was a good guy with a good heart. Born and raised in San Diego, with a 99-year-old mother, he'd give you the shirt off his back. He really would.

"Also, there's thirty thousand of my brother's money in there," he continued.

"Fuck, the guys on Storage Wars love people like you."

"I'll take care of the bill, counselor."

On the way back from the storage facility, a police car tailgated us, then the siren was turned on.

Robert looked in his rear-view mirror. "Fuck, my left taillight is out. Fuck, it's a K-9 unit."

Robert pulled over to the curb. The police car followed us. The siren was turned off, but the lights were left swirling and blinking.

I exhaled and looked at the glistening ocean to my left, spotted with sailboats.

We were across the street from the hotel, in front of Waterfront Park, a haven for the homeless during the day. Since it was a public park, there could be no arrests for trespassing or loitering. But, if the cops wanted, there could have been many arrests for open containers and a few for masturbating in public. I saw an example of the latter with my own eyes.

"Well, it's just a fix-it ticket," I said.

He took his wallet from the console of his used BMW, which he had just bought from a friend who had just been given six months for domestic violence. He took his license and registration out of his wallet.

"Let's hope it's just a ticket," he said.

I didn't feel too good about that sentence. Something was about to go down. But I was sober and drug-free, and that's what I focused on. A drug test, and even a hair follicle test, would reveal nothing bad about me. But there was the outstanding warrant from the crash on the way back from Vegas. Shit. Fingers crossed.

Guitar was in the back seat making eye contact with the officer's German Shepard. I wondered if dogs fell in love at first sight. If they did, there was no such thing as an intelligent breed. "No barking, Guitar," I said. "No bow-wow."

"Counselor?"

"Yes?"

"Not to alarm you, but there's an ounce of coke in the glove box and two grams in my wallet."

"Goddamn it, Robert."

| 5 |

As soon as I woke up, and before Alison did, I called my lawyer buddy, David Canon, who practiced criminal law. Now and then, he'd take a case in the worst practice area in the world – family law – and he'd always regret it.

People getting divorced and battling over children are the most disgusting clients I had ever met. There was always some petty gripe at the top of their list. And you'd always be the one to blame for a bad outcome; it was never their fault, always the lawyer.

Like Cecilia Cabrinha – she lost custody of her daughter and then hired me to get it back to at least shared custody. After the court-appointed psychologist had interviewed both parents, including the child, she reported to the court that Ms. Cabrina was "the main problem" and the majority of custody should remain with the father. Of course, it was my fault that she was an unfit parent. It's always the lawyer's fault in family law.

Then there was Evan Lionell, a semi-handsome black wannabe comedian, who had had six children with six different women. In open court, he said to the judge, "I am paying child support to six different women, Your Honor. Please, stop this madness!" Sometimes, family law was funny.

David answered my call in an upbeat mood. "Hey, how are you?"

"I'm hanging in there."

"That's all we can do, buddy," he said.

David was a big guy with dirty-blonde hair and an oversized body because he loved the food so much. There was an obvious beefiness to him, but he had an oversized heart. He helped Alison and me whenever we needed money to avoid sleeping in our car, or whenever we needed money for food. On top of that, he'd send some cases my way to help the cause. A great person. Another one who would give you the shirt off his back. He knew what I was going through because he and his father had handled some cases of ex-NFL players who were experiencing brain problems in retirement. It would have been helpful if my sister had handled some cases like that.

Anyway, I considered David a lifelong friend. I met him ten years ago when I was helping him pass the California bar. A strong friendship developed during our tutoring sessions. He was always ready to help however he could.

"How've you been?" I asked.

"Working too much."

"At least you're making money."

"Some," he said.

"Anyway, something weird went down last night."

"What happened?"

I told David we were pulled over for a busted taillight and cocaine was found in the car, in which I was a passenger. Robert and I were both taken in, but, because I knew the criminal procedure, I was able to persuade the arresting officer, who took us both back to the station, that there was no reason to place me in a cell.

"Yes, I realize I have no standing to object to the search of the car. It's not my car," I said. "But the cocaine wasn't mine. Even my friend told you that. There is no legal reason to book me. You need to let me walk. I was just a passenger. Just do me a small favor. I don't need this nonsense."

David said, "If you weren't a lawyer and you hadn't shown them your bar card, you'd be in custody with your friend, only because cops are so stupid. And misdemeanor warrants usually don't cross over into other jurisdictions. That's why it didn't show up in San Diego. The judge helped you on that one by reducing it. She cut you some slack because you're a lawyer."

I shrugged on the other end of the phone. "Well," I said, "can you help me with Robert? His dog's at the animal shelter now, and his car was impounded. And I have no idea what bail was set at."

"Probably, ten thousand. I know a guy downtown who'll take five-hundred bucks."

"Okay, let's get that going," I said. "I'll handle the bail for him. He has enough money for you to take care of him. I don't want his case.

Friends are the worst clients, you know. But he'd be cool for you to work with."

"I'll charge thirty-five hundred since he's your friend," Peter said. "But that doesn't include trial."

"Of course not," I said. "All right, man. Thanks. I'll let him know."

"Hey, did you hear about the virus from China?"

"Of course. What's going on now?"

"We'll need to start wearing surgical masks pretty soon."

"Yeah, I heard something about that."

"San Diego County is going to be on lockdown pretty soon. You can only leave your residence for certain stuff."

Except for the news about the virus, it was a good start to the day, but then Alison woke up.

"Leave me alone until I get myself together, Peter!" she barked from the kitchen. "Let me have my cup of coffee and wake up! Make sure there are no pee drippings by your toilet! Did you open your window last night?! And why the hell did you come home at two-thirty in the morning?!!"

Every morning. She was relentless in her disdain for me. But could I blame her? I gambled away a seven-figure fortune during the time we were together, not to mention all the money I lost before we met, which could have been used to buy us a home. Instead, we always lived in apartments. And, now, we're living in a hotel and had been living in our car for a while. All because I had insufficient cash reserves to weather the storm of the car crash. It was all my fault. I was surprised she hadn't murdered me yet, with the traces of Azteca warrior blood flowing through her veins and her severe sense of holier-than-thou-ness spawned from her lacking childhood. I wished she dared to try to kill me. Then I could kill her in self-defense. Not really.

I crawled back under the covers and put my face deep into my pillow. How am I going to get myself out of this bullshit? I thought. I don't think I can. I think I need to just kill myself. Fuck it.

Alison barged through my bedroom door. "Why the hell did you come home at two-thirty in the morning?!!"

"Shut up!" I yelled out.

I refused to move from underneath the covers. I continued daydreaming in the twilight of sleep:

OPRAH: What made you write "American Discontent"?

ME: Death.

OPRAH: Death?

ME: Yes, death.

OPRAH: Can you explain that?

ME: Death is always a possibility, correct? Just like anal leakage from eating tortilla chips. So, I wanted to do what I was put on Earth to do – write. I got tired of seeing talentless people – like the Kardashians, the YouTubers, the TikTokers, and the Instagrammers – achieving fame and wealth without offering anything to the world.

OPRAH: Hmm.

ME: Frankly, Oprah, I have no idea why you're rich and famous. You're an overweight, unattractive Black woman with zero charisma. I mean, zero! I've never understood you, like I never understood Regis Philbin. Why in the world was either of you famous? The same goes for Kathy Lee and Ryan Seacrest, and Jimmy Kimmel, the most untalented late-night personality there ever was. What the hell are any of you doing in the public spotlight?! Why are any of you making millions of dollars providing the world with, really, nothing at all?!

OPRAH (*looking taken aback*): We'll be right back after this commercial break for Preparation-H.

ME: Yeah, Oprah, you can brush your teeth with it.

Hurricane Alison's cup of coffee was speeding its way through her veins. "Home at two-thirty in the morning?!" she barked. "Were you drinking beer again, like the loser you are?"

"What do you want?!"

"Get out from under the covers, you coward!"

I slowly sat up in bed. "What do you want?!"

"Who were you with last night?"

"Robert and Guitar."

"The great Robert," she said. "When are you going to realize that guy's too low for you to be hanging out with?"

"He's a good guy. He has a good heart, Alison. You know that. He's helped us out a lot. He helps me out with rides every now and then. It's not like he's an awful human being."

She tucked her floral pajama top into her underwear. "Whatever, Peter," she said. "I'm just frustrated, you know? This is just an awful life right now. Can you blame me for blasting out and breaking down every now and then? Maybe just be nice to me."

"I wish it was only every now and then." I sighed heavily. "I know it is an awful life right now. And it's all my fault." I wanted to tell her that I was stuck, that I had no solutions in mind, that I wished I weren't alive, but I didn't have the heart. I'm sure she already knew that anyway. "Things will get better."

Alison sat down on the bed, but not close to me. "How?"

"They'll just get better," I said. "I know they will. Just keep praying and thinking positive."

"That's all I do. That's all I ever do."

I accidentally grazed her right forearm with my hand, and she instinctively jerked it away.

"We'll be okay," I said.

She exhaled and dropped her shoulders. "I hope so."

"I'd like to make love to you."

"Now?"

"Not this second. Someday."

"I'm the ugliest I've ever been. I haven't had my hair done in over a year. All I do is eat. You see what this has done to me?"

"I think you're beautiful. You're a goddess."

"Please, Peter. That is ridiculous."

"You look like Audrey Hepburn. You're elegant, charming, sleek, and gorgeous, Alison."

She dropped her shoulders even lower and put her face in her hands. "I've never felt uglier."

"But you're not ugly," I told her the truth.

She looked me straight in the eyes, with sad eyes. "Also, I just don't like you right now. I'm sorry, okay?"

"When can we?"

"I don't know."

"I get it," I said. "I probably wouldn't even be able to get it up. I feel like a fucking loser. I don't deserve someone as beautiful as you."

"You don't," she said.

Alison stood up and began to slowly walk out of the room. Tears started in her eyes. I looked away. I heard the door close behind her.

| 6 |

I was on the phone with Eddie. I was sitting in my bed, looking out the window, across Pacific Highway and Waterfront Park, as the sun relentlessly painted Mission Bay with a golden-white glow, static except for the movement of the waves.

"I should be asking you that," I said.

"Well, it's going. That's all I can say," he said in a weak and tired voice. "It's going."

"You holding up?"

"Yeah, I'm okay, but I'm afraid of losing Heather, man."

"I know."

"And my life."

"That's not going to happen."

"I'm counting on you, man," he said with great expectation in his voice as if I was Jesus himself.

I ran my free hand through my hair. "Well, there's only so much I can do, Eddie. It's all about the law, the facts, and the jury."

"But you said ..."

"We have good arguments because of your PTSD, but I cannot guarantee a certain outcome."

"PTSD?"

"Yeah, post-traumatic stress disorder."

"Yeah, yeah, I know what it is," he said. "I have that?"

"Yeah, man," I answered. "That's why you freaked out that night."

"Yeah, I guess."

"It's not a guess, Eddie. It's a fact."

"Okay, I see. I understand. I'm with you."

I wished I were on one of the sailboats on the bay. I fantasized about a one-way trip to Tahiti. I'd never come back, I thought. And with that thought, I realized there was something very, very wrong with me. I was always running, running away. I never stayed around for the fight.

"All right, Eddie, I don't have my calendar with me, but I'll let you know the date of the arraignment," I said. "It's in about three months."

"All right, bro. Thanks. God bless."

"Have Jerome call me."

"How can I do that from here?" he said. "What's going on with the Trubbles?"

"It's moving along," I said. "I don't know much about it."

"All right. Good-bye."

I realized I needed a beer. Actually, during the phone call, I realized I needed a beer. Truthfully, before the phone call, I realized I needed a beer.

Anyway, I ended up at Princess Pub & Grille in Little Italy, a traditional British Pub. It served European ales and ciders, plus local craft beers. It had the reputation for serving the best fish and chips in town. It was named after the ill-fated Princess Diana. Her picture hung on a few of the walls.

The bar was stacked with cans of every beer that was served, as well as bottles of hard liquor. Also, there were about a dozen taps of delicious beers, including Guinness, one of my favorites. There were various signs nailed onto the walls, with my favorite being, "Wine is what classy people drink to get drunk."

It was a comfortable, unpretentious place. You felt like you were in England. The staff was truly friendly and engaging.

I told the stocky 30-something bartender who was wearing a Ben Hogan golf cap on top of light-brown hair, "I'll have a Michelob Ultra and a glass."

"No problem," he said.

He was on the muscular side and a little on the shy side. Like many, I sensed he didn't care for his job or lot. He placed the can and glass in front of me.

"Bingo," he said.

There was a woman in her mid-thirties who sat on the stool next to me. Wearing a pink top and blue jeans, she was slightly overweight, wore no make-up, had dirty-blonde hair, and was on the wrong side of plain; but she seemed pleasant: she smiled at me as she sat down. "I'll have a glass of chardonnay," she said to the bartender.

"Wine, at this place?" I said to her.

"Yeah, I know, especially here, right?"

I smiled. "Yeah."

"I'm in a wine mood. I usually drink Guinness," she said.

"Well, there you go."

Her wine was placed in front of her. She took a sip and said, "Yeah, I need this."

"That's why I'm here," the bartender said.

She took another sip, this time a larger one. "Work is awful," she said to me.

"Always."

"Not always, but this job is," she said.

"What do you do?" I asked.

"I work for Amazon in a distribution warehouse. A fulfillment center."

"It's bad?"

"It's slavery."

"What goes on?"

"Nothing any good."

"Really?"

"I walk about ten miles every day in the warehouse, and quickly. My feet are always in pain. And get this: there's a vending machine full of over-the-counter pain medication near the breakrooms."

"That ..."

"And there's always a long line outside the nurse's office."

"I believe it."

"They should have a psychiatrist's office, too. The high quotas and the speed they impose on us are unbearable. And get this: breaks are encouraged, but they're never scheduled."

"If you're behind on your quota, you won't take a break, will you?"

"Cheers!" she said and held up her wine glass.

I held up my beer glass and we exchanged smiles.

"And the pay isn't much, either. It just keeps you on the hamster wheel."

I took a deep gulp. "Yeah ..."

"Yeah, I'll never get anywhere. Both sets of my grandparents owned a home. And my parents own a home. And none of them were doctors or lawyers. One of my grandfathers worked in a factory while my grandmother stayed home with their kids. They were able to buy a home and a Cadillac. I remember all my grandparents. I used to love visiting them. We used to always go over for dinner and every holiday."

I pictured Nat sliding into home plate. "It's different now," I said.

"Tell me about it. I'll never own a home of my own. I can barely make car payments."

"The new American Dream is renting an apartment."

For effect, her head dropped, her shoulders slumped, and she sighed. "Yeah. That's sad."

"But we do have people eating Skittles in spaceships."

She raised her head back up and shook it all around with passion. "And people are sleeping in gutters."

"All they give a shit about is whether or not they're trending on Twitter."

"Don't get me started."

I took another gulp as if my lips had forgotten how to sip: beer spilled down my chin and onto my shirt.

"Social media. The Festival of Ignorance and Narcissism. People engaging in that stuff are mentally ill. All they want to do is be heard and seen. It's disgusting," I said. "The last thing I'd want is to be famous. Even if had abs, I wouldn't be posting pictures of them. Absurd."

"Did you hear the entire state is going to be in lockdown in a few days?"

"Yeah, I heard."

"We'll all have to wear masks, like surgeons," she said. "Supposedly, it can kill you, this virus."

"I don't believe that for a second."

"You'd better get to the store. I've heard they're running out of toilet paper." She chuckled.

"Only in America."

"I heard it's the whole world."

I saw our reflection in the mirror behind the bar. We'd make a good couple. I'd be the more attractive of the two, which means we'd be happy.

"Well, we'll see what happens," I said.

She took a sip of wine. "I'm sure we will. I hope it's not bad. I'm Judith."

"I'm Peter. You want to split an appetizer?"

"I can't. I don't get paid for another ten days."

"We'll split the appetizer but not the bill," I said. "I'll pay. How's that sound?"

She smiled. "I like shrimp. Is that okay?"

I called out to the bartender. "Can you bring us an order of the chili prawns and two plates, please?"

"You got it, buddy," he said.

He walked to the register and began punching in numbers as if he were dialing a phone number on an oversized tablet.

"All set," he said.

"So, what about you, Peter? You like your job?"

ADDICT'S WAY

"I'm kind of a retired lawyer. It's a long story. I'm not doing much right now. I've got enough money, so I'm thinking about getting a part-time job in a restaurant, so I can write."

"You're a writer?"

"Yes. No. I used to be. I want to be," I said. "You know what I mean."

"Like me and my acting."

"Life gets in the way."

"We get in the way."

Suddenly, a tattooed server, with huge earlobe holes because of some circular inserts, and magenta-colored hair, who looked like an MMA fighter, placed two plates and two sets of silverware, wrapped in paper napkins, in front of us.

"It's coming out soon," she said, then turned away.

"Would you like some more wine?" I asked.

She softly shook her head. "I have an early shift tomorrow."

"How early?"

"I get up at three o'clock every morning."

"That's a tough schedule."

"You deal."

Six medium-sized prawns, with three buttered pieces of small, oblong, sourdough toast came to the table.

After a few bites, we resumed talking. "Well, you've still got some time in front of you, Judith. If you've made any mistakes, you've got some time to fix them."

"How are old you Peter?"

"Sixtyish."

"I'm thirty-one."

I put two shrimp on top of one of the oblong pieces of toast. "Those were the days," I said. "Actually, not really. I was in law school."

"My only mistake was getting married to a man who beat the crap out of me."

"I'm sorry."

"We divorced last year, but he still bothers me."

"What does he do?"

"He sends me awful texts and e-mails."

"You can get a restraining order," I offered.

"I think that would just make him act crazier."

"It's just a piece of paper. It doesn't stop a knife or a bullet, or a madman from going crazy."

Judith slowly put some food in her mouth and then gently chewed. "It is what it is," she said.

"Well, I hope it works out. If you need any help, I have a good friend who handles them," I offered again. "Think about changing your phone number."

"I try that. It never works. He finds the new one."

"Did you guys have any children?"

"Thank God, no," she said.

"Well, that's a plus. Kid's always get the worst."

"I'm sure you've seen it all."

"Too much."

My cellphone vibrated with an incoming text. It was Alison in her all-caps glory: "YOU WORTHLESS LOSER!!! WHERE ARE YOU???"

"Anything important?" Judith asked.

"Nah," I said. "Just some mental patient."

| 7 |

When I got off the phone with Jerome, I called Dr. Guessner for our scheduled phone session.

"A lot is going on with you," he continued. "It's going to take a lot more than positive thinking and writing down your goals."

"Of course, it will. You'd have to be an idiot to think that's all it takes."

"I'm looking at my notes," he said.

"I can see that," I said playfully.

"When you were about seven, you said your mother found you passed out on the sidewalk. You were running on a wet sidewalk with tennis shoes, and you slipped?"

"Yeah, that's what we think."

"Then, when you were about ten, you were hit in the head with a golf club and were knocked unconscious?"

"Yes."

"Then the car crash that knocked you out of life"

I nodded. "Yes."

"All that head trauma has had a cumulative effect," he said. "That's why it's important for you to not keep beating yourself up."

"I don't know ..."

"Then there's the severe ADD, which was never medically addressed."

"Not really."

"Speaking of ADD, let's go through some questions together."

"All right."

"Just listen. I'm going to read off a shortlist to you and see if they fit."

"All right."

"Not following through on longer tasks or not starting them. Getting distracted by other tasks or thoughts. Seeking out risk or activities that provide an immediate reward. Restlessness, either outwardly or internally. Interrupting other people without wanting to interrupt them."

"Except for the last one," I said. "If I interrupt them, I want to interrupt them."

"So that's how your brain has been operating all these years. ADD makes life very, very difficult. There's no cure. It is a brain disorder. Specifically, it's a neurodevelopment disorder. It's not your fault. Don't let anyone tell you otherwise."

"My brain is broken."

"I'm going to read you something from the National Institute of Mental Health."

"My online memoir will have a link to their site."

"'ADD is a disorder marked by an ongoing pattern of inattention and/or hyperactivity-impulsivity that interferes with functioning or development. Inattention means a person wanders off task, lacks persistence, has difficulty sustaining focus, and is disorganized. These problems are not due to defiance or lack of comprehension.'"

"Me."

"Now a brain like yours smashing against a windshield and cracking the glass. That's quite a cocktail."

I yawned. I wanted to fall asleep. "Yeah."

"That's why you were always self-medicating. That's why you were drinking beers at the top of your street. That's why you had that stint with crack. That's why you gambled every day for 40 years," he said. "How did the gambling make you feel?"

"Good. Then awful. Towards the end, about the last 10 of the 40 years, I couldn't have a winning day to save my life. I mean, I'd have three or four winning days a year. That was about it," I said. "When I went, I knew I was going to lose. But, in the back of my mind, I was waiting to hit the Pick 6 for a million dollars. Overall, I came within six inches of making about four million dollars. There were at least four

Pick 6s where the horses I needed to win came in second by less than an inch or so. It was tormenting."

"How did you feel when you were at the racetrack?"

"I did not think about life when I was betting on horses. You were in your own little world. You didn't think about how fucked up everything was. It was a total escape. Like heroin, from what I've heard about heroin."

"ADD is devastating," he said. "Bankruptcy. Divorce. Infidelity. Jail or prison. It's pretty hardcore. Your family is going to think ADD is complete nonsense. People like them always will."

"Right now, I feel like I'm caught in a slow-moving whirlpool, and I can't swim my way out of it, and I know I'll probably drown. I can't reach out to them."

The call ended. I could hear Alison out in the kitchen, talking to herself.

"This Marriott is such a dump," she said

"It's awful being able to see the ocean water from my bedroom window," I said loudly, behind my door. "I hate being so close to so many wonderful restaurants and attractions."

"Shut up, Peter!"

"I sure feel like I'm living in the projects somewhere in Watts."

"You like living like this!" she snapped. "You have no ambition!"

"I want to go to sleep for thirty years, I need some fucking goddamned beers," I belted out, country rap-like. "That's the beginning of my new country song. You like it? It'll be dedicated to you."

"Shut up! You're such a loser! I'm taking a shower!"

When I heard the shower turn on, I left. I headed to Karl Straus for a few pints.

| 8 |

In the morning, I made the one-mile walk to the nearest Ralphs for a couple of 24-ounce beers: Steel Reserve 211 had the most alcohol content, so it had become my favorite choice. When I walked through the sliding door. I was met by an armed Mexican security guard, dressed in all black. He was pudgy, yet muscular, with tattoos on both forearms.

"You can't come in without a mask," he said friendly enough.

"Oh, that stuff has already started?" I asked.

"Yes, sir."

"Are you providing masks?"

"No, sir."

"Do you sell them?"

"No, but the 7-11 does," he offered.

I came back with a mask and walked inside the medium-sized Ralphs, which had a diverse mixture of people, many of them homeless. Alison couldn't stand the place because of the clientele: "All the homeless make me sad. Plus, it's a small store with an awful selection," she said.

I liked the place. At least it had a great selection of beer, and there was always a decent selection of made-on-the-premises sushi.

I liked it just fine. I felt more comfortable here than in all the sterile Ralphs up in the Carlsbad area, with all the fake people, with their fake white teeth, fake tans, fake breasts, their perfectly-pleated pants and skirts, their shiny, happy Range Rovers. Go fuck yourselves.

This Ralphs was full of real people, full of real life. The only problem was the check-out lines were always so long, but that's how it went in downtown San Diego, which was congested with people, including a substantial number of tourists, many of them international. People from all over the world loved downtown San Diego, so much so that they'd spend thousands of dollars to get here and stay here. I made my way to the beer cooler.

I ended up at Pantoja Park, San Diego's oldest park, just down the street. It was built in 1850 and named after a Spanish explorer. It offered a nice break from the city's asphalt and concrete, from the hustle-and-bustle. It was not a crowded park.

You'd see people walking and playing with their dogs among the many large mature trees, which offered shade to the homeless or anyone looking for a place to rest or nap. There was an olden-day feel to the park, even though it's surrounded by bland high-rise corporate apartments that remind you of today, and 3-Day Notices to Quit. The park was named an official San Diego landmark in 1969.

I sat down at a bench across from a colorful drinking fountain, which was stuck on top of a square block of concrete with hand-painted tiles on all four sides. "Don't worry, be happy" one of them said. Yeah, I thought.

I cracked open one of the beers, careful to keep it concealed by a brown paper bag, which screams, "I'm drinking a beer!" I counted on the cops, who sometimes slowly drove through the park, giving me a break because I didn't look homeless.

I took a deep gulp and stared at a natal plum tree that stood in the middle of the park, the crimson fruit and white blossoms catching my eye.

"You can eat that purplish fruit," I heard a voice behind me remark. "Some days I have to, man."

I turned around. A Black man was standing there, with a light-blue surgical mask on. He had friendly eyes and soft features, and it seemed as if he was smiling. He was wearing a red flannel shirt, faded blue jeans, and a yellow knitted cap. His clothes and shoes seemed new, but his skin was tired and cracked. He was at least in his eighties, shuffling slowly through the city.

"Yeah?" I said.

He sat down next to me with a little bit of difficulty. His eyes were squinted. There was a bright sun shining down and bouncing off all the windows of the high-rises.

"How are you today, young man?" he asked.

"I'm okay."

"You got another beer?"

"Yeah. I even have a bag for you. They doubled me up."

I handed him the bag-covered beer. He cracked it open.

"Thank you so much." He took a sip. "Just what this old man needed. So, how are you today?"

"I'm okay. You?"

"Hey, every day's a blessing, right?"

I took a sip. I shrugged. "Yeah."

"You know we can get arrested for this, right?"

"Drinking a beer in the park and minding our own business?"

He smiled. "You ain't killing anybody drinking a beer, right?"

"Not if I'm walking or sitting down. What's the problem?"

He laughed. He pointed to the tree in the middle of the park. "You know that tree out there is from my country?"

"No, I did not know. Yeah?"

"Africa."

"Really?"

He nodded. "You can eat that fruit."

"You're from Africa?"

He took a quick sip. "We all are."

"That's what they say."

He squirmed a bit on the bench to get comfortable. "So, you're sitting on a park bench drinking a beer?"

"Aren't we all?" I laughed.

He laughed. "Yeah. I get that."

"I'm just trying to relax, and get a little sun."

"I'm Timothy," he said.

"Peter. Nice to meet you."

"Hello, Peter."

"Hello."

He smiled, then looked me straight in the eye. "An old man can always recognize a young man in love and a young man in distress."

I sighed heavily and blew air through my lips. "Yeah."

"You're the latter. How'd I know?"

I shrugged. "I don't know."

"Your body language is awful, son," he said. "You need to raise those shoulders, proudly."

I shrugged them. I took a gulp of beer.

From our right, a police car was slowly coming down the wide walkway, making its rounds through the park. I've seen them here before, and they don't seem interested in very much.

The car stopped in front of us, and the young Black officer lowered his window. He was muscular, with broad shoulders and a chiseled face. He smiled widely. "How are you today, Timothy?"

"Another day in paradise."

"Hello, officer," I said.

"How are you?" he asked.

"Not bad."

"Good to hear," he said. "Now, I know you're both sipping orange juice. Am I right?"

Timothy smiled. "Absolutely."

He pulled away from us. "Carry on, gentlemen. Stay safe."

"He's one of the good ones," Timothy said.

"How are the cops in San Diego?"

He fiddled with the bag around his beer, then took a quick sip. "They're fine. They don't go looking for trouble. They'll leave you alone. Especially now."

"It seems like they leave the homeless alone."

"Unless they see someone hitting the pipe, they'll just keep on driving," he said knowingly. "If you and I were sitting here sharing a crack pipe, things would have gone a whole lot different. I've never seen them bother anyone for beer. But I don't even jaywalk."

"No police contact."

"Sometimes, some of us don't have a choice."

"Yeah, I know," I said.

My cellphone vibrated. It was Alison. Hurricane Alison: "WHERE ARE YOU??? COME BACK NOW!!! I NEED YOUR HELP WITH SOMETHING!!! COME BACK NOW!!!"

All caps. Probably cycling, I thought.

"All right, Timothy I have to hit the road. Duty calls," I said. "Nice meeting you."

"Take care, young man," he said. "I'm sure we'll see each other again."

I stood up and opened my wallet. "You need some help?"

He shrugged.

"Here's eighty dollars."

He took the money. "God bless you," he said softly. "This helps."

"All right."

"I'm staying at the Salvation Army over on Fifth."

I started to walk back to the hotel, slowly. There was no need to rush my way into another one of Alison's onslaughts. I'll just take the blame for whatever it is, I thought.

We just don't go together. My Dad was right. It's all about compatibility. Not one word of my fiction had ever been read by her. All she does is read the legal nonsense I write for her. And she always finds something wrong with that. I'm just a moron to her. Time for more beers.

I ended up at Karl Strauss, where the beer fueled some protracted thinking: "There's no way out of this. Satan listened to me when I dared him to possess my life. How else could this awfulness be explained? Sixty years old and absolutely nothing done, nothing accomplished. Well, there were a few things done. I won those writing awards in high school. And my college professors told me I'd make a living as a writer. I passed the California Bar Exam on my first attempt. I helped many people pass the exam because of my expertise and insight. I have a beautiful wife with a heart of gold, which I turned into pyrite. I have a sweet, handsome son, who, because of me, wants nothing to do with me.

ADDICT'S WAY

You don't have a dime to your name. Your life is a fucking mess. How in the hell do I get out of this? There's no one to help me. But I need help. I need a lot of fucking help. I'm lost. I'm going out of my mind. There's no one to talk to."

My waiter glided over to my table. Twenty-something, tall, white, thin, and always wearing some tie-dyed t-shirt.

"Another one?" he asked.

I nodded. "Also, I'll have a few sirloin medallions."

"Three?"

"Yeah, three."

"Medium rare?"

I nodded. "Yeah."

"All sliced up like always?"

"Yes," I answered. "Smothered in the herb butter."

"All right, man! You got it! On the way!" he said with youthful enthusiasm, unaware of all the meaninglessness that surrounded and awaited him. "I'll bring you a few samples, too. We just brewed a couple of new batches. I think you'll like them."

I saw a couple of lawyer-types walk down the street: crisp suits, perfectly combed hair, expensive-looking briefcases – and sadness pricked me. I should still be a licensed attorney, I thought. That car crash ruined me. I can outthink and outwrite all those motherfuckers! I'd make judges consult the Evidence Code: "Yes, Mr. Panelli is correct." It wasn't a passion, but I liked practicing law well enough. I liked the intellectual challenge of it and the feeling that I was smarter than most people, which is true – you did need an IQ in the top ten percent to pass the California Bar Exam; I don't think the same can be said of many other jurisdictions. California's exam was the toughest, by far.

I also liked the fact that a law license put you in a position to make much more money than the average person. Riches weren't guaranteed, but if you knew how to live life the way it should be lived, you'd do okay: you'd be able to eat in restaurants and take vacations, here and there. No guarantee of a mansion but you could sufficiently house yourself. Unless, of course, you suffered from a pathological gambling addiction.

In my heyday, I'd chase money to gamble with the way a heroin addict chased his next fix: I'd do whatever I could to get my hands on money to bet with, even though I knew I was going to lose. In the early years of my horseplaying, in high school and college, I'd overall win, but only an insignificant amount every year. In my late twenties, I became a compulsive gambler, which is another way of saying perpetual loser. Yet, in the back of my mind, there was always a voice telling me: "You'll hit the big one. You won't have to do the cubicle life. You're smart enough to beat this game. Just be focused and disciplined. Stop the compulsive insanity."

But I couldn't stop the compulsive insanity. Eventually, betting on horses, for 40-plus years, became a way to punish myself. There are 14,600 days in forty years. I was at the racetrack for 8,760 of those 14,600 days. I'm certain, of those 8,760 days, I had gone to track 2,000 times with $1,000 in my pocket and walked out with nothing. Yeah, there's $2,000,000.00 right there. Even if had kept 10% of my overall losses, I'd have at least $400,000 in the bank right now. And if I had never become a horseplayer, I'd be flush: I'd be retired living in a home I owned outright. But I'm a member of the sheltered homeless. From Passing the Bar to Living in My Car. That's my memoir title!

A pathetic life. I wished I had never stepped foot inside Santa Anita Racetrack. My father took me there one Saturday afternoon when I was in the third grade. But what ensued after that fateful day wasn't his fault. I was enamored by the whole scene: back then, men wore suits, and women wore hats and sometimes long gloves. People held martinis, careful not to spill a drop as they cheered their horses down the stretch.

After that fateful day, I wanted to come back again. And I did: not just my father and I, but the whole family. Every weekend during early high school, we'd all pack a picnic basket and sit out in the infield. I loved the way the fog would hug the San Gabriel mountains in the winter months. It was like looking at a postcard photographed by God himself. I'd spend every Friday night making my calculations. I became notorious for having a knack for it. My father would proudly say things like, "Peter picked six winners last Saturday." I felt like I had found my life's calling.

I finished my food and then slowly headed back to the hotel. I surveyed all the high-rises. *You should be living here in a paid-for million-dollar condo, with a view of the bay,* I thought.

Alison heard me using my key card and opened the door for me. "I need you to call a new client for me," she said in an anxious frenzy.

"All right. When?"

"Well, it's too late now. In the morning."

"Okay, I'll do it for you."

"He's a prison inmate. You'll be on a three-way with him and his wife. I'll get the call started for you. We'll be on speaker, so I can listen in. Okay?"

"What time?"

"Sometime before two o'clock."

"I'm tired," I said. "I'm going to go lay down for a little bit."

"Beers?"

"Plus, a sudden, dark onslaught of depression. Gee, I wonder why," I said and turned toward my bedroom.

"I'm going to go to sleep right now until tomorrow. I don't know what time I'm going to wake up. This arthritis is killing me. I'm dead."

"All right."

"I'll email the names and phone numbers to you. I might not make the call after all."

"Okay."

"Call them anytime in the morning."

"I will."

"The wife's name is Violet. The husband's name is Marco."

I tossed myself on my bed and curled up into the fetal position.

I thought about the scene in "Pretty in Pink," where the face of John Cryer's teary-eyed character had consumed itself with sadness and disappointment when he knew he'd never have Molly Ringwald's heart.

| 9 |

After I had finished the call with Violet and Marco Gonzalez, I fell back onto my bed. Clients exhaust me. There wasn't much stress to the call, but my energy levels had been evaporating quickly, lately. Every morning, I wanted to just go back to bed. If I had any beer or wine left over from the night before, I'd quickly chug it down to ease my way back to sleep.

That's what I did this morning: I drank two Michelob Ultra Lights in less than one minute. I felt the gentle snap of relaxation and then I put my head back on my pillow. I looked forward to the few-hour escape. Especially since I had been dreaming very vividly lately as if I was in another dimension while asleep. Plus, I felt safe and comfortable in the fetal position. I was the perfect candidate for a long-term stay in a sanitarium or insane asylum.

My dream state was rudely interrupted when Alison barged through my bedroom door like a lethal virus. "Did you even make the phone call?!" she barked, unprovoked.

"Yes!" I barked back. "What the fuck is wrong with you?! All you do is drain my spirit."

"Do you blame me for not trusting you? You never follow through with anything."

Finding the silver lining in anything just wasn't in her personality. All she knew how to do was complain. About everything.

ADDICT'S WAY

I sat up in bed.

"Fuck this!" I said. "Who writes all your motions? Who writes all your complaints? Who writes all your answers? Who handles all your discovery? I do nothing?! This is bullshit!"

"Did you make the phone call?!"

"Yes. How many more times are you going to ask me?"

"So, you made the phone call?"

"Yes!" I snapped.

"What happened? Wait! I'm not ready yet. Let me have my coffee. Let me wake up first. Just leave me alone right now."

I hugged my pillow. If life is a gift, point me in the direction of customer service – I need to return it: it's broken.

"Peter?" she yelled out.

"Yes."

"Get out here."

I got out of bed and sat on the couch. "What?"

"We'll talk about the phone call later."

"Whenever."

"I want you to get me a #19 from Mona Lisa, with avocado, and oil and vinegar on the side."

"Okay," I said.

"Oil and vinegar on the side."

"Okay."

"With avocado."

"Okay."

"A #19."

"Okay."

"You got it?"

"Yes."

"Let's see," she said. "Do you want me to write it down for you?"

"No, I got it."

"What?"

"A #19 with avocado, and oil and vinegar on the side."

"Okay, let's see if you can follow directions."

"I'll be back."

"Today?"

"Unfortunately."

"Go to hell, Peter."

I left the room, took a few steps toward the elevator, then immediately returned. "I forgot my stupid mask," I said.

"Of course. That's Peter."

"Whatever, Alison."

"Hurry back. I'm starving."

"Do you want anything to drink?"

"No! Hurry!"

"Okay!"

"Aren't you going to comb your hair? You look like a mental patient."

"I don't comb my hair anymore. I'm using that energy on other things."

In the elevator, a man was wearing a U.S. Navy t-shirt, the kind only a Navy insider would be able to get. He was a heavy-set white gentleman with large forearms and gray hair.

"My Dad was World War II Navy. He's 94. Still alive," I said.

"That's amazing," the man answered. "I served 22 years."

"Fantastic. My Dad went to the south pole with Admiral Byrd. He has beautiful pictures. He even had a pet monkey down there."

He smiled with genuine interest. "How wonderful. I bet he appreciates you talking about him."

Mona Lisa is an old-school sandwich shop found at the top of Little Italy on India Street. There's a glass display under the sandwich-ordering counter that highlights Italian meats, cheeses, vegetables, and signature salads. On the wall behind the counter, there's a chalkboard with all the different foods that can be ordered to eat here or take home. Like a liquor store, there is a vast refrigerator section full of beers and wine, some straight from Italy.

Before COVID, it was a crowded place with red-and-white-checkered-tabletops indoor and outdoor seating. Now, everything is take-out. A mask must be worn to go inside, and I was scolded by one of the sandwich makers because mine wasn't covering my nose!

I was hungry now. I bought two #19s and a six-pack of Michelob Ultra.

On the way back to the hotel, I gave a beer to my friend, Tim, a 70-year-old Black man who is homeless because of a manslaughter conviction now over 50 years old. "I've never even been given a chance," he told me the first time we had met over pizza.

"Thanks for the beer," he said. "Can you spare any paper, Peter? My phone's due."

"Not right now. All I have is my debit card. I'll find you tomorrow. How's that?"

"It's thirty dollars. Thanks, Peter."

We have Adopt-a-Highway, but we don't have Adopt-a-Homeless Person, I thought.

"Where do you think you'll be?" I asked him.

"I'll be around the 7-11. You'll be able to find me."

I walked inside the hotel room. I handed Alison the bag with the sandwiches.

"Let's see if he got it right," Alison said.

"It's right."

She examined the sandwiches and small containers of oil and vinegar. "All right," she said. "Did you get a receipt?"

"Is there one in the bag?"

"No," she said.

"I don't know."

"You know I always want a receipt! Pay attention to details, Peter!"

"You're relentless. Yeah, I know," I said. "I'm sorry."

I just didn't understand her receipt obsession. She had Del Taco receipts in plastic, see-through storage containers that were over 10 years old. Anyway. Her problem, not mine. Well, mine too, actually.

"Why do you have such trouble paying attention to details?"

I sighed loudly. "Just give me my sandwich. I just want to eat my sandwich, drink a beer, and run then my suicide note through Grammarly."

| 10 |

In the morning, I could hear Alison's coffee brewing. Then, I could hear her footsteps frantically pounding toward my bedroom door, which she angrily opened with more force than necessary.

"You forgot to tell me about the phone call with the inmate!" she yelled.

I slowly sat up in bed, the day's spirit already broken. "Come on, man. Come on. Give it a rest."

"You were given a task and you didn't do it!"

"I made the phone call."

"Did you report back to me?!"

"I went and got us sandwiches."

"Then you forgot. Then you went into your room to eat your sandwich and drink beer!"

"What do you want?"

She slammed the door shut. Then yelled, "I need to wake up first! I need my coffee!"

When she was finally ready, I told her about the phone call. "Your guy got screwed by the system. It's really corrupted," I began.

"Okay! What else?!"

Marco Gonzalez had been charged by the state court as a felon in possession of a firearm. Thus, a federal hold had been placed on his case, which means the federal government had an interest in him as a known career criminal. Once the state charges had been dismissed against him, the federal government would pick up the case and charge him under a more-harsh federal statute and guideline. At the state level, he had been told the state charges would be dismissed, which is why he denied a plea-bargain offer from the state of 16 months. The only reason the state charges were dismissed against him was so the feds could pick up the case. Had he known the feds would thereafter pick up the case, he certainly would have accepted the state plea-bargain offer.

"He should have been told by the state public defender to accept the plea. Failure to do so was malpractice," I explained. "Are you telling me his defense attorney knew nothing about federal holds? Now, he's facing 15 years instead of 16 months! What a crooked system!"

"What do you mean?" Alison asked.

"What I just said!"

"I wasn't able to process it, Peter."

"What didn't you understand?!"

"I don't know. Just say it again."

"I can't explain it any more clearly than that."

"Just say it again."

I explained it again, almost word for word.

"How could that be done to someone? I didn't think I was hearing you right."

"You heard it right."

"So, what can we do for him?"

"Not much"

"Anything at all?"

I wrinkled my brow and scratched my head. "He could sue his state public defender. He wasn't properly apprised of his rights."

Her eyes turned suddenly fierce. "How do I even know what you're telling me is right?"

My shoulders and the very essence of me dropped. "Why do you have to treat me like this? What the hell is wrong with you? Can't you be nice for more than just a few minutes at a time?"

"You're just mad because you lost your law license," she taunted.

I slammed my bedroom door closed behind me.

"No, I'm mad because you're such a bitch!" I yelled out. "What the fuck did you know about federal holds before I told you?!"

Eventually, I heard her bathroom fan turn on. I left. I ended up at Princess Pub & Grille, which had quickly become my favorite place to waste time. There was always an English grunge-type welcoming vibe and a great mix of music playing, from country to Motown. Today, Heather was behind the bar. Shapely, blonde, attractive, arms covered with colorful tattoos, she was nice, energetic, and cautiously friendly, with a shy smile. I sat at the bar, where I could see all the television screens.

"Hey, buddy," she said.

I smiled. "Hey, Heather."

"Michelob Ultra with a glass?"

I nodded and handed her my debit card. "Keep my tab open."

"You got it."

I poured myself the beer. I drank half the glass with one deep, quick swig. I noisily smacked my lips and exhaled deeply. "Thanks, I needed that."

"Rough day?"

"Always. Married."

Her eyes rolled. "Yeah, tell me about it," she said. "Are you hungry at all?"

I shook my head. "Not yet."

Heather stood by the cash register, looking at her phone, facing India Street, and the symmetry of her hourglass silhouette was on full display, I wondered if she was standing this way for the benefit of me. I laughed at the thought. You're over with, I thought. You had your day in the sun.

I took a deep swig of beer and was glad there was some still left. Look at yourself, I thought. You're so lost. Your life is pathetic. You may as well be on Death Row. At least, there you wouldn't have to worry about room-and-board or calls from creditors. Or Alison. You could be miserable in peace.

Heather turned around to face me with an inviting smile. "So, what kind of lawyer are you?"

I'm the disbarred kind, I thought.

"Criminal defense and family law. It's not like on television," I said. "It's mostly tedious. I'm not a fan of the profession. It's just a way to make a lot more money than the average person. I'd rather be a movie star."

"Right?" she said.

"So, do you have to work at another restaurant after you're done here?"

"No, I don't do double shifts anymore. Too old for that."

"Yeah," I said. "When I was just out of law school, I'd work 14-hour days. Now, I'm lucky to get in 4 hours. Always tired. Always bored."

I wondered if Heather had an extra bedroom. I wanted to rent a room somewhere and live off the grid. You know, use a P.O. Box, a burner cellphone, and just disappear, and hide in plain sight. I was done, there was no way out of this mess.

"What's going on?" she asked.

I laughed. "Where would you like me to start?"

She smiled. "I hear you, Peter."

"I should have followed my heart. I didn't. I went to law school instead."

"Another beer?"

Another life, I thought. "Yes," I said.

"Is it too late?" she asked.

"I hope not. Probably."

"Are you hungry?"

I nodded. "I'll have fish tacos."

"Corn or tortilla?"

"Corn."

She started tapping on the screen of the cash register, then turned back toward the bar. A small diamond between her breasts caught my eye because it was not hanging from a chain. "Is that diamond connected to your bone or just the skin?" I asked.

She laughed heartily, and her tight ponytail swished from side to side. "It goes all the way through, to my spine. You have no idea how many people ask that."

"Funny," I said.

"I got it when I was a teenager."

"You graduated high school in 1998?" I guessed.

"1990."

"76," I said. "I'm old as dirt."

"That's not old," she said.

I finished my fish tacos. "When do you work next?"

"Tomorrow. I always work the day shift. I'm usually off at 5 here. When I'm not here, I'm at Coronado Golf Course, working."

"I heard that's a nice place."

"It is. But it's an older crowd. Yesterday, a grandpa-type told me that he'd never hire someone like me because of my tattoos."

"All right, close me out, Heather. I'm sure I'll see you soon."

I lunged toward another bar: the one inside Born and Raised, just up the street. There, you'd find the fanciest and most elegant restaurant in all of Little Italy. There was a Great Gatsby theme in place, according to the restaurant's Website, with all the waiters and bartenders dressed tuxedo-style in felt bow ties. To me, the place was like a mob joint, where murders were planned over drinks and food. There was something about the décor reminiscent of the Titanic's. Exquisite woodwork throughout. I've always felt good in places like this.

I took my place at the bar. A few moments later, a tall, elegant twenty-something, with reddish-brown hair, bright blue eyes, and smooth features, appeared before me. I could feel my dopamine rise.

"Hello. I'm Courtney. Have you been here before?"

I nodded. "Once. I really like it."

"What are you in the mood for?"

"I like appetizers."

"Anything to drink?"

"Any light beers on tap?"

"We have Modern Times Ice."

I nodded. "And I'll have the shrimp cocktail."

"I've tried it. It's my favorite. I'm glad they give you so much."

Suddenly, the place stopped working: a wave of emptiness fell upon me, and I realized I had no idea how to get from point A to point B. And I didn't even know what the point was, of getting from point A to point B.

Now, what the hell am I going to do now? I thought. Become a paralegal? A busser? Maybe I'll just spend the rest of my life pretending to be an out-of-work actor.

"Would you like another beer?" Courtney asked.

"No, I have an audition in the morning."

| 11 |

As I walked by the 7-11, I noticed my homeless friend, Sheri, laying on the concrete with her eyes closed. I could see her breasts lowering and rising, so I knew she was still alive. I gently nudged her shoe with mine. She opened her eyes and sat up. She was chubby, with short blonde hair and a suntanned face. She could usually be seen on her stomach scratching off a lottery ticket against the sidewalk.

"Oh, hi Peter," she said.

"Sorry I bothered you, Sheri. I have a few bucks for you."

"Okay, thanks," she said. "I was having the weirdest dream. I was at a rehab facility that was having a Happy Hour. I was sipping wine and nibbling on cheese before the 12-Step Meeting."

"That's funny." I pulled a few bills out of my wallet. "Here's $12. It's all I have right now."

"Thanks, Peter. God bless you. You're one of the nicest people around here."

I need to buy her a sleeping bag, I thought. "Okay, Sheri, I'll see you around. Be safe," I said.

I was walking through Downtown with a sense of doom, in a state of sheer panic. There was a strong ringing in my ears. The medicines aren't working anymore, I thought. I need a beer.

I ended up at the Princess Pub & Grille. Heather was behind the bar. A bottle of beer was placed in front of me with enthusiasm, making a sound as it hit the bar, as if the territory were being marked with a flag during wartime "Here you go," she said.

"How's today going for you?" I asked.

"Like shit. Not all that great. The owner's shutting down the place because of COVID."

"Same. When?"

"Tomorrow, I think. Soon, anyway."

"Why?"

"The city says so," she said. "It's being done to all the bars and restaurants."

"Fucking bullshit," I said.

"In a couple of weeks, we might be able to sell drinks to-go and, maybe, take-out food. Keep checking our Web site."

I couldn't sit still. I quickly finished my beer and headed to our office to pick up the mail.

On the way, I ended up at Karl Strauss. I needed more beer. I went with a pint of Follow the Sun.

Since my stomach was empty, I quickly drank the entire pint. There has to be a better way, I thought.

"Would you like some food?" the tie-died-t-shirt-wearing waiter asked me. Some of these Millennials think they're hippies. Maybe it's the reruns of That 70s Show.

"God, no. I don't want anything to interfere with the beers," I said. "I'll have another one. This time, a Boat Shoes."

I was suddenly afraid of everything. I wondered if I was transitioning into schizophrenia.

I took a sip of the new beer. I felt I was just biding my time until some kind of tragedy developed.

I looked up at the big-screen television above the middle of the bar, hoping to see a breaking-news report about the imminent end of the world.

I started to hyperventilate. The wonderment of downtown San Diego had disappeared.

At the office, there were three pieces of life-sucking mail. Even though I could tell it was all junk mail, Alison would want to see it herself – as if I didn't know what junk mail looked like. I was trusted with very little, even tossing junk mail into the trash. This is no way to live, I thought.

ADDICT'S WAY

I walked to the nearby G-Street Ralphs, which was already in full mask-wearing mode. It was always full of the homeless, and the downtrodden, which wasn't surprising, as there was an awful Skid Row-type neighborhood just a few blocks away, near an old U.S. Post Office. It's only a matter of time, I thought.

I grabbed a couple of 24-ouncers. The lines at all the check-out stands were too long, so I walked toward the back of the store, to the men's room, which needed a code for entry. I knew the code. I quickly guzzled one of the beers in the lone stall.

The door to the restroom opened and someone said, "I need to use the porcelain, buddy."

"All right," I said.

I walked out of the stall to be greeted by an elderly-white homeless guy standing by the dirty sink, holding a dirty backpack in his right hand. Everything about him radiated a life gone wrong. Grey hair, unshaven face, and sun-cracked skin. I wondered if he had anybody who cared about him. Yeah, sure he did.

I took a $5 bill from my wallet and handed it to him. "Here you go, buddy."

He took the bill. He nodded. There was no eye contact.

"All right," I said. "Have a good one, brother."

At the register, I paid for both beers – it wasn't the first time I had handed the cashier a full beer can and an empty beer can.

Depression was winning today in a rout. I had nothing to fight back with.

I ended up at Pantoja Park, where I quickly guzzled the second beer and took a nap on the soft grass underneath the shade of a friendly tree.

I dreamed Alison and I were living in my Grandma Dina's house in Montebello. It was a modest tract home built after World War II, with two bedrooms, two bathrooms, a den, a living room, and a dining room, modestly furnished, with green-and-yellow shag carpeting. There was vintage peach-and-blue marble plastic tile in both bathrooms, which, if seen today, would bring you back to the 1950s.

Everything about their home spoke of that decade, which my Uncle Cliff called, thirty years later, the last great decade in America's history. I'd say he was right.

Today, all the media does is create racial division and hatred of the police. I can't stand more than 3 minutes of CNN, which truly seems intent on destroying America's values by replacing them with their lunatic-liberal-left propaganda.

Now, don't get me wrong, we sure have evolved as a country. Thanks to the great Obama, men, and women can now share the same restroom. That's what I call meaningful progress. (Have I just been canceled with this paragraph? Fuck off!)

Back in the day, every Friday night my sister and I would spend the night at Grandma and Grandpa's, which was something we both looked forward to during the week of not-that-much-fun Catholic school. We'd sit on the couch with Grandma, and Grandpa would sit nearby in his recliner, and we'd all watch, usually, either Gunsmoke or The Lawrence Welk Show. Sometimes Mario Lanza records were played. We'd be allowed to stay up late. In the morning, Grandma would make us all a big breakfast of eggs and pancakes, and we'd be allowed to drink coffee out of light-green coffee cups – half milk, half coffee, half sugar. Usually, either food or coffee fell onto the speckled linoleum, put there by either my sister or me. Usually, me.

Great days. Grandma was a cute butterball of a woman, and Grandpa was a tall, dark, handsome man with the looks of a movie star (looks which Cousin Michael inherited). He always wore a suit and tie even though he labored in a battery factory for a living. He and Grandma looked sharp driving around in their mint-green Cadillac, which they proudly parked in the unattached garage. Uncle Cliff was right.

Anyway, in my dream, Alison and I were living with Grandma Dina. Grandpa Giuseppe had already passed on. While Grandma was standing at the stove tending to some marinara sauce, she said, "You guys can always live with me." She wiped her brow, then turned from the stove. Leaving her wooden ladle in the deep silver pot, she walked over to the kitchen table where Alison and I were sitting. She placed two door keys on the table. "Nobody's homeless when there's family," she said.

Then, the loud sound of a lawnmower woke me up from this celestial nap. There's nobody here anymore, I thought.

Back at the hotel room, Alison was stuck in another one of her high-strung frenzies.

"Did you finish the mediation brief for me?!" she barked.

"It's almost done."

"It told you I wanted it this morning!"

"I'll do it right now. It'll take me an hour. I just have to polish it up."

"God, you're pathetic! Can I rely on you for anything?!"

| 12 |

"Then I need you to walk in your sleep to the courthouse. I need you to file a proof-of-service and pick up a minute order for me. You may as well get the mail."

"All right," I said.

"Okay, let's get going, Peter. Okay, let's get going," she said. "I'll write down the case number for you. Don't open the door yet. Let me just finish my coffee."

Just another morning in Paradise.

"I'm going to take a shower," I said.

"NO!!!" she snapped like a maniac.

"Why not?"

"I can't handle all of the scents. Your shampoo, your soap, your conditioner, your deodorant. Whenever I smell them, I get a headache. You already know this."

"So, what am I supposed to do, go shower at the Y.M.C.A?"

"There he is, taking everything to an extreme. I know I have problems, but what am I supposed to do?!"

"Just give me the case number. I'll head out right now."

"Don't put on any cologne! I'll choke to death if you do!"

I know God didn't make me fall in love with this woman at first.

The courthouse at Union Street is a modern structure, recently built in 2016, 22 stories and 389 feet high, with a top cornice that doubles as a shade structure for the east-facing corridors. It is 704,000 square feet of modern architecture, with no Classical columns or bell towers, which will undoubtedly last until and through the next century, built for 555 million dollars. Because people can't fucking get along.

There was a long line to get inside. Everyone had a mask on, and you needed one to enter but not until after your temperature had been taken and after you had answered a series of questions about recent health symptoms, including sneezing.

"If I'm sneezing, I might have the virus?" I asked the Sheriff who had just let me inside the front entrance. He was friendly, with an inviting demeanor. A happy Mexican man who loved his food. He rolled his eyes. He knew what was going on.

"Who knows? They say it's one of the symptoms," he said. "Where are you headed today?"

"Probate window."

"Third floor."

I made my way through the metal detector. Stricken from the roll call of attorneys, I thought. I gathered my belongings from the provided grey tub which looked like something you'd see at a restaurant's bus station.

I took the elevator – faster than the escalators – up to the Probate office, where you pull a number from a dispenser as if you're waiting to order an ice cream cone or cold cuts. Your number digitally appears on a large HD screen that hangs from the ceiling; a male computer-generated voice sounds it as well. There's never much of a line for the Probate window, but you still have to pull a number. Today, the Probate office was empty.

I approached the window without a number in my hand and was instructed by the heavy-set Black woman behind the counter to pull a number anyway. I rolled my eyes to myself.

"How can I help you today?" she asked flatly.

In general, courthouse clerks were no different from DMV clerks: there was always an attitude from them, that you were an interruption to their daydreaming or their inherent laziness. Rarely, would you meet a friendly one. I can't imagine court clerks are paid much of a salary, so I do my best to not respond to them in kind. Everybody's poor, I thought.

"How can I help you, sir?" she asked again.

"Yeah, I'm ready," I said.

"What do we need to do today?"

I handed her the proof of service. "Here to file a proof-of-service and pick up a minute order. I have the case number for the minute order."

She carefully examined the proof of service, running her middle finger across every line of type. Her fingers were stubby, and her forearms were thick. So were her glasses. She looked strong, more than she looked overweight. She reminded me of Alison's grandmother, the way she looked in photographs when she was much younger. Everything about Grandmother Obdulia was a testament to strength and courage. Her father was a nasty, abusive man, infecting the female lineage, spiritually, with acts of unspeakable abuse, both physical and sexual. Alison believed her own DNA had been infected by these unspeakable acts; the reason why she had always struggled with sexual intimacy. Eventually, our marriage became sexless, but she blamed that eventuality on my addiction-fueled misdeeds. "Who could even like you?" she'd say to me.

"I'm sorry, sir," the clerk said. "I find the signature on the proof-of-service suspect."

"'Suspect?' What does that mean?"

"I think the signature is forged."

"How would you know if a signature was forged?" I asked with a friendly tone.

"It looks like a fake scribble."

"Look, it's just a proof-of-service," I said. "It's not a verification, it's not a declaration, it's not a complaint. It's a very innocuous document."

"I understand. I'm going to flag it as suspect and let the judge determine what she wants to do."

"What does that mean? I'm just here filing something for an attorney friend of mine. I'm in family law, I have nothing to do with probate."

"I'm just going to make a note on the file, that's all," she said. "It probably won't be a big deal."

"Then why even bring it up?"

"Anything else?" she asked.

I handed her a Post-It note. "I need the minute order for the last hearing on this case. Thanks."

She turned to her computer screen and did some typing after repositioning her glasses. "When was the hearing?" she asked.

"Just a couple of days ago, I think."

"It won't be in the system yet."

"When will it be?"

"I'd check back at the end of the week."

"So, it's not available yet?"

"No."

This exchange is why they check everyone for weapons when they enter a courthouse. As if awful judges weren't bad enough. In San Diego, they're also crooked, not just awful.

The judge on Richard Stearns' case, Timothy B. Taylor, the pompous, bow-tie-wearing scoundrel, ordered attorney's fees of over $100,000 when the awarded amount should have been no more than $10,000. News Flash: Judge Taylor awarded over $100,000 to the law firm, Shepard Mullins; interestingly, Judge Taylor worked for Shepard Mullins before he had been appointed to the bench by Arnold Schwarzenegger, I learned after the fact. I suspect Judge Taylor had an ethical obligation to reveal this fact on the record, as judges in other cases I had been involved with had done so under similar circumstances (like noble Judge Silberman in Pasadena), but Judge Taylor didn't. He ordered $100,000 in attorney's fees to Shepard Mullins for 33 pages of work!

It's a crooked profession. Even the State Bar is crooked. Just look at what Attorney Tim Girardi was able to do to his clients, for decades, under its watch. You're telling me nobody knew? Fuck the State Bar.

Outside in the hallway, I heard a woman speaking loudly to the Probate clerk: "Why doesn't anyone help me? Why am I always told no one can help me? All I want to know is what forms I need to file. That's not legal advice, is it? Doesn't anyone around here want to work?"

I stepped back inside the Probate area. There was a Black woman with long hair, wearing a long dress that fell gently to her feet, wearing brown sandals. Her black hair was straight and cascaded to the small of her back. Her frame was thin.

I waited for her to leave the Probate area. "What's going on?" I asked her.

"I think this is being done because I'm a black transgender," she said.

"What's being done?"

"No help at all. I just need to start a probate case."

"Okay. I'm a lawyer," I said. "I'll write down all the forms you'll need."

"I'm Patricia. Do you have a card?"

"Not with me. I'm Peter. I'll write down my cell for you. Just send me a text if you have any questions," I said. "A friend of mine, she handles probate cases. You'll definitely need a lawyer for this."

I was in the mood for sushi, so I headed over to Sushi 2 on Broadway and First, which has an unbeatable Happy Hour for beer:

a pint of Sapporo Draft for only $2. Decent sushi on top of that. I always ordered several pieces of Salmon Nigari because of the Omega-3 fatty acids, but I had no idea why I was trying to prolong my life through diet.

I ordered eight pieces. I drank the pint in less than 30 seconds. I patiently waited for the sushi, and I was feeling great.

I ordered another beer. I speared a piece of sushi with one of my chopsticks.

I saw a text from Julio come through. Ah, shit, I have to catch up with the Indio crowd, I thought.

When I got back to the hotel room, Alison was looking at her laptop, sitting at her desk, and scooping up some hummus with a blue-corn tortilla chip. The curtains were drawn open, and I could see the sun's rays falling on the Recorder's Office and the bay.

I told her about the suspected forgery.

"What is she involving herself for?" she snapped. "A notation to the judge?! What a bitch!"

"What else do they have to live for?"

"Exactly. Did you get the minute order?"

"Not yet. It wasn't available yet."

"Who told you that?"

ADDICT'S WAY

"She did."

"That's a lie."

"I'm not lying."

"I bet she was lying to you just to screw me."

"I doubt that," I said.

"You don't know anything about women, do you?"

"Like, this woman knows who you are?"

"I'm sure I've filed something with her before."

"She made a point of memorizing your name?"

"Probably."

I sat down on the couch and looked out the window at glimmering the bay.

"Why would she do that, Alison?"

"I had a run-in with her before."

"Gee, you had a run-in with someone? How surprising."

"Shut up, Peter."

I stood up. I wished I was out on one of the sailboats I could see slowly moving in the bay.

"Stay here!" Alison snapped.

I sat back down. "What the hell is wrong with you?"

"I have three trusts that I need you to create."

"All right, I will."

"Did you hear?"

"Yeah, I heard you."

"Not the trusts, the lockdown. Did you hear about the lockdown?"

"Yeah. Kind of."

"Everyone has to stay inside for the next 6 weeks. You can only go to the store, get gas, or go to work. It starts at midnight. All restaurants and bars are closed."

"This is fucking nonsense."

"Now what are you going to do? Now you can't frolic around Little Italy anymore. Hmm. Maybe now he'll get some work done."

I silently took and exhaled a few deep breaths. "I'm resting my eyes for a little bit," I announced.

I crawled into bed. I closed my eyes. I thought of distant night skies, full of falling stars that warned you to never wish upon them.

| 13 |

Buzzed on a six-pack, I started my memoir, The 30 Days Leading Up to Me Slitting My Wrists. I decided to get some writing done during the proposed 6-week lockdown.

"I think when I was a young boy," I wrote, "there must have been a reverse exorcism, or something, performed on me, where all the goodness and innocence was driven from my body. I mean, when I was 9 years old, I already knew it was all bullshit. Destiny's momentum is an inescapable riptide, taking us wherever it wishes, no matter how hard we try to swim toward goodness, no matter how hard people pray to keep us from drowning. We're all fucked. I'm sorry to be such a downer, but it's just what I know to be true."

"I hope that's the sound of you working on a living trust!" Alison bellowed from the kitchen.

"Yeah."

"What are you doing?"

"Typing on my laptop."

"What?"

"Stuff."

"I hope it's stuff that can make us money."

"I don't care if it does or doesn't."

"Peter, what is wrong with you?"

"I'll get your trusts done. There's a learning curve with the software. That's all I'm dealing with right now."

I could hear the sound of her cooking. I opened my bedroom door.

Alison was using the spatula on some egg whites. I sat back down on my bed.

"Can I have some?"

"I'm making these for me."

"Whatever."

"Look, Peter, you're a good-looking guy, you're personable, people like you," she said. "You were voted President of your law school. You're intelligent but there's something really wrong here." She paused to sprinkle on some grated cheese and grind some pepper on the eggs. "All those big-time lawyers we know, they have nothing on you from a personality standpoint, a looks standpoint, or a charisma standpoint. Clients would easily sign up with you instead of them. But."

"When are you going to stop with the punitive stuff? Every chance you get, you beat me down, one way or another. Stop."

"I need you to load the dishwasher. I'm tired of being the only one who does it," she said. "Contribute to the unit."

ADDICT'S WAY

I ended up at Princess Pub & Grille. I couldn't sit inside or outside, but I was able to order a to-go beer from Heather from the counter next to the entrance, and chat with her a little bit.

"Weird, huh?" she said.

"I don't believe any of it."

"I don't either. We'll see, I guess."

"If Biden gets in, we're going to see a shitstorm coming our way," I said. "He and that joke of a V.P. choice will ruin this country. They'll ruin this country, trust me."

"It'll be sad," she said. "I'm going to Vegas after my shift."

"Where are you guys going?"

"My brother and I are meeting a group of friends."

"Is Vegas even open?"

"So far. We're staying at Aria."

"I've been there. I like the Wynn."

"So, what are you going to be doing the next few days?"

"I'll be taking Prozac and Wellbutrin. I might ask my doctor to add an anti-psychotic to the mix. When will you be back?"

She smiled. "It's a 5-day trip," she said. "You're hilarious. Do you ever just want to hang out with me?"

"We already do hang out with each other."

She playfully grinned. "When I'm not working."

"I must warn you."

"What?"

"I demand the friend zone. I'm just not sure if intimacy is a thing of mine anymore."

She rolled her eyes. "All right."

We exchanged numbers. Now, I'd probably never come back to the place.

"Good luck in Vegas, Heather," I said. "Number 9."

I couldn't sit still. I went to Karl Straus.

Already, the streets seemed empty of people connected to any kind of commerce, other than collecting bottles and cans. Only the homeless were shuffling around. I wondered where they'd be during the lockdown.

Despite the pull of the beer, my thoughts were racing: "I have to get in touch with the Indio crowd. I have to get out of this fucking mess. I have no idea what the fuck I'm doing. The days are just passing by. I'm stuck in survival mode. I can't live in a hotel forever. I feel like shit."

As I waited for another beer, a Black homeless man approached my table, one of the many wooden picnic tables that had been placed out in the street, due, no doubt, to the forthcoming no-dining-inside mandate.

He stood before me and matter-of-factly said, "The world is going to end."

He seemed firm in his opinion, wearing combat fatigues and a purple-knit beanie. His facial skin was unusually smooth-looking, but there was no smile on his face; it was painted with a little bit of anger.

I was interested in the topic he had just brought up.

"When?" I asked. "When is it going to end?"

"Before midnight, I'm afraid."

I nodded. "Would you like to have a beer with me?"

He slowly sat down across from me, as if his entire body were sore.

"I haven't had a drink in over 20 years. But in light of what will be happening by midnight, I will."

"So, then, we just drink. There's no need for food," I said.

"Well, I am hungry," he said. "Perhaps we can refer to it as our last meal, the way the prisoners do before they take their seat in the chair?"

"Okay then, my friend," I said. "What is your last meal request?"

"I'm Thomas."

"I'm Peter."

"I would like a rack of lamb. And a dry martini," Thomas said. "And, for dessert, some high-end vanilla ice cream. I would also like to be wearing a tuxedo."

"Marvelous. Do you know if the lockdown is already in full effect around here?"

He shook his head. "Some places are still open, I've heard. What will you eat, Peter?"

"Four shrimp cocktails, with jumbo shrimp," I said, thinking. "And, yes, four Long Island iced teas, or beers. Ending with vanilla ice cream does sound good."

He gulped some beer. "I have no money for any of this. Thank you for the beer."

"I will pay for everything. Soon enough, money will no longer be needed."

"Is that kind of food here?"

"We will need to head somewhere else," I said. "First, though, we will have two more beers each before we embark on this tour of magical mystery."

Thomas raised his pint of beer. "God bless us all," he said.

We took an Uber to a tuxedo shop in Barrio Logan, which touted itself as a Historical Cultural District but was nothing more than a modestly-interesting Latino ghetto. It often made the news for weekend violence, including murder, occurring usually after the last call of the bar in question. I didn't feel safe because of my white skin, but the owner of the shop assured me that she "knew everybody around here" and I would not be harmed.

"I am the owner. You are safe with me." She was a skinny, 70-something Mexican woman, with a jet-black bee-hive hairdo. Her skin was smooth and taut. Her deep-set eyes looked like two turquoise marbles that had been dipped in watery milk. "I'm Isabella," she said. "How can I help you?"

"We need a tuxedo for my friend," I said. "We'd like to buy one."

"All I have are rentals," she said.

"Can we buy just one?" I asked.

"Si."

"Okay, Thomas. Let her measure you up, and I'll go outside and get some air. Hopefully, I don't get killed. Just kidding. Can I sit down here, Isabella?"

"Yes."

I sat down on a metal card-table chair. I looked around the place. All the walls, except the walls behind the cash register, were covered with hanging tuxedos. There were a couple of long mirrors stuck between them on each wall so you could see how unattractive you might be. There was a yellow pinata hanging from the ceiling above the cash register, with a small sign on it that read, "En venta. Más atrás. Solo pregunta." No idea what the sign meant, but I liked being in a Mexican tuxedo shop with a pinata. Maybe I could punch it and get some candy.

"Is this for a wedding?" Isabella asked.

"No, just a special occasion," Thomas answered.

"A graduation?"

"Kind of," I said.

"Shall I get a bag for your clothes?"

Thomas shook his head. "I won't be needing them anymore," he said.

After I handed Isabella a fistful of tens and fives, we took an Uber to Mister A's, the fanciest restaurant in San Diego, situated on the penthouse floor of the Fifth Avenue Financial Center.

When we walked inside, I was not impressed with the décor nor the ambiance: plain powder-blue chairs, white tablecloths, and restroom doors you'd find in an office tower. There was, however, a magnificent view of downtown San Diego and the ocean beyond, with vivid sunsets, not to mention a stunning wine display. From every table on the patio, you could see San Diego Bay, Balboa Park, Coronado Island, Point Loma, and even the San Diego Zoo. Jetliners zoomed by at eye level. It would be a nice place to jump from.

After a little while, an attractive, brown-haired, middle-aged woman appeared with menus held against the wealth of her breasts.

"Would you like to sit inside or outside?" she asked.

Her smile was put-offish and all-business, with her looks, likely, dictating such a façade.

"We have seating available on the outdoor patio," she said matter-of-factly.

"What do you think, Thomas?"

"Outside," he said. "I like to watch the planes."

"I don't even see or hear them anymore," the woman said.

A roasted Rack of Lamb was placed in front of Thomas. Pan-Roasted Ora King Salmon was placed in front of me. Even though I was a self-proclaimed pseudo-Nihilist, I, inexplicably, made sure to intake a sufficient amount of Omega-3s. Thomas had a martini to consume. I had a draft beer.

Whenever I was dining, or drinking, at a restaurant, I didn't care how fucked-up the world, or my life, was. It was like being, and betting, at the racetrack. A Racing Form and a stiff drink were like a heroin escape. It was exactly like a heroin escape, even though I had avoided that other-worldly experience through the years. I had researched the heroin high on Social Media, and it had always received 5-Star ratings. One try, and I knew I'd be hooked. On that note, I was glad I didn't live in a country with opium dens. I'd be in one of them watching television, or porn, all the time. Know thyself.

"Don't you wish we could just sit here with bazookas and blow up all the planes?" Thomas said, taking a knife to his lamb, and looking at a landing plane.

"You mean like in a video game?" I said.

"No, in real life," he said. "You know what else would be cool?"

"Oh, I don't know, blowing up buildings?"

"Killing all white people would be a good thing. And a fun thing."

"I don't think I'd find it much fun."

"Well, you're white."

"Yeah."

"I'm just messing with you, Peter. How's your food?"

"Really good," I said. "Why so much violence on your mind, even if joking?"

"I don't know. What day is it?"

"Tuesday."

"Yeah, that makes sense."

"What makes sense?"

"I don't just know how to be happy on Tuesdays. Tuesdays always get me down. I haven't been able to figure out Tuesdays yet."

"How are Mondays?"

"I don't have any problems with Mondays. Mondays are okay. And Thursdays between 4 pm and 6, I have not mastered those two hours yet. How about you?"

"Mine's more numerically based."

"Yeah?"

"Yeah, I don't do well on the 29th day of the month."

"Then Februarys are good for you."

I took a quick gulp of beer. "Yeah," I said. "I think you're right about that. Though, the 5th, the 8th, the 11th, the 14th, and the 17th are problematic too. Realistically, though, it's 1 through 31. Life gets in the way of happiness."

"So, no months are good for you," Thomas said. "Maybe you should circle those dates on your calendar and stay in bed. You know, take a sleeping pill as soon as you wake up."

"I've tried that already."

"How'd it go for you?"

I shrugged. "You still wake up."

"It can't be that bad, Peter."

"I only have peace of mind when I'm on the toilet."

"Well, you can't sit on the toilet forever."

"Not yet. Someday maybe we'll have the technology for that," I said. "Hey, I'm in the mood for a Tiger Woods."

"What's that?"

"You know what an Arnold Palmer is, right? Iced tea and lemonade."

"Yeah, yeah."

"A Tiger Woods is iced coffee and orange juice."

He nodded. "Hey, I like that. I'll have one too. I've never had one."

"I don't think anyone has," I said. "I just made it up."

I'd end up seeing Thomas a few days later. He'd be in the fetal position in front of the 7-11 on Cedar Street, still wearing the tuxedo. He'd look like he was about to be wheeled into surgery for a lobotomy. "Hey, Thomas," I'd say.

"You ruined my life, Peter!"

"What are you talking about, man?"

"Because of this stupid tuxedo, nobody gives me any money for food anymore. I'm dying out here. I might have to strip down to my underwear. Even the soup lines are turning me away. This is very problematic, Peter."

| 14 |

"Suicide, like anal leakage, is always a possibility," I said.

"Well, that's a fine way to answer the phone," Dr. Guessner remarked. "How are you, Peter?"

"I'm awful," I said. "I wasted my life. I was possessed by a gambling compulsion for over 40 years. It was like I was in a trance." I shrugged. "This went on while everyone in my family was busy creating a life for themselves."

"You can't get that time and money back. There's no way."

I sat up in my bed so I could look out the window at the San Diego Bay and the toy-sized sailboats. The sky was full of thin see-through clouds that looked like slowly-moving streaks of powdered sugar.

"I feel like I'm in a holding pattern right now," I said. "I'm just waiting for time to pass until I'm dead. It's game over. I'm done. What can a disbarred 60-year-old attorney do with his life? Not to mention the half-million in IRS debt."

There was a pause. I could tell he was thinking. "Handle the warrant situation. That's not that big of a deal. Take whatever actions you need to take with the bar. It won't be easy, but you need to take some common-sense actions right now."

"Yes."

"You're not going to end up on Death Row. If the bar says no, then change your name and get into a different line of work. Google's not a friend of yours anymore. You need to do whatever you need to do, Peter."

"Yes."

"Massive action needs to be taken," he said. "Wait a minute. I need to take this. My wife is beeping in. Wait."

I looked out across San Diego Bay, at Point Loma, where there are no beaches, but you can see waves majestically crashing on cliffs if you look hard enough. It's a place known for its tidepools full of marine life. I had only been there once, to eat at a Denny's. Someday, I wanted to go there for whale watching, which is another thing Point Loma is known for, along with sport fishing. From what I could gather, it was a great place to hang out. Maybe take Heather. I knew it was a place where I'd like to eat and drink. A few beer buzz would be a great way to spend the day there. I heard there was dive with great Mexican food.

"Are you still there?" Dr. Guessner asked.

"Yes."

"You only have about 7,000 productive days left. You still have time for an impressive tombstone. We need to get started on some inner-child work."

I heard Alison bust her bedroom door open. It was never gently opened; she always had to bust through it like a bulldozer that said, "Here I am!" to the trees and the dirt about to be plowed over.

"Peter!" she shrieked. "Peter Panelli!"

"Dr. Guessner, I'll call you back later if I can. There's an Alison situation over here."

I ended the call: "What now!?"

"I'm hungry. I need food," she whined. "There's no food in this place. Do you see what you've done to me?"

"I'll get it for you."

She walked inside my bedroom, her anger spitting out all over. "Why are your curtains open? Do you enjoy looking at all the filthy homeless people walking around?"

"Yes. I do."

"Everything you do is so wrong."

"Yeah."

"I'm closing these curtains right now. It helps keep out noise."

"What do you want?"

She walked out of the bedroom. I followed her. She sat at her desk, looking down at a cup of coffee. I sat on the couch.

"I want you to go to Burger Lounge."

I stood up. "All right," I said.

"You don't even know what I want."

"Yes, I do. A turkey burger with no cheese and no sauce."

"A free-range turkey burger."

The refrigerator started to quietly hum.

"I hate that awful noise," she said. "This place is just awful, Peter."

"I'm going to Burger Lounge. I'll be right back."

"No! Wait!" she snapped. "How are you going to place my order?!"

"In-person."

"No! What are you going to say to the person taking your order?!"

I wanted to yell at her but the wiring in her brain was all wrong. All my fault, of course. "I know how to come back with what you want, Alison. I always do."

"What precisely are you going to say to the person to make sure you come back with what I want?!"

"What I always say!"

"What?!"

"'I'll have a turkey burger with no cheese and no sauce.'"

"No! I want a free-range turkey burger!"

"All they have are free-range turkey burgers!"

"Still ask for one! I want you to order it like this: 'A free-range turkey burger with lettuce, tomatoes, raw onions, and pickles.'"

"Isn't that what I always come back with?"

I wanted to fall to the ground.

"I want you to say my exact words to the person! I want you to order it just like that! Those words!"

I imagined shooting myself through the roof of my mouth. Then turning the gun on her.

"I'll be right back."

"Bring me back the receipt!"

Christina was behind the counter. Pretty eyes, friendly smile, round face, black hair pulled up in a bun. Always full of niceness. "The usual, Peter?"

"Yeah. Where's Victoria been?"

Her essence dropped a bit. "Her mother died."

"Oh."

"I can't even imagine."

"I need separate receipts. One for the burger. One for the beers."

"I got you, Peter."

"I'll just be sitting outside."

I took the beers with me. I scrolled through the news feed on my phone. COVID is going to kill us all. Elon Musk wants to build condos on Mars. And everything is Whitey's fault.

Of course, the turkey burger didn't please Alison.

"You need to bring this back. This is undercooked. Where are the pickles? There's like only two little ones"

"What's the big deal?"

"I paid nine dollars to cook it myself?"

On the walk back to Burger Lounge, I gave the "undercooked" burger to a homeless woman whom I had not seen before. Elderly, limp grey hair, meth-user skinny, I was sure she wasn't about to complain about the patty. I wondered what her story was. There were so many stories around here. A lot of sad ones.

| 15 |

"Hey, Dr. Guessner, I'm sorry I couldn't call you back the other day."

"That's okay. I figured you were in discussions."

"Yeah, 'discussions.'"

"So, how is everything?"

I looked out the window at the San Diego Bay. It was glistening with sunlight and dotted with sailboats. "I'm married," I said.

"That's a tough one."

"Any advice?"

"Don't buy a gun."

"I thought that very thought the other day."

"You don't want to end up in jail for murder."

"The best thing about depression – I wouldn't have the energy to follow through with the murder. I mean, getting rid of a dead body? That would be harder than the murder itself. Too much commitment is involved. And the ones who take the time to dismember and use a woodchipper? That's commitment. I admire those people."

Dr. Guessner had a good laugh. "So, what's on your mind, Peter?"

"For a while, Wellbutrin gave me an energy boost, but it didn't last long."

"I'll call in a higher dose for you."

"All right."

"So, what's on your mind?"

I glanced at the sailboats. I wished I was one of them. In college, my best friend Chris and I would take his father's 27-foot sailboat out all the time, from the Marina Del Rey Harbor. We'd usually drink to excess and smoke hash as if a DUI on ocean water was an impossibility. One day, Chris had set the rutter to go around in a continuous circle as we partied. We both passed out and were woken up three hours later by the Harbor Patrol. "What are you going to make us do, see if we can walk a straight line on water?" I asked the officer, tan, muscular, with the mustache of a 70's porn star. He grinned and just shook his head. "Be safe, boys." Those were the days.

Years later, my friendship with Chris ended when I asked him to borrow $7,500 after a day of $16,000 in losses at Santa Anita Racetrack one Breeder's Cup. He refused, and I became indignant. It's hard for a compulsive gambler to have a best friend, unless he's a compulsive gambler, too.

I finally answered Dr. Guessner. "I'm still feeling down, you know? I wasted so many years."

"Yeah. I've been thinking about you. I think you've been in a perpetual state of childhood your entire adult life."

"Alison would agree."

"I have a theory."

"Okay."

"You've lived in a state of perpetual potential instead of committing yourself to become someone with a societal label. Growing up to become something specific, that's what society calls on us to do. We cannot stay in a state of being potentially anything. Childhood is a magical place because the possibilities are endless."

"After I had passed the bar exam, I resented being pigeonholed into being a lawyer. I said to myself, 'This is all I'm going to do with my life, be a lawyer?'"

"Some say we don't mature beyond the moment of our most-hurtful childhood wound. When you were 9 years old, that certain Saturday morning happened. Since then, you've been going through life with a 9-year-old brain. I'm not saying you never stopped fingerpainting or playing dodgeball."

"I understand."

"Chronologically, you entered adulthood. But you've been traveling through life anchored to a wounded 9-year-old soul. Just like a child, you've been in a perpetual I'm-gonna-be mode. With you, it's been 'I'm gonna be a writer.' You never really committed to a defined actuality. You went to law school just to put a respectable label on yourself."

"Yeah ..."

"Subconsciously, you've been trying to protect yourself by staying in the safety of childhood. As time goes by, though, you end up dealing with the long-term consequences of living like that."

"There's always been something wrong with me."

"I've mentioned that I liken the mind to a computer. The virus wants to kill you. It's almost like a dream-eating, life-eating virus. Ironically, when addicts are self-medicating, they're self-destructing."

"It never gets better."

"I have a colleague – whom I agree with – who thinks all compulsive gamblers lack the confidence or courage to bet on themselves."

I saw a lone seagull swooping down across the parking lot, spraying shit all over the cars below, incoming dark clouds in the backdrop.

"I'm struggling," I said.

"That's enough for today. Before our next session, I want you to start reading The Gulag Archipelago, by Aleksandr Solzhenitsyn."

When the call ended, I heard Alison open the refrigerator door. "There's nothing in here," she said.

"I know," I said.

"You expect me to be happy?"

"Marriage is when two small rings turn into a pair of invisible handcuffs."

"I agree with that."

"What are you trying to achieve right now?"

"An empty refrigerator doesn't make me happy."

"There's all kinds of stuff in there."

"Nothing that I want!"

There was no use matching her anger and disgust. "Of course not," I said calmly.

"I need something to eat, Peter!" she continued. "There's nothing to eat, Peter! I need food! I'm starving! You're starving me to death! This is domestic violence, Peter!"

"Will you calm down? What do you want me to get you?"

"I guess another stupid turkey burger! It better come back right! I'm going to trust you!"

ADDICT'S WAY

I walked out into the hallway of the hotel, with the signature, almost psychedelic Marriott carpeting, full of exploding orange, yellow, red, and dark turquoise. I wished I were walking to Born and Raised instead, with a pocket full of cash, enough for several appetizers, gin-and-tonics, and a medium-rare Rib-Eye. I wished I were walking into a different dimension, a rabbit hole that lead to a magical galaxy where everyone was pleasant and nice, with no way back.

I passed the Jack-in-the-Box on the corner of Cedar and Pacific Highway. A homeless man was sleeping in the middle of the right lane, traveling east. He was a light-skinned Latino, with a bowl cut and a thin mustache, wearing grey sweats, and a pair of grimy white socks. I could see his torso slowly rising and lowering. There was an overwhelming smell of alcohol.

"Hey, buddy," I said. I touched his shoulder. "Hey, buddy."

He didn't move one bit. I didn't nudge him again: he might be dreaming, and I didn't want to interrupt his brief unit of pleasure. I had seen him before a few times, sleeping in the planters at the end of the drive-thru. I stood in front of him so I could wave off any oncoming cars.

I called 911: "I'm at the Jack-in-the-Box across from the Recorder's Office. There's a homeless man in the middle of the street. He's breathing but he hasn't moved. He's passed out. Very, very something. He's in danger of being run over. I'll waive off the cars."

"Be careful with that," the operator said. "A unit will be on the way."

I stood in front of the man. I turned on my cellphone's flashlight. I waved it about in a circular motion.

Soon, a police car arrived, with its lights flashing, reflecting off the windows of the Jack-in-the-Box and the Recorder's Office.

I made it back to the room with Alison's perfect order.

I closed the bedroom door behind me to listen to some music. I turned on some country, and put my headphones on.

Alison barged through the door. "I can hear the music buzzing through the headphones! It'll give me a migraine! Turn it off!"

| 16 |

I woke up sweating, trembling, and shaking. I calmed down on my way to Ralphs. My brain knew beer was on the way.

Everyone in the place was wearing a mask. I grabbed two cold 24-ounce Coors Lights. I wanted stronger malt liquor, but the homeless crowd always depleted the supply. I couldn't blame them: a large can of malt liquor made you take a nap.

On my way to pay for the beer, my mask slipped below my nose. Some pretty, long-legged Millennial standing in line at the in-store Starbucks, wearing a colorful USD sweatshirt, yelled at me, with a scowl, "Cover your nose! Do you want to kill people?!"

I made my way to the 15-items-or-less Express line. There, a friendly black-haired Filipino in nursing scrubs, with a Dutch Boy haircut, dark-brown eyes, and lots of make-up in the eye area, told me a vaccine was on the way. She insisted I take any vaccine offered, to save my life and the lives of others. "This isn't all about you, you know?" she said. Apparently, she had received the Hoax Pandemic Panic Memorandum.

I walked to Little Italy. I sat on a bench across the street from Burger Lounge, which was empty. The entire street was empty. A week ago, it was bustling with energy. Now every bar was empty. Every restaurant was empty. Every liquor store was empty. Every hair-cutting place was empty. Every gym was empty. Everything was empty.

Suddenly, I started to sweat, tremble, and shake. My breath shortened. It felt like the world was ending. I managed another gulp of beer, the can trembling in my hand. I heard the loud wail of a nearby ambulance as if it had been called for me. I sensed suffering everywhere.

I closed my eyes and took a few controlled breaths. Then I called Dr. Guessner: "You have a little time?"

"You sound like you're in the middle of a marathon."

I quickly described my symptoms. "I feel like collapsing," I ended.

"Where are you?"

"I'm sitting on a bench."

"Is there any pain in your left arm or shoulder?"

"No."

"Good."

"So, what do you think?"

"Anxiety attack. How've you been feeling lately?"

"The constant ringing in my ears is the loudest it's ever been. My head is constantly pulsating with a headache. The left side of my

ADDICT'S WAY

face is always tight. Alison is killing me. There's something wrong with her."

"This is the question, Peter: 'What do I have to do to have a meaningful life?' No one knows the 'meaning' of life. There's no 'meaning' in just being alive. Are you with me?"

"Yeah, I understand," I managed to say.

A loud street sweeper passed by across the street, spraying a large cloud of water and mist all over the sidewalk and the clean windows of Burger Lounge. A stray cat raced down the middle of the street. A large rat followed. Twilight was on the way. I imagined the fluorescent-orange sun slowly setting behind Point Loma.

I stood up to stretch my legs and walk a few feet, and I nearly slipped on a piece of dogshit. Instantly, the stench ran for cover inside my nose. The bottom of my left shoe was plastered with an orange-colored smelly goo.

"All right, Peter. We'll talk soon. You know how to dial 9-1-1."

The stench of the dogshit became stronger. I tried to breathe a bit shallower.

I walked to Jack-in-the-Box, where I was going to wipe my shoe clean on a patch of grass that bordered the parking lot. There were too many homeless people sleeping on it, and I didn't want to interrupt their naps. I went inside the Jack-in-the-Box and left with a cup of water and some napkins. I headed over to Marriott's dog-poop area and cleaned the bottom of my shoe.

Then I called Eddie: "Yeah, do not sweat the court date. It's not going to happen right away because of COVID."

"I'm just stressed, man."

"Of course, you are."

Then I called Jerome: "Hey, man, how are you?"

"Professor, I'm glad you called. I have something to tell you. First, what's going on with my sister's case? She wants to know."

"Tell her that a big firm in downtown L.A. is looking at it right now. I know the owner. He's got millions and millions of dollars in the bank. He has the money to play with FedEx."

"I get it. FedEx is powerful."

"What do you have to tell me?"

"I'm being fucked with at IHOP."

"What's happening?" I asked.

"My boss is calling me 'boy'," he said matter-of-factly.

"All of a sudden?"

"Yeah. We used to be cool. We used to get along. Then, he started calling me 'boy' one day, which is just a different way of saying 'nigger.'"

"Have you spoken with him?"

"He just laughed. I don't want to get fired, man. Me and Teisha, we will be on the streets. Maybe he just gets to call me 'boy.'"

"No, he doesn't. I'll come up with a strategy."

"Thanks, man. Hey, Julio wants you to call him. He says he has money for you."

"I'll call him right now. Sit tight, Jerome. I'll be in touch. Soon."

"My man."

I called Julio: "Julio. Brother. What's up?"

"Professor."

"How are you, brother?"

"I have some money for you, and I have another case for you."

"Sounds good."

"We need to hook up soon."

"All right. We will," I said.

I bought a cold six-pack at the 7-11.

Alison's bathroom fan was on. I took out two bottles and put four in the refrigerator. I closed my bedroom door behind me. I took a refreshing gulp. I placed a pillow against the headboard, and then I leaned on both.

Then Alison violently busted through the door. I thought a small plane had crashed into the roof of the hotel.

| 17 |

It was midnight and getting ready to rain harder. Seagulls were circling, squawking, and shitting.

I was standing on the sidewalk in front of the Jack-in-the-Box. I finally flagged down a police car.

I walked up to the passenger door. The window lowered.

"How can I help you?" the officer asked, looking at her glowing laptop screen.

Her tone was friendly and inviting. She had dirty blonde hair up in a bun, and her round freckled face was free of makeup. The various multi-colored lights on her dashboard were nervously blinking and flashing.

"I want to turn myself in on a warrant," I said.

She quickly turned her head toward me. "Because of COVID, we're not taking anyone in right now. What's the warrant for?"

"Hit-and-run."

"Where?"

"Victorville. Barstow."

"What's your name?"

"Peter. Last name, Panelli. P-A-N-E-L-L-I."

"Date of birth."

"11-14-58."

She quickly tapped on her keyboard. "Nothing's coming up, honey."

"Really?"

"Nothing at all. Is it a felony?"

"No. The judge reduced it."

"That's probably why," she said. "Plus, it's from another county. What's going on with you tonight?"

"We had a blowout, me, and my wife. I need a place to sleep."

"I'm on my way to a call, honey. I'm sure you'll be okay. I'm sorry."

My cell phone beeped. It was a text from Alison: "All your stuff is at the front desk in a big white trash bag. I left it with Michelle."

I retrieved my belongings from Michelle without any fanfare.

I had grown to know Michelle – who was an accountant acting as a front-desk worker because of COVID – from the nights I had spent drinking wine in the dining area of the hotel, where breakfast and wine nights had occurred before COVID. There was a big-screen television where I mostly watched sports. There was a pool outside the glass back door that glowed fluorescent blue in the evening. It was a comfortable place to pass time: Alison was always up in the room.

Michelle handed me the unscented trash bag over the front-desk counter.

"Here you go, Mr. Panelli," she said matter-of-factly. "Ms. Tradgett told us to not let you inside the hotel again, and not accept any calls from you to her room."

"It was nice meeting you, Michelle. I had too much wine and it's that time of the month for her," I said bluntly. Hormones rule the world.

I made my way outside and then to the back of the hotel, next to an air-conditioning unit and a large trash dumpster. I positioned myself so I was out of the rain. It was cold. I leaned against the back wall of the hotel. What the hell was I going to do with an empty debit card and a dead cell phone? Above me was California Street, where a small population of homeless perpetually camped out. I could hear them talking, but I couldn't decipher any dialogue. Well, I'd be one of them tonight. I had no way to pay for a hotel room. Where would I try to make it through the night?

Eventually, I saw the beam of a flashlight pouring into my space, dust floating in its shine. It was the hotel's nighttime security guard, a thin grey-haired white guy with a crooked nose, wearing a pair of black-rimmed glasses, dressed in dark blue, holding a flashlight in his right hand and a clipboard in the other.

"You can't stay here, sir," he said.

"I'm just taking a breather. I'm in room 432. Me and my wife had a blowout," I said.

"I know. That's what the front desk said. Your wife called the police. She wants you off the premises."

I was ready to stand up. "The police are coming?"

"I'd just go somewhere else right now. I'm sure things will straighten out."

The bright lights from the parking lot, which Alison claimed hurt her eyes when she slept, made his name badge visible. "Thanks, Robert," I said.

I slowly stood up. I picked up my laptop and grabbed the clumsy white trash bag. I situated myself, then dragged myself through the parking lot and made my way to the 7-11, looking like one of them. I was offered a bag of small chocolate donuts by a Camp Pendleton Marine. "No thanks," I said.

What a bitch! I thought. She does this when it's raining? Whatever came out of my mouth during the blowout was probably a shitload of truth she couldn't handle. She's not well. I need to get the hell away from her. At most, she's stable 5 days a month. The other twenty-five are dreadful. According to her, there's always something wrong with me and the world. You gambled away a fortune, but you don't deserve to be treated this the rest of your life. Who is she to set forth your never-ending penance? Like she's fucking perfect?

I went inside the 7-11 and stole two $1-dollar breakfast burritos, which was easy to do, as I had been a professed lawyer and an upstanding customer for the past several months to them. There were never any eyes on me, but the homeless-looking were surveyed with great daily suspicion.

I needed to use a restroom, but all the restaurants were closed, and 7-11, smartly, offers none. I had to head down to the portable-toilet units on Broadway that were provided for the homeless. I had been in one before, and the smell made me wretch. This time, the smell wasn't too bad: there was only an unbearable stench of urine to deal with.

I had to leave the white trash bag outside on the sidewalk, otherwise, there'd have been no room for me, and the bottom of the trash bag would have gotten wet with urine.

I looked down at the collection of toilet paper and floating globs of shit as I pissed. I don't know how the homeless do this every day, I thought. I'd put a gun to my head. This is no way to live. I couldn't do it. These homeless are strong people.

When I stepped outside, my white plastic bag had been stolen. It's a good thing I had taken my laptop inside with me, which had all my meds in its bag. What a lowlife move to steal someone's clothes. You need to get out of the rain. I turned around in a circle and quickly surveyed the streets. There was nothing safe about them. People were plenty. All homeless. All sketchy. All on the prowl for something. Everyone was prey. There was not a good feeling to anything.

I started walking back toward the Little Italy 7-11. I knew I'd feel more comfortable there.

I was livid. I slammed my feet down on the sidewalk with each step, like Godzilla, raising my feet high, then lowering them loudly. I figured if I seemed mentally off, people would stay away from me. So, I stomped my way through Downtown San Diego.

I found shelter from the moderate rain in an alcove between two restaurants on India Street. I called Dr. Guessner: "Peter?" he answered

"Sorry to call so late. It's kind of a 9-1-1."

"It's fine. I'm up reading."

"Me and Alison had a bad blowout. I was bombed on wine. She called the police. I left."

"What's the situation now?"

"Empty debit card. Dead phone. No cash. I'll be sleeping in the streets. I told you there's demonic stuff going on with me."

"Is it raining down there, too?"

"Yeah."

"Any chance of begging Alison to let you back inside the hotel tonight?"

"It's that time of the month when she's insane," I said. "I'm not sure if I ever want to go back in there. I'm going to try to find a way to make it up to my parent's house. See what happens with that."

"Okay, keep me posted. You can call me all night long."

I called my lawyer buddy, David Canon: "Well, hello."

"Hey, David what's going on? Did I wake you?"

"I'm looking at the rain trying to put out our campfire."

"Oh, you're camping?"

"I needed a break from the god-awful clients. You know how it is."

"Yeah, I know."

"What's going on with you?" he asked. "How's Alison?"

"Well, I'll be sleeping on the sidewalk somewhere tonight. That's why I called."

"What?!"

"We had a blowout. I had too much wine. She's who she is. I have no idea what I even said. Oh well. It is what it is."

"We're not coming back for another full week. We just pulled in tonight."

"Okay, I'll give you a buzz when you get back."

"You know I'd come to pick you up if we were home."

"I know you would," I said. "All right. I'll figure something out."

"Head to Little Italy."

"Yeah, that's where I am."

"Stay away from the Gaslamp Quarter. That place just isn't safe anymore at night," he advised. "Call me tomorrow. I can figure something out. Maybe Tom will let you sleep on the couch in my office. I'll see."

"Thanks. I'll buzz you tomorrow."

"If I don't pick up, it's because the service can get be bad out here."

"Got it. Thanks, David. You're awesome."

I sent Alison a text: "You send me out to the streets when it's raining? What a bitch!"

I made my way to the 7-11. I needed something to eat. "Hi, Laura," I said.

Wearing her signature red lipstick, she waved and smiled, like always. "Hi," she said.

We were the only people in the store.

"How are you?" I asked her.

"Fine," she said.

"What happened to the door?" I asked, pointing at it. The glass on one of the double doors had been replaced with plywood.

"Some crazy homeless person last night. He banged a big rock against the door and screamed, 'You're mentally ill. You have a mental problem.'"

"He was probably looking at his reflection."

Even though she had her mask on, I could tell she smiled. "Yeah."

"When did it happen?"

"Two o'clock. In the morning."

"Was it just you working?"

"Yes. I called 911," she said.

"You shouldn't be working by yourself, Laura."

"I know. I told the owners. I won't be alone at night anymore. Somebody's coming."

I had met the owners. They seemed like nice people. They were a middle-aged Hindu couple who were always friendly to their customers. There were times when I'd see them give food to the homeless. Other times, they'd just let it be blatantly stolen by them. Good hearts.

"Laura, do you mind if I stay inside here for a little while?"

ADDICT'S WAY

Part THREE

| 1 |

I woke up tired. I found it difficult to sleep on cold concrete. There was no way to get comfortable. There was no way to fall asleep. There was a biting wind, from the nearby bay, which surged through the streets all night long.

I thought about the Santa Anita Turf Club era: heading there right after Judge Silberman's morning calendar, drinking gin-and-tonics, eating bacon-wrapped filet mignon, hobnobbing with all the millionaires and trust-fund babies, knowing I should be anywhere but there.

I walked to the Santa Fe Depot, an old train depot, built in 1915, with Spanish-style architectural influences. It was too early in the morning to meet with anyone who might be able to help so I bought a ticket for the Coaster. It was a coastal commuter train that took you as far north as Oceanside, and then back to San Diego, with various stops along the way, both up and down. It was a scenic ride, with views of the ocean along the way. I bought a round-trip ticket from the kiosk to have a place to rest for about an hour and a half. I didn't look at the ocean once. It was the same the way back down to San Diego. I sat in my seat and rested my head on the top of the seat in front of me. The train was COVID-empty.

I was able to nap a little. I stepped off the Coaster hungry and tired. I walked to the Starbucks across the way. On the way, I ran into a new character. There was an elderly grey-haired Asian man who looked close to 80 years old. He was shirtless, only wearing khaki shorts. He was talking out loud about a war he had survived with a dead compatriot. There was another big one on the way, he told me. My debit card was declined.

I had to ask Mindy, the general secretary at our office building, for some help. I took the elevator up to the fourth floor of Emerald Plaza. Mindy was looking at her computer screen, wearing a mask.

"Hi, Peter," she said. "Do you need a mask?"

"I've got one in my pocket," I said. "I'm not used to putting it on yet. Sorry."

"I know."

I put on my mask. "Hey, Mindy, can I talk to you in private somewhere?"

Her face suggested she knew something serious was going on. "Sure."

We walked into the lobby right behind the reception area. We stood across from the big-screen television. There were four turquoise-colored couches, four orange-colored soft chairs, a couple of futuristic-looking privacy pods, and a view of the stately-looking

<u>Edward J Schwartz Federal Building</u> across the street. We ended up sitting in one of the orange chairs. The place was empty.

"Mindy, I have to ask a favor of you?" I managed to say.

"What's going on?"

"Is it okay if we talk in one of the conference rooms?"

I followed her. I closed the door behind me.

"The look on your face is not good."

"Alison and I got into a blowout last night, and I spent the night on the street."

"I'm sorry."

"Anyway, I'm out here with no money and a dead phone that needs to be replenished. I can't call anyone. I need to make arrangements."

"Okay."

"Can I borrow $50 to get my phone back on and get something to eat? I promise I will pay you back."

"Of course. I might have to find an ATM but let me go check my purse."

"Thank you, Mindy."

She returned with a $50 bill. "Here, you go. I'm sure it'll all work out for you guys."

I took the elevator down to the lobby. I sat in one of the soft-green chairs next to the security desk, which was always staffed with a particularly-friendly Black man named Robert. He had a shiny bald head and an engaging smile. I'd speak with him often about current events, ranging from sports to Black Lives Matter. His take on things was always colorblind. He'd say things like, "The BLM stuff, they're just pawns, and they have no idea they're being played. All this hatred doesn't help."

Today, we talked about George Floyd.

Robert shook his head. "No, I don't think he was trying to kill him," he said. "I think he was trying to show him who's boss. Maybe they had an encounter before or something like that. I don't think the cop was trying to kill him that day."

"If George Floyd was white, though, he'd probably still be alive," I said.

"I agree with that. Everything's a mess right now. Too much anger."

"Too many people stoking the fire," I said.

"Amen, Peter. I feel you. We all need to calm down."

We switched to COVID. "I don't think there was a need to shut down every Mom-and-Pop in the country," he said. "My brother owns a rib joint in Inglewood. He can't handle this."

"It feels like some kind of power grab."

He nodded. "It doesn't add up," he said.

At 7-11, I bought a Verizon pre-paid card and a couple of hotdogs. Then I headed back to the lobby.

I had sunk deep into the same chair. I wanted to lean back and close my eyes for about three weeks. What a nightmare life you made, I thought.

Robert walked over to me. "You holding up okay?" he asked.

"Yeah. I'm okay."

"You look stressed."

"I'm just really tired."

"All right, Counselor. Hang in there. That's all we can do."

"So far, it's been a tough century."

"There have been worse. Just ask my great grandparents, God rest their souls."

"True," I said. "Yes."

David's phone went straight to voicemail. I pictured him sleeping on a hammock, high on THC gummies, his preferred method of escape – a lot less expensive than gambling. "You can live in a campground," he'd tell me.

I scrolled through my phone for homeless shelters. I called a few before someone finally answered. "How can I help you?" a man's voice answered.

"I need a place to sleep."

"Are you homeless?"

"Right now, yes."

"Long-term or short-term?"

"I'm hoping short-term. Yes, I think short-term."

"Well, right now," he said, "San Diego is putting people up in hotels because of the COVID crisis."

"Okay. Thanks. How can I make that happen?"

"Well, you'll have to submit to a TB test, and you'll need a valid ID, and you'll have to answer a confidential questionnaire," he explained.

"My ID's not valid. Right now, the DMV is closed."

"Do you have a way to write down an address?" he asked.

I had to shoot up a flare to my mother. I'd have to somehow take a taxi up there. "That's awful, Peter," she said. "Is there a Catholic church close by? Maybe you can go there for some help."

"I don't know. I only have $12 on me, Mom. Alison controls it all. I'm guessing, it'll probably be about $300 for the cab," I said.

"That's fine. We can do that. Oh, Peter."

I expected the worst. I knew Thomas Wolfe was right.

| 2 |

I negotiated a price of $280 cash. I had to give the cab driver my laptop and cell phone to hold as a down payment. I handed them over, and he placed them on the passenger seat. I'd pay him when we made it up there.

He said, "You don't know what's going to happen when you get up there to your family." He had overheard the cellphone conversation I had with my mother in the backseat. He was a dark-skinned man from Guatemala, with a kind face who looked tired. His eyes were a dull brown. I could only imagine what Uber had done to his taxi-cab driving life. "Maybe nobody gets along where you're going," he finished.

"I hope everything is good," I said. "I hope it'll be okay."

I could feel my heart beating. I could feel sweat accumulating.

"My name is Abelardo. In America, I am Abel."

"I'm Peter."

"By law, I have to keep the meter on. But don't look at the meter. The meter doesn't matter. All that matters are the masks. We're both good with that."

I nodded to his eyes in the rear-view mirror. "Okay, I got it."

After getting gas at the Shell on 10th street, we were headed north on the 5.

"What do you think about all this crazy stuff?" he asked.

"They're just trying to hurt everybody."

"Because my kids can't go to school, my wife has to stay home with them all day long now. We can't afford that."

"What does she do?"

"Bartender."

"That's awful," I said. "Bars are shut down now."

"Yes, this is going to kill a lot of people."

I looked at the cars in front of us. Traffic wasn't bad yet. That would change as soon as we made it to Orange County.

"It's what they want," I said.

"I wear the mask for my clients."

"The virus is real, but the reaction to it is designed to destroy."

"What do you do, Peter?"

"My wife and I are lawyers, but the phone isn't ringing off the hook right now."

"I heard they closed the courthouses."

"Calling a lawyer isn't on anybody's mind right now," I said.

"No."

"This isn't going to be good for anybody."

"Except for the rich people," he said, glancing at his side-view mirror. "What can you do? I feel bad for the children. Look what their world will be."

"Awful."

"Do you mind if we stop for some snacks? I should've got some already."

Abel pulled into an AM/PM. I waited in the cab. He came back with a Slim Jim and a Red Bull. He held up the Red Bull.

"I can't make it through the day with these," he said.

"I used to drink them all the time, then I looked at the ingredients."

"Oh, I know."

I looked to my left. Del Mar Racetrack in all its glory, looking like a picture-perfect postcard. What a bunch of wasted time, I thought. Before simulcasting and the proliferation of online betting, you'd have to visit the actual racetrack where the horses were running. I made the drive down from Whittier hundreds of times, sometimes traveling on the left shoulder of the speed lane if I thought I'd be late for the first race. Now and then, I'd take Amtrak down and catch a cab to the track. I didn't like doing that, because you'd have to leave before the last race to accommodate the Amtrak schedule. The trip back was always miserable if you lost. After winning days, I'd visit exclusive downtown Del Mar, with all its spectacular restaurants, and walk around like I belonged, like I lived in one of the mansions on the beach. I knew someday I'd score a couple of six-figure Pick 6 payouts and join the neighborhood, eat lobster every night, buy a Jaguar, and have a stunningly-beautiful wife who enjoyed and appreciated the life I provided her. The big score never came, but it was a magical place to spend time and lose money. From the seats in the grandstand, you could see the ocean and feel its breeze. Across the track itself, there were expensive homes and condos on the hill looking down on everything. Everyone was usually well-dressed, but many of the locals dressed like a day at the beach: flip-flops, shorts, t-shirts, beer in one hand, Racing Form in the other. It was only a summer meet back then, and college kids were everywhere. There were plenty of young co-eds who were dressed for stares: revealing halter tops, short shorts, high-heels, or flip-flops. Some of them dressed like they'd be called to walk down a runway any minute. Their beauty added to the scenery, but I had no interest: I was there to flirt with disaster instead.

In all my trips to Del Mar, I squandered over a million dollars. Still, the place made me feel alive, and I knew I'd always win next time. There wasn't a better racetrack to chase the impossible. I always felt like I was in the middle of a grand celebration whenever I was there.

Win or lose, seafood and drinks were often part of the after-party. I miss those days.

"Abel, I think I'm going to rest my eyes for a little bit," I said.

"Okay, you relax, Peter. I know where I'm going. I plugged it in."

I put my headphones on and clicked on an ADHD link Dr. Guessner had sent to my phone. I leaned back to listen. An enthusiastic male voice began: "Here is why you should worry about adult ADHD. These are the reasons you want to get your adult ADD handled. This is why you want to take it seriously. If you don't know what's going on, Attention Deficit Hyperactivity Disorder can wreak havoc with every area of life."

Then another voice took over. The nurturing, caring voice of a female: "ADHD is a highly impairing disorder. ADD can ruin your life. Non-treatment leads to all kinds of problems. We do know that rates of pathological gambling in untreated adults with ADHD are much higher. Does it lead to other medical problems? Yes. As an adult, you have an increased risk of depression and anxiety. There's the risk of substance abuse. You will self-medicate with illegal substances. You can end up dead. You will engage in high-sensation-seeking behavior. Your risk for suicide is high. Sadly, our prisons are full of people with undiagnosed untreated ADD. It can ruin your family, ruin your marriage, ruin your childhood, absolutely cause chaos in your life, your entire life."

I had had enough. I turned off my phone. I removed my headphones. I fell asleep the rest of the way. There was no dreaming.

When we got to the entrance of Friendly Hills, Abel surveyed the golf course to our left and right, then the expensive houses lining both sides of the street we were on.

"This is a very nice neighborhood. This is where you grew up?" he asked.

"Here and Montebello."

"When I grew up, we collected cans and bottles just so we could eat."

"That sounds like downtown San Diego."

I called my mother to let her know we were minutes away. "Okay, sweetheart," she said.

Jay, still in courtroom attire, came up to the driver-side door with a stack of twenties and handed them to Abel. "Here's $300," he said.

"Thank you very much," he said to Jay.

"Thank you," Jay said.

Abel handed me my cell phone and laptop.

"Thank you very much, Peter. I hope everything is fine. Hopefully, I'll see you in Little Italy again."

I grabbed my tote bag.

"You will. Drive safe, my friend," I said.

Jay and I ended up on the backyard lawn, talking. I looked at the lush fairway. There was nobody playing golf. Through the years, we'd always hit golf balls from the backyard to the 4th green. Once, my father shanked a shot and broke one of my mother's prized statues which served as a planter for roses. It was only six feet away. Nat and I couldn't stop laughing.

"I don't know what's going on," Jay said.

"What do you mean."

"You seem lucid and all there. Did you just hit rock bottom?"

"No, I did not. I hit a car stopped at a red light going 40 miles per hour without breaking," I explained. "I tried to enlighten everyone by sending links about traumatic brain injury. Remember, I told you I was impotent the very next day. Fell off the bed when I was about to cum, with the worst pain I had ever felt in my life, shooting through my head, which my doctor said was a bleeding brain. I told you guys everything, but nobody was interested in helping us."

"I get it. We have a TBI case," Jay offered. "Sheriff beat the shit out of a client of mine."

"There's no way he suffered the impact I had to deal with."

"So, what happened between you and Alison?"

"I drank too much wine. I had to sleep on the streets last night."

"Are you going back?"

"Yeah."

"When?"

"I just have to give her some time," I said. "It won't be tomorrow. I can tell you that much."

"Yeah, I know."

"Tough love on someone with a brain injury? What the fuck is wrong with you guys?"

"All right, we need to get you tested," he said. "Everybody's freaked out about it. Especially Amanda. It's over by Whittier Hospital."

After the test, Jay set me up in the Vagabond Inn on Whitter Boulevard for two nights, until I got my results back. It was a Motel-6 type establishment, cheap and clean.

Through the years, many struggling families with children had called it their home. Occasionally, a prostitution sting would happen, with the names of the Johns ending up in the Daily News. Overall, though, the Vagabond wasn't really about that. Mostly, it was frequented by high school and college kids for coke-snorting and sex, and by those inclined to cheat on spouses. There was always lonely energy that wrapped itself around the Vagabond.

My room was basic. It had a double bed, a cheap nightstand, an oversized upholstered chair, and sounds of sex coming from the other side of the wall. I needed something to drink.

After I emptied my duffel bag, I walked to the liquor store across the street for a six-pack. In high school, it's where we bought our beer. We'd call the owner The Man. He'd sell alcohol to kids who looked 12 years old. And there was a Mexican restaurant in Uptown Whittier that would serve us margaritas when we were just high school freshmen. It was called Los Portales. It was owned by a gregarious man named Francisco. Always friendly, Francisco looked the part of a restaurant owner. He was a handsome man with jet-black hair and a carefully-manicured mustache who enjoyed acting as a backup waiter for everyone, clearing tables, and pouring drinks. One night when he had been drinking too much, he revealed a secret desire to be a rodeo clown. Supposedly, he owned a horse ranch somewhere in Mexico, which he had inherited from his father. Occasionally comping our meals, he never looked stressed for money.

The Man. Francisco. Beer. Margaritas. Free food. The 70s were great.

| 3 |

There's no way out of this, I thought. Nothing can be done. You lost your license to practice law. You lost the respect of everyone. You're dead-broke. A high-school kid working at McDonald's has more money than you. Kill yourself, man.

I took a gulp of beer. It felt good sliding the back of my throat. I took another gulp. I could hear the hum of traffic on Whittier Boulevard. People had places to be. People had things to do. People were alive out there.

And another gulp. I need something to do, I thought. I don't have anything to do now. There has to be something. Ghostwrite motions for other lawyers? Become a process server? Change my name? Become a busser? I pictured myself bussing tables at Princess Pub & Grille. I'm sure I'd join in on conversations about custody and divorce, or murder.

My cell phone chirped. "Hello?"

"Is this Peter Panelli?"

"Yes."

"This is the testing center calling."

"Okay."

"Can you please verify your date of birth for me?"

"11-14-58."

"Your test came back negative."

I called my parents.

My mother answered. "Hello?"

"Hi, Mom. My test came back negative."

"Oh, wonderful. I'm so glad to hear that, Peter."

"All right, Mom," I said, trying to sound upbeat.

"Do you want us to come to pick you up?"

"No, I have the room for another night. May as well use it."

"Okay, but let us pick you up for dinner."

"All right."

"I'll make the baked chicken the way you and Alison like it."

I called Dr. Guessner.

"I'm alive," I began.

"Everything okay?"

"I'm in a hotel in Whittier."

"Yeah. How is that?"

"There's not much energy in Whittier these days."

"Well, maybe, some downtime will be good, you know?"

I looked around the room. It offered no dopamine release at all.

"I just don't see any way out," I said.

"Hold those thoughts for next time, Peter. I have an appointment beeping in."

I tried to take a nap but couldn't fall asleep.

My mind wandered to my high school days.

High school was like a teen movie. I was a mere extra in my freshmen and sophomore years because I didn't know a single person when we moved here from Montebello. Virtually, all the other students had been in school with each other since kindergarten. In junior year, I was a supporting actor, as I had made many friends by then. In my senior year, I was one of the stars, having finally come out of my shell. There were friendships all across the social strata – with the Stoners, the Jocks, the Soshes, the Cheerleaders, and the Cool Teachers, like Mr. Davis who was having sex with 14-year-old girls at his ranch on Turnbull Canyon. Senior year was the most magical year until it got close to the end when I fully realized only the deluded were genuinely happy. Soon after we throw our caps up toward the sky, the magic in the air became polluted by the haze of an uncomfortable and undeniable realization – that there'd always be something or someone to get in our way, including, mostly, ourselves.

We all graduate high school not knowing how to live life. That's why we need to rethink our country's grade school and high-school curriculums. We need to add some practicality to them: The Kind of Person You Should Marry 101; How to Overcome Childhood Wounds 101; Why You Should Use a Condom Even When You Think You're Dating Your Soulmate 101; Home Remedies to Relieve the Pain of Herpes Lesions 101; Why Your Marriage Will End in Divorce 101; Exploring the Benefits of Mood-Altering Pharmaceuticals 101; etcetera. Classes like these should be made automatic additions, with no board meetings necessary. And when it comes to grade school, replace all the books on Critical Race Theory with age-appropriate, illustrated children's books, like Why Sally Shouldn't Become a Street Whore.

Despite its educational deficiencies, high school is still an iconic time of American life. But college is better. College, even more removed from everyday life, is magical. It really is all about sex, drugs, and rock-and-roll. Especially in the 70s, when we could smoke a joint, snort a line, and listen to Led Zeppelin on the radio. Something which Nat envied. "Damn, Dad, Led?" he'd say. "Our music is shit. You guys were lucky."

We were lucky. And there were mushrooms, LSD, and beautiful sorority girls whom I partied with regularly. Magical was spelled with a capital M. There was Nancy Drury, and Molly Hartman, to name just a couple. They were my two favorites. Probably the two most beautiful girls to ever attend Whitter College. Nancy was a long-legged blue-eyed blonde who looked like a Ralph Lauren model, while auburn-haired Molly was a seductive girl-next-door type who looked like a Guess model. Still, I have never laid eyes on anyone as beautiful as the raven-haired Alison. Two more inches of height and Alison could have worked for Victoria's Secret. And I don't mean as a checker.

Whittier College wasn't all wine and roses, though – especially when it came to affairs of the heart – so, I paused the trip down Memory Lane. I promised to visit the nearby campus before I headed back down to San Diego. Maybe I'd visit my old fraternity house and my favorite sorority house, where I lived my freshman year. A Time Machine would be nice.

I sighed. I turned over onto my back. I stared at the ceiling trying to find the faces of animals or people, the way we do when we look at clouds.

There's always some disaster, I thought. Things are always headed to Shitsville. Things never turn out well. I rested my right forearm across my forehead. I wondered how all my friends had turned out.

I'm sure Doctor Ray Dominquez had made his family proud. If I had kept a couple of high-school relationships intact, I'd be sitting on Easy Street. I could have followed my best friend back then into a spinoff of his family's business, which made all the children of Tony and Mary Neumann millionaires. If I had followed through on a few opportunities offered to me by members of the country club when I was a senior in high school, I'd be living the life now. One member, Fred

Glassman, had invited me to create advertisements for his business, which designed spectacular high-end lighting fixtures for many fine restaurants and various opulent homes throughout southern California. I came up with a few clever ads. One of them was a picture of the Milky Way, with the following copy: "God isn't the only one who makes spectacular lighting. See for yourself. Come visit our showroom. Fred Glassman." I never followed through with Mr. Glassman. Two months later, I ran into him in the Men's Grill. I was there for a sandwich and a gin-and-tonic. "I thought you were going to design some ads for me," he said. His tanned face wrinkled into a bewildered scowl under his jet-black furrowed eyebrows. If I had told him the truth, I would have said, "Sorry, I've been involved in a marijuana-fueled masturbation frenzy, and I lost track of time. I kept thinking today is yesterday." I walked away as if I hadn't heard a word he had said. A shining moment at the beginning of my successful life journey.

Back home, almost thirty years after I had lived there with my parents, made for a surreal experience: I achieved absolutely nothing during the interim. Three decades of gambling my life away. Now everybody knew. There was no hiding my colossal failure. It was almost cinematic: "FOCUS IN: Peter Panelli, disbarred, dead-broke, suicidal, homeless horseplayer …"

I've always felt like I was hopelessly stuck in a B-movie that had no end – just an endless series of mediocre moments, which the audience looked at with horrified fascination. It was a suspenseless horror film that interested moviegoers, the way the aftermath of a fatal car crash makes us take our eyes off the road. It was filmed in grainy black-and-white and looked like the dreams a troubled soul might have before the daily nighttime meds kicked them into frenzied-kaleidoscope mode. I'm starring in the movie but I'm in the audience as well. There's always been an out-of-body feel to my existence. I rarely feel in control of an outcome – kind of like a dead leaf slowly floating down a stream.

I wasn't feeling the dinner tonight with my parents, so I sent a cancellation text to Jay: "Hey, tell Mom I'm under the weather tonight. I'm just going to hang out in my room. I'll eat the baked chicken tomorrow for lunch. I'll call her in the morning. I have to check out by 11. All right. See you soon."

I turned on the free Internet TV. I ended up watching YouTube – a debate about transgender people.

WOMAN: Do you think transgender women are real women?

MAN: What do you mean by 'real women'? What does that mean?

WOMAN: Is a transgender women a women? Simple question.

MAN: No, they are not.

WOMAN: Why do you say that?

MAN: Well, women have wombs. They can give birth. They can breastfeed. Their chromosomal makeup is different from a man's. Women are women. Men are men.

WOMAN: So, you're saying chromosomes determine a person's gender?

MAN (nodding): What else does?

WOMAN: Many, many things.

MAN: There's only one thing. What sex a person feels they are does not determine what sex they are.

WOMAN (disgustedly): No wonder Twitter is so outraged over you. You're such a bigot.

MAN (smirking): And I'm racist too, right? One last thing. Why do transgender women have to take female hormones?

I turned off the TV. I walked across the street to the liquor store. I looked both ways before crossing. I couldn't just feel like no cars were coming.

| 4 |

I wanted to sleep a bit little more, but I had to check out. I grabbed a beer from the small refrigerator and turned the TV on to the news. Mostly, I watched it for entertainment value only. Whenever I did, I knew our 98-average-IQ nation was in trouble. There were too many unintelligent people tuning in for the propaganda onslaught. Too many people discounting chromosomes. Too many people that thinking everything is Whitey's fault. Too many people thinking BLM's looting, destruction of property, and overall stance rooted in violent disruption is a good thing. Too many people labeling another person's views as racist when their views aren't unequivocally mirrored. Too many people who were suddenly legal experts whenever a factual verdict doesn't align with their feelings. Too many people on Instagram focusing on their external appeal. It's all bad news. When a CNN "Breaking News" headline flashed at the bottom of the screen, I turned off the TV.

I took a gulp of beer. I walked over to the window. I parted the curtains with my beer-free hand. There was a Mexican family swimming and playing in the pool, happily.

I looked out at Whittier Boulevard. There was a homeless man slowly shuffling his way down the sidewalk. I recognized him. It was the infamous Richard Concannon. He was a year ahead of me in high school. He was voted Senior Homecoming King. Back then, he had the looks of a matinee idol. Light brown hair, strong chin, high cheekbones, deep-set blue eyes. The kind of guy all the guys wanted to look like. For a while, there was a rumor floating around that he had just had a bad acid trip, and he just couldn't snap out of it. That's why people surmised he was walking the streets soon after graduation, talking to himself. He was severely schizophrenic beyond the reach of medicine and therapy. That was all she wrote for King Richard.

Jay sent me a text: "I'll be picking you up at 10:45, after golf. I'll honk for you."

I texted him back with a thumbs-up emoji.

After I showered and stuffed everything into my outdated Pierre Cardin tote bag, I could hear Jay's honking.

I left the room.

I got inside a black Mercedes I hadn't seen Jay in before.

He smiled at me with great enthusiasm.

"Hey, what's up man?!" he said.

He took a swig of amber liquid from a small bottle.

"Scotch. Want some?"

"All right."

I took a swig. I looked at the impressive dash of the car with thin strips of eye-catching purple and blue neon lights, with a bit of envy.

"New car?"

"I don't buy them new," he answered. "Payment's not high. Put the bottle in the glove box."

I placed the bottle of scotch on top of a puffy bag of marijuana buds.

Jay looked good. The beer belly that used to make him look pregnant had disappeared, and his face had thinned considerably. Almost 60 now, he still resembled Kevin Costner – at least a little bit.

"You lost a lot of weight," I told him.

"Yeah. Still going bald. You hungry?"

I nodded. "Yeah."

"You in the mood for Eggs Benedict?"

We ended up at the country club.

Jay drove like a drunken maniac to get there. Engine revving, tires screeching, my stomach turning. There seemed to be no concern about the police. I was reminded of my DUI 40 years ago.

We pulled into the parking lot. We both took another swig. Then Jay rolled a joint, which he took a few deep hits from before putting it into the ashtray. One more swig. Then we headed into the clubhouse.

We sat in the downstairs bar and grill, at a table close to the crystal-clear panoramic window next to the practice putting green.

There was a great view of the 1st tee, the 18th green, and the lake that surrounded the 1st tee. Several mud hens and ducks were always moving around. There was a small, yet dazzling waterfall at the far-left end of the lake, where many errant drives ended up. In high school one night, stoned out of our minds, my friends and I thought we had seen the Loch Ness monster in the lake – back then, Thai sticks were dipped in opium. I'll never forget the Saturday morning when my Dad had instantly killed a duck with a worm burner off the 1st tee. Tragically, the ball squarely found the beak area.

Our server, a pretty twenty-something, modestly dressed in black and white, with a friendly smile, took our food order after bringing us scotches. Her brown hair cascaded softly to the middle of her back. I casually wondered if she was working here in the hopes of finding a husband. Back in the day, it happened a lot. There were a few provocative servers who had ended up as members themselves because they had caught the eye of a wealthy member. "Homewreckers" is what my mother called them. "Hot pieces of ass" is what me and my friend called them. Now we call them milfs.

"Okay, let me know if you guys need anything," our server said before gliding away.

"I miss the country club days," I announced.

Jay raised his glass.

"To Peter," he said. "I know he'll get back on track and pull out of this."

I raised my glass.

"Thanks," I said. "It's been a nightmare. Especially for Alison."

"I know, I know. I'm sorry, man. Amanda was on some crazed mission. She still is."

"It was a long buildup. I know that. I've never been the best person on planet Earth, that's for sure."

"We all have our stuff, man," he offered.

It took me over an hour to tell Jay about all the gory details of the last few years. "I never thought in a million years," I ended.

"The crack-house stuff is out of this world, dude."

"It was insane."

"It's unbelievable Alison's still with you."

"She's the only one who knows how sick I've been," I said.

"We'll all get past this. Amanda's still on a rampage. I'll get her to come around."

"I don't think I should have been vilified after the Vegas crash."

"It was all a build-up."

"It's not like we're the only dysfunctional family in America."

"How is it between you and Alison, really?"

"Unbearable. More on that later."

"Okay," Jay said standing up. "I need to hit the head, and we need a couple more."

Our server appeared, and I placed the order. Then, I drifted over to the trophy case in the nearby hallway, which featured various cups and plaques, dating back to the late 60s, when the club was founded. In recent years, whenever I was at the club, I always looked for my name on one of the trophies. It was always there: "Peter Panelli, Junior Club Champion 1976." Seeing the trophy always took me back in time to the greatest decade of rock-and-roll in the history of the world, when Led Zeppelin ruled the airwaves. Back then, we all listened to KLOS and the legendary DJ, Jim Ladd. We listened to him interview the likes of John Lennon, Grateful Dead, Pink Floyd, Rush, U2, Joni Mitchell, Stevie Nicks, Crosby, Stills, Nash & Young, Eagles, and, last but not least, Led Zeppelin. In the 70s, there wasn't much for teenagers to do other than smoke weed and listen to Led. Now and then cocaine, mushrooms, and LSD would make it into the mix. Throw in fantasizing about sex with cheerleaders, and that was about all we had. There weren't any soul-sucking social media for us to waste our time on.

One of the plusses of the 70s was our parents. Because of all the LSD use in the 60s, they didn't mind us smoking pot or coming home drunk. I'm sure they were all glad we weren't dropping acid and staring at the sun until we went blind. Also, there was the most-anticipated 4th of July celebration ever – our country's Bicentennial. Because there were no social media, it was celebrated with pride and enthusiasm. There wasn't any faction of malcontents telling us that we should all be ashamed to be American. There were no obvious corporate-media agendas yet intent on destroying our very culture like there are today. At least they weren't obvious about it.

Though much calmer than the 60s, which included three notable assassinations on American soil, the 70s were a tumultuous time in their own way. There was still a fight for equality, led by women, African Americans, Native Americans, gays and lesbians, and other marginalized people, while many Americans protested against the ongoing war in Vietnam. In a way, the decade was a repudiation of the 60s. There was a "New Right" mobilized in defense of political conservatism and traditional family values, and President Richard Nixon made many people realize our government was capable of outlandish corruption. The divisions and disappointments of the 70s set the stage for public life that is still with us today – only today there's much more name-calling, disrespect, and a media-manufactured hatred of the police and whites. Nowadays, you're a White Supremacist simply because you're white, and you're a bad police officer simply because you're a police officer.

All I cared about back then was weed, Led, and finding concert tickets at face value. I guess, because of my white-privileged upbringing, the latter was my only real struggle. I didn't have to worry about cop cars driving slowly through the neighborhood. If one did, there was no reason for me to worry about a confrontation. I'm sure that's what a BLM would tell me with great disrespect.

Jay approached me at the trophy case. "Did you get the drinks?" he asked.

"Yeah, I did."

"Travelling down Memory Lane?"

We went back to the table. Jay ordered us shrimp cocktails. We kept talking.

"There's not much action here today," I said. "Not one person has walked through the grill."

"There's not much going on here during the week now. There's no way it was like it was back then."

"What's it like here now?"

"Older. Mostly Asian. Not that many kids," he answered. "There's a cool group of guys I hang with. I still like the club."

"You and Amanda are living the life."

"You reap what you sow."

"If you know how to sow," I said.

"You know how to sow."

"You'd think I'd know. That's where everybody's wrong"

"I'm going to give you this audiobook I just finished. It's called Stop Self-Sabotage."

"All right."

"I never thought you'd be this far off the rails," Jay said.

I looked around. It was over 35 years since I had been a member under my father's membership. When you turn 27, you're no longer a member. The overall décor of today's bar-and-grill wasn't much different from when I was a fixture. The pastels were still in use, as was the understated furniture. Friendly Hill Country Club was no match for Wilshire Country Club, found in the heart of the Hollywood area; but, still, it was a club that made you proud to belong. If you were able to walk these grounds as a member, you were living a privileged life, but one which you had earned. The Whittier Daily News often referred to the club as "exclusive."

I loved growing up at the country club. Of course, I wanted to provide the same for Nat, but I was hopelessly lost in the addiction to gambling. I was generating enough cash flow to provide him with such a life, but when you're caught in the whirlpool of gambling addiction, all that matters is what you have to do to make your next bet. Shamefully, my focus did not extend beyond that. Owning a home and supporting a family just wasn't on my list of things to do, because I wanted to hit it big at the racetrack.

In the stands with my laptop, I'd bet horses online at Nat's baseball games. I was always preoccupied with betting. It's easy to understand why he has disowned me. After divorcing his mother, all I did was live in apartments, never owning a home again. I knew this bothered him by the things he'd say to his friends. I'd be driving the gang home from practice: "My Dad is poor," he'd say. "He just lives in an apartment with my stepmom." Graciously, his friends would come to my defense: "What does that matter, Nat? There's nothing wrong with living in an apartment." Well, to Nat there was certainly something wrong. I'm sure he was always thinking to himself, 'Why does my Dad have nothing?'"

"I think we should have a couple more," Jay said. "Then we should check you into the Vagabond for one more night. I'm too buzzed for any family fireworks right now."

"That's fine. Are you okay to drive?"

"As long as I don't fucking run someone over."

On the way to the Vagabond, the driving was the same, but the conversation had turned to politics, with a drunken Jay leading the way.

"That motherfucker Biden had better not make his way into the Whitehouse!" he yelled.

"Trump's not going to get re-elected."

"I hope you're wrong!"

"I'm not wrong. There are too many lowlife puppets," I said. "There's a concerted effort to oust Trump, the only President since Reagan who cares about the country. The corporate media know the majority of the liberal left isn't that quick on the uptake. They're all anti-White reactionaries. CNN and MSNBC are disgusting outlets. How do Don Lemon and Chris Cuomo keep a straight face?"

"They've sold their souls."

"Biden and Harris will turn this country into a Third-World cesspool. Just watch."

Jay missed a green light by several seconds. I heard the tires of another car screech. I looked around for cops. They were pretty rare in Friendly Hills. The only time you'd see them is when they'd be given orders, at the end of the month, to write tickets for rolling through a stop sign. They'd hide on the side streets of Youngwood and Lindante, the two main streets of the neighborhood. Everybody was outraged by this general targeting of resident motorists. Often, it was a subject at city council meetings. In high school and college, I had more than my fair share. I once got two tickets in one day. I simply handed the first ticket to the officer writing the second ticket. We both had a good laugh.

| 5 |

Someone knocking on the hotel door woke me up. I walked over to the door in my underwear. "Yes?" I said without opening it.

"I'm here," a young female voice said.

"Here for what?"

"Our appointment."

I peered through the door's peephole. There was an overweight teen-aged Black girl, with a round pretty face, wearing an orange bikini top, fluorescent-blue shorts, and white sandals, standing there. Her expression revealed a state of distress. "I don't have an appointment with anybody right now," I said.

"I'm here to give you your massage."

"I didn't order a massage."

"I guess it's a mistake. Can I come in? Would you like a massage?"

"No, I'm okay."

"Please, sir. I'm just trying to make some money to buy some formula for my babies."

"I don't have any money. I'm sorry."

"You don't care about Black people."

"I do but I'm not opening this door."

I heard her walking away. Then I heard her knocking on the door of the room next to mine. "I'm here," she said.

I crawled back into bed. I turned on the TV. I didn't have the energy to do anything else. There was a closeup of a Black woman shaking and crying hysterically. "They had no right to take my baby," she wailed. "He did nothing wrong. I love him so much. The police murdered him. This has to stop." The camera moved to a BLM higher-up, going back and forth with an attractive white reporter. Blonde hair, blue eyes, the kind BLM hate. There was a burning police car in the background. "I understand what you're saying," the white-skinned reporter said to a dark-skinned Black man. "But what about all the killings of Black people every weekend in Chicago at the hands of other Blacks? I haven't seen any protests on those streets." "You're talking about apples and oranges," the man answered. Someone off-screen yelled: "Blacks are 13 percent of the population, and they commit 50 percent of the murders!"

I switched the channel and listened to a "Breaking News" story about how crabs, lobsters, and octopuses feel pain when they're being boiled for human consumption. Then I ended up listening to a Black professor talk about the origins of the political ideology of White supremacy: "White supremacy is far more encompassing than simple racism or bigotry," the professor said.

I turned off the TV when the remote happened to land on The View, which has been void of actual journalists since the departure of Barbara Walters.

Jay sat down at the light-green upholstered chair by the window and pulled out a fat joint he immediately lit. "Are you sure you don't want any?" he asked.

"I'm good. All it does is summon paranoia."

"I was thinking," he said.

"Yeah?"

"You seem very lucid. You don't seem out of it. You never really did. Every e-mail you sent us was perfectly written."

I had to hold my anger. "Still with this shit?" I said. "I couldn't deal with anything. I wanted to be dead. There was no way out. You should have seen me try to work up my caseload. I was completely clueless. I didn't even remember how to do basic stuff. I had to Google stuff all the time. I had to engage other law firms for free consultations, acting like I was a potential client just to figure out how to handle matters that I had done hundreds of times before. I was in a coma."

Jay was staring intently at a spot on the wall above the TV, which made me wonder if the joint had been laced. "Yeah, man," he said slowly.

"Are you talking to me?"

Jay's eyes darted away from the spot on the wall to the small trashcan full of beer bottles by the sink area. "What? Yeah."

"What's that laced with?"

Jay took a deep drag on the joint, then coughed out a plume of smoke that slowly floated through the room. "I was just somewhere else. I don't remember where."

I revisited an old joke between us. "What color is the wall?"

"You mean, now or when you asked the question?"

After we laughed for a bit, Jay said, "It'll get better. You just have to shift into clean-up mode."

"There's a warehouse full of trash I need to clean."

"Just get going on it," he advised. "The audiobook will help you. Right now, you're frozen solid. I'll help you however I can."

"All right," I managed to say.

"We need a change of venue," Jay announced.

We ended up at the country club's bar-and-grill. This time, the drive there was much more mellow and subdued.

We sat outside, just on the other side of the window in front of the always perfectly-manicured practice putting green. Shots of scotch were placed on the table, by the same server as last time. "Hi, again," she said. "Ready to order?"

"Eggs Benedict again?" Jay asked me.

"I love it."

There was an unusual calm in the air. The sun danced on the surface of the lake and glimmered like a million diamonds on the waterfall. The ducks peacefully floated. The scotch warmed my soul. I wanted to sit here forever.

"So, how do you feel overall?" Jay asked.

"Scotch helps."

"In general."

I took another sip. "There's a constant headache where my forehead smashed into the window shield. The left side of my face is always tight. There's a nonstop ringing in my ears. There's not much energy. It's hard for me to get going. I do feel frozen solid. I feel like a failure. I feel like it's all over."

Eggs Benedict was placed in front of us. "It's not over," Jay said. "It's time for you to do what you were born to do. I've got some great story ideas."

Jay clinked his glass against mine, which was still on the table next to my plate.

"There are only about seven thousand days left for us."

I splashed some scotch on the back of my throat. I broke the yolk of one of the eggs. "I've wasted about twenty-thousand, so far."

"Not every day was a waste."

A man wearing white shorts, a blue golf shirt, and a red MAGA hat, slowly walked onto the practice green holding a mallet putter in his right hand. His steps were labored, as if painful. His face, arms, and legs were thin, but his stomach was enormous, which made him look like he might tip over at any moment. He dropped a few balls near the apron and stroked one toward the nearest hole, just missing. "Fuck," he said.

I recognized the voice. I looked closer. It was Timmy Green. He looked like he had gained over forty pounds since the time I had seen him, about 7 years ago at a party in Jay and Amanda's backyard.

"I think that's Timmy Green," I said to Jay.

"Timmy!" Jay said loud enough.

Timmy looked our way. "Hey," he said. He strained to pick up his three golf balls. Maybe he was going to tip over. We'd need a forklift. He walked our way in a crooked line and almost fell into the empty chair at our table. He reeked of alcohol. "I need another drink."

"All right," Jay said. "I guess your suspension's up?"

"Fuck them."

"Timmy was suspended 30 days for falling flat on his face in the grill area after yelling obscenities at a table of Asian members," Jay announced. "I had to drive him home, or the police were going to be called."

"Fuck those COVID motherfuckers. Fuck this club," Timmy slurred. "I need another drink, Jay. What the fuck, Peter?!"

"Hey, Timmy."

"I heard things went sideways," he said.

"Yeah?"

"Your sister told Carol."

Jay didn't miss a beat. "Hey, Peter, will you get us some more scotch? Just grab a bottle from the bartender."

"A bottle?" I asked.

"It won't be a problem," Jay answered.

"You might have to drive me home again, Jay."

I came back to the table with an unopened bottle of Jack Daniels. I twisted off the top and filled our glasses to the brim.

"Guess what this COVID bullshit is doing to me?" Timmy asked. "I'll tell you what it's doing to me. Fuck Gavin Newsom. You hear me?"

"What are you talking about, Timmy?" Jay asked.

"My fucking renters don't have to pay rent anymore. How's that for some liberal bullshit?"

"It already started down in San Diego."

"What started?"

"This COVID bullshit," Timmy said.

"What about the rent, Peter?"

"Yeah, I know what he's talking about."

"I still don't," Jay said.

"Tell him, Peter. I need to take a drink."

"Because of the lockdown, a lot of people can't earn a living right now. There's no income for them. So, right now, until further notice, they don't have to pay rent," I explained.

"What if the landlord has a mortgage payment?"

"Exactly," Timmy said. "I'm lucky, all my stuff is bought and paid for."

Timmy had made all his money from dealing marijuana and cocaine out of wherever he was living in Uptown Whittier at the time. Mostly, he sold to the local high school kids and the students and professors at Whitter College. When he had accumulated enough paid-for income property and had enough money in the bank, he retired, about twenty-five years ago. In retirement, he drank enormous amounts of alcohol in all his free time and played a lot of golf.

"Newsom said everyone's rent will be paid," I said.

"Fuck Newsom," Timmy said. "All of this bullshit because of the Ching-Chang-Chongs!"

"Timmy," I said. "Shh. Relax. There's no need to talk like that."

"Yeah, Timmy, tone it down. You want your name brought up at the next board meeting?"

"I don't give a fuck about that. This is the beginning of one of the biggest shitshow ever planned," Timmy said. "You know it, and I know it. Only the fucking idiots don't know it. America has way too many fucking idiots, with all the Snowflakes, the Millennials, and the dumb-fuck AOC types. We're all fucked!"

Jay raised his glass. "To being fucked."

I raised mine. "To the beginning of the biggest shitshow ever planned."

Timmy raised his glass, then slammed the fist of his free hand down on the table, startling our glasses, plates, silverware, and us. "That's fucking right!" he yelled.

| 6 |

Satan was trying to possess me. I kept screaming out The Our Father in my dream. Thankfully, the golf course lawnmowers woke me up. When I tried to get out of bed, I immediately fainted and fell to the ground, unconscious, I was later told.

I had spent the night in my sister's old bedroom, which had remained untouched for the past 35 years. Everything was still in place, from the canopy bed to the pictures on the walls to the green-and-yellow shag carpeting – even the pink Princess rotary phone. When we were growing up, her bedroom was on the other side of the wall from mine, which had a view of the 4th fairway, from tee to green. Since then, my bedroom had been turned into a home office for my father.

My mother found me motionless, next to the bed. I was roused awake by her and my father. I ended up in the emergency room of nearby Whittier Hospital, taken there by ambulance. I was wheeled into a small room in the ER, with grey walls and a tan linoleum floor.

Almost thirty minutes later, a nurse appeared. Her name badge read Elva. She was a middle-aged Mexican woman, who looked like an old gang-banger from the 60s – the kind you'd see cruising on Whittier Boulevard back then. Harsh eyeliner, and thick make-up all over her slender face. She checked my heartbeat, took my blood pressure, and checked my lungs. "What happened?" she asked, holding a clipboard.

"I fainted."

"How do you feel now?"

"A little bit of a headache," I explained. "My forehead cracked my windshield in a car crash a few years ago. The left side. There's always a headache there. I've been having brain surges lately."

"How long ago was the car accident?"

"About five years ago."

"How've you been feeling recently?"

"The brain surges. Lots of fatigue. Brain fog. Loud ringing in the ears. Anxiety. Depression. The usual stuff. Constant headache."

"Are you on any medications?" she asked.

"Wellbutrin."

"Anything recreationally?"

"Beer. Scotch. Mostly, beer."

"How much?"

"Probably too much. I use it to relax."

"Thank you," she said, scrawling on the clipboard. "I'm going to track down a neurologist for you. It might be a little while, but it shouldn't be too long."

"You might want to track down a psychiatrist, too," I said.

There's no way I'm going back down to that personality, I thought. Alison's mental and emotional ailments were synergistically operating at an unbearable level, on mine. I couldn't leave the hotel room in the morning when I was hungry if I wanted to grab some breakfast from the free buffet downstairs. Why? COVID. And she just didn't want me to leave the room. I couldn't grab a midnight snack from the refrigerator. Why? She was afraid I'd leave the refrigerator open and drop food all over the kitchen floor. I guess she thought all the food inside the refrigerator would spoil as we slept. And I couldn't watch TV with the sound on (closed caption only). And I couldn't watch TV during working hours even if the sound was muted. Why? "Because I just don't want to hear anything," she'd state. Hear what? I couldn't relax and listen to music with my earbuds on, even when the door to my room closed. Why? "Because I can still hear it," she'd complain. I was not allowed to interject my thoughts during a conversation with her. I had to wait until she had finished with what she was saying before I could speak a word. Sometimes, I'd have to wait thirty minutes before voicing my thoughts. Why? Because she didn't want to lose her train of thought. There's more to this list, including, but not limited to, our marriage was sexless. Any man would be driven insane. She just carried too much disdain for me, for the gambling, for the car crashes, for the disbarment, for the fact we were dead-broke and homeless – all because of me. Her stated forgiveness was rarely evident. Her implied insults were obvious and always aimed at how broken and useless I was. Life is a worthy foe for love. Life wins.

I adjusted the hospital bed with the touch of a button. I leaned back and closed my eyes. I tried to slide into the place between being awake and being asleep, but the noises of the ER were persistent. People screaming, moaning, crying, barking, and lashing out. I just stared at the back of my eyelids, trying to see the blues and the turquoises. I was stuck in an orange-black mode. It was difficult to find that nice feeling between being asleep and being awake. Especially since I could hear a conversation on the other side of the curtain.

MAN: I told you not to leave the house.

WOMAN: I know. But we needed powdered milk.

MAN: Do you know what you've caused?

WOMAN: I'm sorry, Sergio.

MAN: No insurance on the car. No health insurance. Now more madness for me to deal with.

WOMAN: It wasn't my fault. I got cut off.

MAN: That's what everybody says when they smash into a telephone pole. It's your fault for leaving the house.

WOMAN: I didn't do anything wrong.

MAN: You left the house. You waited until I was taking a nap. That's not proper behavior.

WOMAN: I'm sorry.

MAN: You should have walked to the store.

WOMAN: In the neighborhood we live in?

MAN: Stop insulting me. I'm doing the best I can. I'm sorry I'm not some guy who wears a suit to work.

WOMAN: I didn't mean anything.

MAN: Next time you want to leave the house, ask.

WOMAN: Okay. I will. I'm sorry. Maybe I should get a job.

MAN: Stop insulting me, Daisy.

WOMAN: I wasn't.

MAN: Sergio Castillo's wife will not be working!

WOMAN: But nobody's working.

Suddenly, someone's face was being slapped.

WOMAN: Stop! I'm calling the police!

MAN: Shut up. All I did was slap. I'm leaving. Look at what you've done.

I heard the man walk away with angry and forceful steps.

"Are you okay?" I called out to the woman.

"I'll be fine," the woman answered. "He has too much stress. His restaurant was shut down because of the virus."

"That's awful."

"I don't know what's going to happen to this world."

"Nothing good," I said.

"I think you're right. We have five kids."

"Does he always hit you?"

"Not always," she answered softly.

"Don't be embarrassed."

"I'll be okay."

"How old are your children?"

"All under 10."

"Sounds like a busy life," I said.

She needs to leave, I thought. I knew she had been hit in front of her kids.

ADDICT'S WAY

A doctor appeared at the foot of my bed. About my age, with greying hair, light-blue eyes, bland features, tall and lanky. He's what we'd call a pencil-neck back in high school. You wanted to know a few in case you'd ever need help with math. He had the smooth skin and the perfect haircut of a rich person.

"Mr. Panelli, I'm Doctor Wyse," he announced.

"It was nice meeting you, Daisy."

"It was nice meeting you. Thanks."

"The nurse filled me in a little bit. You fainted. There are residual effects of a brain injury. That'll be my main focus. I'm a neurologist and a neuropsychiatrist. I play golf with your brother-in-law."

I nodded. "You've made it to the right cubicle," I said.

"Is there anything you did yesterday that might have caused you to faint this morning?"

"No." I shook my head. "I've been having brain surges lately."

"How long?"

"About three weeks."

"When do they happen?"

"Whenever. When I'm sitting. When I'm standing," I said. "Mostly, when I'm sitting on the toilet counting the tiles on the floor, for some reason."

"Anything else going on?"

I nodded. "When I'm sitting up in bed, a tingling feeling makes its way through my legs."

"Painful?"

I shook my head. "No. It's like a pleasurable tingling. It's not bothersome."

He disappeared for a few seconds and came back with a black-and-brown padded office chair. He placed it at the foot of the bed.

"Tell me what's been going on since the car crash," he said.

"How much time do you have?" I asked lightheartedly.

"I've got time." He sat down. The chair sounded comfortable. "It's either this or a pile of paperwork. Jay asked me to go deep with you."

They play golf together, so I crossed off the doctor-patient privilege. I told him everything. It took nearly an hour. He listened intently without taking any notes. I'm sure it was a billable hour for him, and the hospital. Another impossible-to-pay invoice is on the way to me. Another stain on the credit report. Another reason to curl up with a good book from the Hemlock Society.

"I'm sorry what you're going through with your wife," he began. "From what you told me, she has an obsessive-compulsive personality disorder. It ruins relationships, friendships, and marriages. She needs help. She'll never admit she needs help. That's one of the many symptoms. Unless you're striving for perfection, there's something wrong with you. That's how she thinks. You're in a tough place with her."

"It's impossible."

"Your life right now isn't helping her at all. The cluster-C varieties react to stress. I'd cut her some slack."

"Okay, I understand."

"I'd also cut your sister and your family some slack," he said. "They don't have any knowledge about what happened to you in that car crash. You're suffering from Post-Traumatic Brain Injury Syndrome. There's always going to be some lingering symptoms for you to deal with. Other people don't understand that. It's an invisible injury to them. Unless you're in a full-body cast, or a chunk of your skull is missing, people won't understand why you couldn't get out of bed for three years. Their knee-jerk reaction is laziness. There's no need to waste any more energy trying to make them understand."

"Still, you don't practice tough love on someone with a brain injury. That's just cruel and hateful."

"You're also dealing with mitochondrial dysfunction and neurodegeneration."

"I believe anything you say. Except what you just said about my sister and my family."

"I'll email you some links."

I nodded. "Links. I'll look at them."

"Of course, the situation with your son is hurtful," he continued. "He's having a difficult time accepting the truth about you. He's having a difficult time respecting you. You can't expect him to have a deep understanding of addiction when all the adults surrounding him certainly don't. You're right, his mother isn't helping any. Right now, just let him get his bearings straight. I'm sure you'll see him again. Things will take their course."

"I think they will."

"The brain surges are concerning," he said. "Usually, they occur only occasionally. Since yours are static, basically, never-ending, from what you say, we need to run some tests. I'm going to keep you overnight for observation. In the morning, we'll run the tests. If everything checks out, you can get out of here."

He stood up, taking a gold pen out of his shirt pocket. "I'll make arrangements to get you into a bed tonight. I'll call your family."

| 7 |

White toast, scrambled eggs, apple sauce, and a small carton of orange juice. That was breakfast. A young, energetic Candy Striper delivered it to me with a side of happiness. She and her smile were pretty. Braces, big brown eyes, a little bit of makeup. She glided over to the nearest window as if she were slowly and steadily being pulled there by an invisible rainbow. "Would you like me to let some sunshine inside?" she asked.

"Sure, why not," I said.

She parted the curtains. Sunshine poured in. "There you go," she said.

This was a welcome change from Alison's morning ritual: "Are you just going to sleep all day, Peter? This has been going on for almost five years now. Why's there a fork in the sink? Did you break the rules and come out and get a midnight snack?"

"Do you go to Whittier College?" I asked.

She stepped away from the window. "I go to Whitter High," she answered. "I don't have my nametag today. I'm Cheryl."

"Hi, Cheryl. I went to Whittier College. I'm Peter. And I went to La Serna."

"When did you go to Whittier?"

"A million years ago."

She smiled and laughed a little bit. She held her hand over her mouth, worried about the braces.

"Oh, I forgot to put my mask on. I'm a sophomore." She pulled her air behind her ears, then put on a light-blue surgical mask.

"My sister was a Candy Striper here when she was in high school."

"I enjoy it," she said. "I think I'll become a nurse. Maybe a doctor."

"That sounds like a plan if that's what you really want to do."

She shrugged. "My mom's a doctor. My dad's a lawyer. So."

"I'm a lawyer."

"Do you like it?"

"Not really."

"My dad doesn't like it, either."

"Where do you guys live?" I asked.

"In the hills above Whittier College."

"Oh, those houses are nice."

"I was thinking of maybe going there, or UCLA."

"I liked Whittier College."

She sat down in the flimsy wheelchair that had been left near the window. "Gosh, my feet hurt today."

"Sure. Sit. Take a break. I don't bite." I smiled.

"Did you hear that President Trump was banned from Twitter? Isn't that crazy?"

"This country's crazy."

"I can't believe they did that."

"Do you like Trump?"

"Not really. No. My parents like him," she said. "I think he's a racist."

"Why?"

"The things he says."

"He's not a racist. Do you know why Twitter banned him?"

She shrugged. "The things he says?"

"He was banned because he knew how to use Twitter. He used it as a weapon against mainstream media. That's how he got elected,"

I explained. "So, now, the liberal idiots took that weapon away from him. They'll do everything to make sure he doesn't get re-elected. Even Facebook is in on it. It's disgusting."

"You sound just like my dad."

"Just be careful what you listen to and what you read," I said. "Everything these days is liberal propaganda. Remember, the media's job is to keep us misinformed so that we make irrational decisions against our interests." I repositioned my ridiculous mask. "And avoid social media like the plague. All that's there is negativity. It's a place where malcontents hang out. Only idiots would waste their time on that stuff. I don't care about celebrities. Like, I need to know what they eat as soon as they wake up in the morning. Instagram and TikTok are the most worthless ones of all. 'Look at me, everyone! Look at me!' Do I care about Selena Gomez's new back tattoo? Everybody wants to be part of the fabric of fame. It's absurd the things people waste their time on nowadays."

"You sound like my dad," she said. "What do you think about the border wall?"

"I'm for keeping our country safe."

"The wall's racist."

You sound like an idiot, I thought.

I felt a brain surge pulsate through my skull flowing from my left eye socket, and my vision blurred for a few seconds. "Cheryl, it was great talking with you, but I'm feeling a little tired all of a sudden."

She got out of the wheelchair, then took my breakfast tray. "Sure, no problem. I should finish my rounds. It was very nice meeting you, Peter. You and my dad would get along."

A few minutes later, Dr. Wyse walked in. I was still tired, inside my forehead. Some dizziness had settled in.

"One more thing from yesterday," he began. "You're not possessed by the devil because of what you did in high school when The Exorcist was playing. You're possessed by your subconscious, and it's intent on destroying your life and killing you. Addiction is a deadly disease."

Someone screamed out from a nearby room: "My TV isn't working! I need some applesauce! Nurse!"

"Was that one of the doctors on staff here?" I asked.

I could tell he vaguely smiled despite his mask. It turns out people don't just smile or scowl with their lips – the top of the cheekbones and the eyes are involved. He continued, unamused. "Now turning to your test results," he said. "You're also suffering from Postural Orthostatic Tachycardia Syndrome. Also known as POTS."

"I've never heard of it."

"I wouldn't worry about it. It's a byproduct of your brain injury," he explained. "That's why you fainted. That's why you're having brain surges. Just drink lots of water, eat smaller meals, and salt your food liberally. We'll avoid medications for now. I want to follow up in about a month on Zoom. I'll have my office call you to set that up."

I silently yawned. "All right."

He wrinkled his lips from one side to the other. He furrowed his brows. Then he looked intently at my forehead as if a bull's eye had been painted on it. "I strongly recommend Jungian Analysis."

"I'm in therapy."

"I'm sure it's not the right kind," he said. "No offense to whomever you're working with, but you need to be working with a neuropsychiatrist. Someone well-versed in Jungian Analysis. There aren't too many of us. It's not too late to be who you were supposed to be." He walked out of the room. He left the door open.

Drained, the hospital sounds began to caress my ears like tiny bits of twilight. There was a police siren wailing in the distance. A gust of wind brushed against the room's window. My breath softly whistled through my nose. I closed my eyes. I listened to the loud ringing in my ears. I dozed off.

ADDICT'S WAY

Cheryl cut short my nap. She wheeled me out to the curb of the parking lot. Jay was waiting there to pick me up. "It's open," he said. I heard the door click open. I slid into the passenger seat. I acknowledged Jay with a nod. There was scotch on his breath. The car reeked of marijuana.

"You okay? What happened? I heard you fainted."

"It'll be okay. It's part of the car-crash stuff," I answered. "I'm dealing with brain surges, too."

"Brain surges are awesome!"

I weakly laughed. "I just have to drink more water, use more salt, and eat less food. It's called POTS. I forget all the letters. Anyway, nothing serious."

"Good. I'm going to drop you off at your parent's house. Then I'm going to play a little golf. Just nine holes. Then we're all eating dinner together. Except for Amanda. She's not ready yet."

I rang the doorbell. "It's me, Mom," I said loud enough.

My mother opened the door. I stepped inside. We hugged. She held me tighter than she ever had. Usually, whenever she hugged me, it felt like she was simultaneously trying to pull away. I looked over her shoulder through the kitchen window at the right side of the 4th fairway, which was a collection of various trees – many that were pepper trees – and shrubbery, the kind you'd find growing on a golf course in Britain.

In high school, we'd hide in the trees and smoke opium-laced joints. I can hear Bob Hope singing.

"I thought I had lost you, Peter," she said. "I love you so much. I know these last few years have been very awful for you."

We pulled away from each other. "I love you, Mom. Where's Dad?"

"He's upstairs taking a nap. He'll be down later. What did the hospital say?"

"I'll be okay. I'll fill you in later. It's nothing to worry about," I said. "How's Dad doing?"

"The same. He doesn't have any short-term memory. The doctor said it'll only get worse. His father had the same thing."

"I didn't know Grandpa Peter had the same thing."

"He did. So does his sister, Anna."

"How he's acting?"

"It's the same him."

"What a nightmare for you, Mom."

"It is a nightmare."

"I wish I lived closer."

"I wish you did, too, Peter."

I glanced down at the outdated greyish-white tile in the entry hall, which had a ceiling over 20 feet above it. The tile was the house's original tile. It looked like something you'd see in a museum featuring things from the 1970s.

That 70s Show, except for their kitchen, could be filmed in my parents' home. The remodeled kitchen was the only modern room in the house. A few years ago, it was given a makeover because my father likes to cook. Granite countertops, a metallic oven, a stove, and a refrigerator ruined the 70s vibe. One room in the house still has the same wallpaper that could be seen in various episodes of the Golden Girls.

I missed the 70s in this place the way a Death Row inmate misses the glow of the moon and the twinkle of the stars. Smoking weed. Listening to Led. Thumbing through the glorious pages of Playboy. Watching Happy Days, The Brady Bunch, and Good Times. Summers at the country club pool.

That was then, this is now.

"Is there any beer in the garage?" I asked.

"You just got out of the hospital."

"That's why I need a beer."

I put my travel bag under the stairs. I walked into the garage.

Two early-model Mercedes-Benzes and various "historic" knick-knacks took up most of the space there. I grabbed a Michelob Ultra from the still-working antique refrigerator that was the color of yellow infant discharge. Another item for the 70's museum. The color choices by the parents of the Me Generation were sometimes pleasing but more often than not hideous. The actual name of the refrigerator's color was Summer Haze. The other choices my mother had considered were Peace & Love (orange-yellow) and Moon Landing (cobalt blue). I had voted for Groovy Gold. The designers in the 70s had certainly been influenced by the previous decade's tie-dyed t-shirts and staring-at-the-sun acid trips. Perhaps the color schemes of the 70s were designed to keep our attention from an oil crisis, rising inflation, and Watergate. Now race and denial of chromosomes are used to divert our attention from the awful obvious. And so, it goes.

My mother and I sat outside at the round glass table that was at the far-left end of the backyard. There was a built-in umbrella in the middle of the table that offered needed shade on hot summer days. The table sat on top of a raised piece of circular concrete that provided an elevated view of the 4th fairway and the tranquilizing Koi Pond of the house next door.

"So, are you doing okay with Alison?"

I took a gulp of the beer. Then put my mask back on. I heard the sound of a golf ball being clipped nearby. "She's an impossible personality," I answered. "I can't take much more of her. She's controlling. She's rigid. She's inflexible. She's too much. Always on high-stress alert. There's not a relaxed bone in her body."

"You have to be patient, Peter. You guys have been through a lot."

"I don't have any more patience. I'm being killed."

"You put her through a lot, Peter."

"I know."

"Maybe you can go to marriage counseling."

I looked down at the tails of the colorful koi slinking through the water. In college, I'd sometimes look at them tripping on mushrooms. "Counseling won't help her," I said. "She's beyond that."

"She's a good woman, Peter. I just wished she'd be more involved with the family. We haven't seen her in a few years now."

"She has clinical problems," I said. "I'm not going to know her much longer. There's just no way to get along with her. It's impossible."

"Don't talk like that." She fidgeted with her mask to make sure her nostrils were properly imprisoned as well as her mouth. "I thought I had lost you, Peter."

I pulled my mask below my chin. I took a gulp of beer. "I was pretty angry, Mom. I was livid. I'm told by Amanda and Jay that I didn't have a brain injury. They dole out tough love to someone with a brain injury? Yeah, they're really cerebral people," I said. "I'm still dealing with symptoms five years later. Me and Alison lived in our car for over nine months. You know, no matter how much you might hate a family member, you help your family. Period. End of story. I don't want to hear anything else."

"Peter, nobody hates anybody."

"You could have fooled me," I said. "I told them a million times the Vegas crash was the eighth one after the La Habra crash. I mean, they couldn't put two and two together? My brain wasn't working!"

"We all have to get along now, Peter. That's what we have to do. Promise me you will."

I wasn't done. Someone needed to know more of the truth. The narcissistic, self-serving psychobabble that my sister had broadcast to my parents and most relatives, held exaggerated falsehoods and half-truths. These lies and semi-lies were designed to reflect the fact that Alison and I had been thrown crumbs when we needed an entire loaf of bread. Okay, maybe, we were given a few slices. Those slices didn't keep us from being evicted. Those slices didn't keep us from living in our car for over three months. Sometimes, a person's familial designation is irrelevant. Ultimately, it is all about dynamics. "I couldn't think straight. I couldn't fend for myself. I shut down. I stopped functioning," I continued. "I couldn't get out of bed. I wasn't just tired. I was dead. And that's the response I get from them? I understand I haven't been a perfect person through the years, but this was not deserved. And I'm staying at the Vagabond?"

"Promise me, Peter," she pleaded. "I want my last few years to be spent with my loving family."

I was disappointed my mother had to endure such dissension, especially at her age. I couldn't imagine a 90-year-old mind and body being able to handle such a thing. Especially when she had my father's cognitive decline to deal with as well. There was a noticeable sadness in her eyes. Her face was sullen now. The last five years should not have been wasted on such resentful conflict. A hummingbird flew by backward. I washed away the subtle taste of rage with a quick swig of beer. I swished it around like mouthwash. "Alright. I will, Mom. This has gone on long enough," I said.

"IRENE!! IRENE!!" my father yelled from the upstairs master bedroom. His talent for yelling at the top of his lungs hadn't left him. It was a talent that had earned him the nickname Crazy George, given to him by the Koi Pond neighbors. "WHERE ARE YOU!?!" he yelled again.

My mother sighed heavily. "I can never just catch my breath anymore. I should have listened to Jay. I should've hired a live-in nurse when all this started."

"You still can."

She walked away from the table, with a noticeable lack of spring in her step. There was an aura of fatigue and resignation in her movements. "No, not now," she said. "You don't know him anymore."

| 8 |

The chirp of a text coming through woke me up. It was Dr. Guessner: "Are we still on for this morning?" I texted back: "I guess I didn't set my alarm. Sorry about that. One minute."

I sat up in bed. Everything in the room assaulted my still-crusty eyes. It was an absolutely-hideous collection of pinks, throw-up yellows, and baby-shit greens. The 70s: when hitch-hiking was safe, and wallpaper was ugly. I wish I still had my metal lunchboxes: the Partridge Family, Brady Bunch, Six Million Dollar Man, and Batman. I'd have some valuable stuff.

"How's your mind been, Peter?"

"If it was a car, it would be in the junkyard."

"What make and model?"

"Shit and More Shit."

"I see you haven't had your morning coffee yet."

"Morning beer. I'm hanging in there."

"Are you still in Whittier?"

"Yes."

"Have you had contact with Alison?"

"No."

"Will you?"

"I'm sure. Eventually. I'm enjoying the break from all the rituals. From all the demeaning and belittling. From the radical controlling behavior," I explained.

"It's classic OCPD," he said.

I arranged my legs Indian-style. "It's a never-ending shitfest."

"The demeaning and the belittling. That's narcissistic abuse," he said. "In marriage, a Narcissist is simply a spouse who discards the other. They make them feel like they have no value."

"Every fucking day."

His voice was genuine and concerned: "It's time to start taking care of yourself, Peter."

"This is a nightmare. The devil did listen to me that night in high school."

"She can't help herself. And she won't," he continued. "That's the problem."

"But I'm always the one with the problem."

"It's part of what she suffers from."

I leaned back against the throw-up-yellow headboard. I massaged the left side of my face. "You know, we drank when we dated. I never got to know the real her, I guess."

"I think all this stress is why you're having the brain surges."

Suddenly, you could hear the soothing hum of the golf course lawnmowers trimming the fairway. I slid open the window above the headboard. Birds chirped and tweeted. A dove cooed nearby. A car honked in the distance. A leaf blower from the bottom of the cul-de-sac joined in. Then a dog started barking. After going through several more examples of Alison's behaviors, I went on to tell him about the fainting spell and Dr. Wyse's POTS diagnosis. "Everything always keeps getting worse," I ended.

He laughed. "At least you can handle your own divorce."

"Yeah, there's always a silver lining. Thanks."

I texted my good lawyer buddy, David Canon: "Hey, David. I've had it with Alison. Will you handle my divorce?"

"WHAT???" he texted back.

"Yeah, it's that bad."

"You just need a break from each other. You need hobbies."

I opened the bedroom door and looked down the hallway at my parent's door. It was open. Their bed was empty. That meant they were downstairs, eating breakfast and/or watching game shows. But I thought I heard their bathroom fan on, so I walked inside their bedroom. Nearly 40 years old, the orange-brown carpeting had none of the usual wear-and-tear. My mother was still meticulously making the bed. The covers and sheets were smooth and flat without any wrinkles. The pillows had even been plumped up like at a hotel. The only thing missing was the gold-and-ruby tasseled bedspread. But I guess it wasn't seen as an aesthetic necessary anymore, as most of the parental neighborhood had died. Jack Book, the 84-year-old across-the-street neighbor, died a couple of weeks ago, supposedly, of COVID. Yvonne Sarnito, just a year ago, had succumbed to Parkinson's. Rene Montrose, who refused chemo and a secret blend of herbs from a family friend, as well as hospital visitors, died from stomach cancer. There were only a few elderly neighbors left, but they were all on their way out. Mort Johnson, two doors up, had been diagnosed with pancreatic cancer. Ron Meyers, next door, was waiting for prostate cancer to kill him. Ms. Sanchez, who had never smoked, was waiting for stage-4 lung cancer to run its course. That's why the house hadn't seen any friends for quite some time now.

All of a sudden, the sounds of police sirens were just outside the house, along with the sounds of screeching tires. The sounds suddenly stopped. Right outside. Quickly, there was a loud banging on the front door: "Police! Open up!"

I quickly made my way downstairs, where my mother was already standing. All the color had left her face. I looked through the peephole, then opened the door.

"Put your hands up!" I did.

"You, too, ma'am!"

Two police officers had guns drawn and pointed right at us.

"What is this all about?" I asked, thinking a warrant was being executed on me.

"A 9-1-1 call came about two intruders inside the home," one of the officers answered. They were both twenty-somethings, fit and ready for action.

"This house?" my mother asked. "I don't think so."

They lowered their guns. "From this address, yes, ma'am."

My father walked out of the kitchen. He was still in his light-blue pajamas and brown slippers. "I'm the one who called 9-1-1," he said. "I don't know these people."

"Dad, it's me, Peter."

"George. Honey. It's me." My mother's voice was heartbroken.

"Can we talk outside?" I asked the officers.

They made room for me out on the porch.

"My father's dealing with dementia. He has no short-term memory," I said. "This is a new development, though."

ADDICT'S WAY

They both understood. Their eyes were sympathetic. They asked if they could walk through the house as a precaution. "Yes, of course," I said.

My mother hugged my father. "George. Sweetheart."

"Why are the police here?" he asked. "What's going on? Who called the police?"

After the police left, I walked back upstairs and made my way to the bed in my sister's old room. I was exhausted. The fatigue was disabling, again. Zero energy.

There was a soft knock on the bedroom door. "Peter."

"Yes, Mom. Come on in."

She slowly made her way to the foot of the bed. Worry swirled through her eyes. Panic tinted her cheeks pale grey. "Your father's sleeping," she said.

"It's really sad," I said.

"That's life when you get this old."

"I can't talk to him anymore, can I?"

"No, not really."

"Seems like an Alzheimer's, Mom."

"Something like this has never happened," she said. "I called his doctor already. She said that you being here threw him off. You know, he hasn't seen you very much in the last 5 years. You look a lot older now, too."

"Maybe. Probably. Could be. Yeah, I guess."

"Before he went for a nap, he asked me, 'Why does that man visiting us have the same last name as me?'"

I shook my head. "Because he doesn't remember me being born," I said. "He wasn't at the hospital."

"Don't talk like that."

"It's true."

"I told Amanda and Jay what happened," she said.

"What did they say?"

"Nothing much. What could they say? Everyone's ready."

I looked around the bedroom. "I can't believe we moved in here 50 years ago, Mom."

"It goes so fast, Peter."

"Nat's already 23."

"Victor's turning 30 this year."

ADDICT'S WAY

"I remember when he was in the incubator at St. Jude's."

"That was a tough pregnancy for your sister."

A man yelled "Fore!" at the top of his lungs.

"We're all getting together for dinner tonight."

I rolled my shoulders against the headboard. "Where?" I asked.

"At Amanda and Jay's house."

"Amanda? Mom, I don't know about that."

"I talked to her. We have to be a family, Peter."

"I don't know."

I remember seeing the same pink-flannel pajamas that she was wearing today, about 40 years ago. Probably the same pair. Another artifact for the museum. It'll feature furniture and clothing.

"What do you mean you don't know?" she said.

"I don't know," I began. "I think somebody should have made sure we weren't evicted from our apartment."

"I wanted to help you guys, but I didn't have very much to say about it."

"It's unforgivable, Mom," I said. "Me and Alison living in our car. Me in a virtual coma. You guys knowing about the car crash. You guys knowing about us being evicted. I have an awful family."

"I know, but Jay's going to be bringing food from Lascari's."

"What time?"

"Amanda's going to call when she gets home from work. Then we'll all go over."

"Alright, Mom. I need to take a nap. I just don't have any energy."

| 9 |

I woke up at the Vagabond Inn. I have no idea how I got there. I only have a vague recollection of last night's Italian dinner, but I clearly remembered Jay was pouring a lot of scotch for us. I do remember yelling, "Fuck you, Amanda! You're so fucking dumb! You're not the least bit cerebral!" Then, I remember Amanda yelling back, "Get the fuck out of my house!" That's about it.

Now, I was in an Uber on my way to the Fullerton Transportation Center to catch the Amtrak. It was a place rich with Spanish Mission architecture, despite a few instances of modernization. There was a one-way ticket to San Diego waiting there for me. Somehow, $500 had ended up in my buttoned shirt pocket. It was placed there by either Jay or my mother.

The kiosk spit out my ticket.

I didn't expect to be heading back down so soon.

I knew Alison's welcoming would not be warm: "They're disgusting!!!" she texted back after I had texted her the reason for the abrupt change in plans.

I quickly gulped down a couple of beers inside the station market, which was half restaurant, half convenience store. Non-traveling locals ate there because the food was so good. And it was. The beers slowed my breathing but only a little bit.

I thought the rhythmic hum of the train would relax me, but I sat between dread and gloom the entire way back down. All I wanted to do was peacefully daydream, but that wish had been eclipsed by an onslaught of unbearable anxiety.

When the train pulled into Downtown San Diego, I wasn't in the mood to walk straight into the den of misery. I ended up at an outside table at Felipe's.

I ordered some red wine and thin-crust pepperoni pizza from my favorite server, Dorothy. Her brown hair was cropped short, and her brown eyes were friendly. She had been serving tables for over 50 years. For the past 10, she had been doing it with a bad knee. In her seventies, she didn't complain. It was in her blood to work hard. Her legs and forearms were sturdy. She grew up milking cows on a farm in Tennessee. She'd often say, "What else would I be doing if I wasn't waitressing?"

I didn't have to wait long for my carafe. "Here, you go, Peter."

I poured some wine into my stemless wine glass. The kind of glass Grandpa Giuseppe used when he was still alive. "Everyday wine should be served without pretense," he would say. I miss him. He worked hard in a battery factory. Owned his own home and a Cadillac, when owning one's own home and a nice car was an automatic part of the American Dream. He had the strong features and piercing eyes of a movie star. On weekends, he'd dress in a full-blown suit. If he were still alive, he'd be ashamed of me. Salud, Grandpa.

Suddenly, there was illegible yelling and chanting in the distance. It grew closer, and the chanting became clear: "Say his name, George Floyd! No justice, no peace! No racist police!"

I looked down India Street. Black Lives Matter was the scene. They march passed in front of Filipe's.

Some people clapped, some people booed, and some people yelled out their refrains: "What about all the Black-on-Black crime every weekend in Chicago? I guess those Blacks don't matter to you!" "You're all corporate pawns and too dumb to know it!" "B-L-M. Blacks loot more!"

I grabbed a slice of pizza. I said nothing. It doesn't matter what I think, I thought. It doesn't matter what anybody thinks, really.

Dorothy appeared. "I did that for Vietnam in the 60s," she said proudly.

I shrugged. "I guess someone has to do it." I took a sip of wine. "There's enough people doing it so that I don't have to do it. I can watch it all on TV."

A text from Alison chirped through: "WHERE THE HELL ARE YOU???"

"I'm walking back," I texted back.

"CALL ME NOW!!!"

My shoulders dropped. My blood pressure rose. If I were a tire, I'd be flat. I called her.

"Where are you?" she answered.

"On my way back."

"Walking?"

"No, I'm flying."

"I need you to get me a brownie from Starbucks."

"All right."

"Also, pass by Burger Lounge."

"I will. I know what you want."

"Let me say it!" she snapped.

"A turkey burger with no cheese and no sauce."

"Let me say it!" she snapped again. "A free-range turkey burger with no cheese and no sauce. You need to say free-range turkey burger."

"That's all they have."

"Say it anyway."

"Alright."

"What are you going to say?"

"A free-range turkey burger."

"What else?"

"With no cheese and no sauce."

"Hurry. I'm starving."

"Okay."

"Remember the brownie! Bring back the receipts! Hurry up! I need food! You don't even supply basic food for the refrigerator!"

On my way back, an elderly homeless Black man was sleeping in front of the 7-11. His grey sweats were soiled. He was laying on his side. There was a small cup with some change next to him. There was a half-eaten hamburger near his chin. He was actively sucking his thumb.

I kept on walking. I looked out at the shimmering bay. The sun was slowly falling to its knees.

About the Author

STEPHEN LIOSI, former President of his law school graduating class and Law Review Invitee, no longer practices law.

In May 2016, Mr. Liosi suffered a traumatic brain injury in a car accident. Because of his gambling addiction, he lacked the cash reserves to withstand the car crash's devastation. In turn, he was homeless for 9 months in his car. Thereafter, he was unable to function for 4 years, with his law practice collapsing along with him, living in and out of hotels.

In 2018, he failed to return approximately $1,700 in court fees to a then-friend client. Recently evicted at the time, Mr. Liosi was living in his car and out of contact with everyone. With no help from his family and only disbelief and vilification from them, his brain injury changed his life — for the worse.

He is repentant, remorseful, and contrite to all those affected by his unintentional downfall. Mr. Liosi lacked the ability even to respond to the State Bar's complaint, where he was disbarred by default. Still, he struggles with significant residual symptoms.

Having written professionally since he was 15-years old, he is now determined to pursue his lifelong dream of becoming a novelist. He hopes to share stories that will inspire others, including blogging about addiction, brain injury, narcissistic family dysfunction, and self-discovery. He began and finished his novel ADDICT'S WAY while homeless.

Made in the USA
Coppell, TX
12 December 2023